Access VBA Programming

WITHDRAWN

R
Reference

About the Authors

Charles E. Brown is one of the most noted authors, teachers, and consultants in the computer industry today. His first two books, *Beginner Dreamweaver MX* and *Fireworks MX: Zero to Hero,* have received critical acclaim and are consistent bestsellers. This year, Charles will be releasing books on VBA for Microsoft Access, and the new Microsoft FrontPage environment. He is also a Fireworks MX contributor for the MX Developer's Journal. In addition to his busy writing schedule, he conducts frequent seminars for Future Media Concepts, speaking about the Macromedia development environment. In 2004, he will also be involved in developing e-learning courses using Macromedia's RoboDemo development environment.

When Charles is not writing and teaching, he is a consultant for many high-profile websites. This year, he is placing a lot of his web development efforts with the Flash MX 2004 Professional environment. He feels strongly that this is the future of web development.

Charles is also a noted classical organist, pianist, and guitarist who studied with such notables as Vladimir Horowitz, Virgil Fox, and Igor Stravinsky. It was because of his association with Stravinsky that he got to meet, and develop a friendship with, famed 20th-century artist Pablo Picasso.

Ron Petrusha has over 25 years of experience in the computer industry and is the author of ten computer books and numerous print and online articles. He is the principal of Howling Wolf Consulting Services, a company that provides editorial services to the publishing industry and also offers application and web development services using Microsoft technologies. He can be reached at ron@howlingwolfconsulting.com.

Access VBA Programming

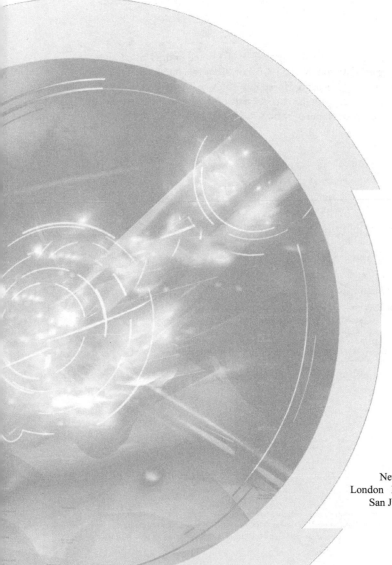

Charles E. Brown
Ron Petrusha

McGraw-Hill/Osborne

New York   Chicago   San Francisco   Lisbon
London   Madrid   Mexico City   Milan   New Delhi
San Juan   Seoul   Singapore   Sydney   Toronto

The **McGraw·Hill** Companies

McGraw-Hill/Osborne
2100 Powell Street, 10th Floor
Emeryville, California 94608
U.S.A.

To arrange bulk purchase discounts for sales promotions, premiums, or fund-raisers, please contact **McGraw-Hill**/Osborne at the above address. For information on translations or book distributors outside the U.S.A., please see the International Contact Information page immediately following the index of this book.

Access VBA Programming

1234567890 FGR FGR 01987654

ISBN 0-07-223197-1

Publisher	Brandon A. Nordin
Vice President & Associate Publisher	Scott Rogers
Editorial Director	Wendy Rinaldi
Project Editor	Carolyn Welch
Acquisitions Coordinator	Athena Honore
Technical Editor	David Schulz
Copy Editor	Judith Brown
Proofreader	Marian Selig
Indexer	Claire Splan
Composition	Lucie Ericksen, John Patrus, Kelly Stanton-Scott
Illustrators	Kathleen Edwards, Melinda Lytle, Greg Scott
Series Design	Roberta Steele
Cover Design	Tom Slick

This book was composed with Corel VENTURA™ Publisher.

Contents at a Glance

Contents

Part V **Application Development**

Introduction

Before the introduction of Microsoft Access, database management systems were synonymous with programming. Without programming, you were unable to tap into the full power of the software. Indeed, some database management systems, like Nantucket Corporation's Clipper, consisted only of a development environment and a compiler. The database developer was responsible for designing the databases and then writing all of the code that constituted his or her application.

The introduction of Microsoft Access in 1991 changed all that. Access was distinguished by its graphical approach to database management, which allowed users to take advantage of some powerful features of the DBMS without needing to do any programming. By using wizards and graphical designers, Access allowed users to design databases, create forms and user interfaces, write queries, and generate reports. It was this power and flexibility combined with its ease of use that quickly made Access the leading desktop database management system.

Although programming is not required to use Access, nevertheless, Access has attracted a huge programming audience. In fact, more programmers are working with Access than with any other database management system. There are two major reasons for this apparent contradiction:

► By providing such an effective rapid application development environment for database applications, Access prompts users to want to learn more about using the software more powerfully, effectively, and efficiently. In fact, many professional Access programmers began as Access users who developed a passion for the product and experienced a frustration over the things they wanted to do but didn't know how to do.

▶ Despite its ease of use, users at some point run into the limitations of the Access user interface and must turn to programming. Although you can do a great deal as an Access user, some things can only be done programmatically.

If you've picked up this book, you're no doubt an Access user who has had both of these experiences. You enjoy using Access, enjoy the power that it places at your disposal, and want to learn more about using it effectively. At the same time, you find that you're running into some of the limitations of the Access interface and suspect that if you're to continue to deepen your skills in using Access, you need to turn to programming. And perhaps you're even beginning to find yourself responsible for developing and maintaining Access applications, possibly in a small business setting, where most users have very little experience with the Access interface. In that case, this book is for you.

Access VBA Programming takes the Access power user to the next level, from using Access to programming with Access, by building on much of what you already know. Part I, "Understanding the Access Environment," introduces some of the basic concepts of program design and architecture (like requirements analysis and naming conventions) at the same time that it reviews what you can do in Access without programming. It includes a refresher course on the major components of an Access application (including macros, modules, and events), as well as a discussion of some of the interface elements you can eventually use to allow yourself and other users access to the code you'll eventually write. This includes using the Switchboard Manager as the menu system of an Access application and customizing Access menus and toolbars so that the user can execute routines by clicking a toolbar button or selecting a menu item.

Part II, "Understanding the Visual Basic for Applications Environment," introduces you to Visual Basic for Applications (VBA), the programming language used by Microsoft Access (as well as by the other Office applications and by Visual Basic). Here you'll learn about basic programming concepts, such as variables, arrays, objects, program structures (looping structures, decision-making structures), functions, and procedures. VBA, however, offers not only a programming language, but a complete integrated development environment (IDE) that allows you to run, test, and debug your code. This part of the book introduces you to the VBA Editor, VBA's IDE. Finally, VBA itself has no language elements that support data access. Instead, data access is handled by a separate library, ActiveX Data Objects (ADO), which can be called from VBA code. Part II introduces you to the basics of ADO as well.

With the basics in place, Part III of the book, "Interacting with VBA," begins to show you how you can put VBA to creative use in developing Access applications. It covers using VBA with forms and reports, creating menus and toolbars programmatically, and customizing the Access environment both from the Options dialog and programmatically. In this part of the book, you learn not only how to use VBA to get Access objects (like forms and reports) to run, but also to configure the Access user interface so that the user can run your application.

Part IV, "Advanced Access Programming Techniques," introduces some of the more specialized areas of Access development. You'll learn about security in Access, an increasingly important topic as Access becomes more widely used in networked and multiuser environments. You'll also learn how to use Access to create Data Access Pages for the web and to import data from other Office applications, like Excel and Word. Chapter 19 covers upgrading to a more enterprise-level DBMS like Microsoft SQL Server while continuing to use Access as a front-end through a technology called Access Data Projects (ADP).

Part V, "Application Development," consists of two chapters, one on multiuser programming and one on programming outside of the Access environment with the skills you've developed while programming with Access. As Access evolves from a single-user, desktop DBMS to a networked DBMS, the demands placed on programmers to write robust, efficient code increases. The chapter on multiuser programming covers some of the techniques you can use to make sure your application performs as expected when multiple users are accessing data. The final chapter, "Beyond Microsoft Access," demonstrates that the skills you have learned in the course of the book are applicable not only to Access, but also to the other Office applications, to the retail edition of Visual Basic, and even to VBScript and Active Server Pages.

Who Should Read This Book?

Access VBA Programming is written for the Access power user who is familiar with the basics of creating database applications using the Access interface. It assumes that you know your way about the Access interface and are familiar with creating tables, queries, and reports using either wizards or Design View, and that possibly you've created forms and run Access macros as well.

It also assumes that you're ready and eager to take the next step—either that you're experiencing the limitations of the Access interface and want to learn more, or that you find yourself in the position where you need to know more in order to create professional applications for other users.

Although we have written this book using Access 2003 in all cases, we have also tested it using previous versions of Access. We've also tried to be as sensitive as possible to differences in Access versions. Because of this, the book should serve as a useful introduction to Access programming as long as you're using Access 97 or a later version.

Understanding the MS Access Environment

Introduction to VBA for Applications

In 1992 a good friend of mine said to me that this new database package, Microsoft Access version 1.0, is never going to last. He felt that it was not a strong enough contender considering the competition that was then available.

Here we are, 12 years later, and evidence strongly shows that my friend was quite wrong. Not only has Access lasted, but it is now serving as the backbone for many large web sites. It has successfully combined a powerful database engine with an interface that is friendly for even the first-time user. In many respects, it now rivals Microsoft's enterprise SQL Server database environment.

With Microsoft Access, you can accomplish a lot without any programming skills whatsoever. However, with a knowledge of Visual Basic for Applications (VBA), you can do a tremendous amount of customization, as well as address a large number of scenarios.

In this chapter, we are going to take a brief excursion into the history of Access. We are then going to examine the Access environment by looking at how to create the various objects that make up a database. We are going to take our first brief look at the Visual Basic Editor (VBE).

Since we are looking at the history of Access in this chapter, we will conclude by gazing, briefly, into a crystal ball and taking a guess as to where Microsoft may be going in the future.

History of Microsoft Access

Microsoft Access came into being in 1992 with version 1.0 and coincided with the introduction of Microsoft Windows. This introduced new software concepts (at least to the consumer market) such as drag and drop, form and report writing capabilities, and wizards to help the beginner get a job done. It also introduced a way for different database packages to talk to each other. This new technology was called ODBC, or Object Database Connectivity.

The following year, Microsoft built on these features with Access 1.1. This is also the year they purchased their competition, FoxPro. Since Access was actually part of the Microsoft Office environment, they introduced the ability for these Office programs to communicate with each other. As an example, users now had easy mail-merge capabilities with Microsoft Word. The program also now had the ability to handle more data.

In 1994, Access 2.0 came out with even more wizards, better development tools, and significant improvements to the Jet database engine that made running queries considerably faster.

With the introduction of Windows 95 came the introduction of Office 95. In addition to the improved form and report writing capabilities, VBA was formally made the development language behind all the Office programs.

In 1997, the Web was starting to grow and Access 97 came with tools that helped it integrate with web applications. It was able to speak with HTML and publish data to the Web. VBA also took a step closer to becoming more OOP (object-oriented programming) friendly, with the introduction of modules to hold the VBA procedures. A number of other development tools were also introduced.

Access 2000 made a significant improvement in programming with the introduction of ActiveX Data Objects (ADO). We will be spending a significant part of this book discussing that very topic. This version also introduced increased capabilities for working with the SQL Server database engine. Access 2002 improved on this capability by tightening something called *referential integrity*. This means that if data is edited in one table, those edits cascade to related data in another table. Also, XML capabilities were introduced.

Finally the present version, Access 2003, has expanded the XML capabilities and added some unique programming and debugging tools.

Developing in Access

As stated in the introduction, Access has successfully combined a powerful database development environment with a relatively easy-to-use interface. It has a number of wizards that will walk you through a variety of actions such as building a table, a form, a report, or a query.

In this section, we take a brief look at the development environment. However, before we begin, we must distinguish between two terms: database and database project (note, the terms database project and database application mean the same thing and will be used interchangeably throughout this book).

In its simplest form, a *database* is a collection of related data held in a structured environment. The data is usually related in order to manipulate it to accomplish a task. Most databases are relational and have tools to easily relate data. A *database application* is programming to help the database manipulate and deliver information. This is where VBA comes into play.

The Database Window

When you first open Access, you are presented with the window shown in Figure 1-1.

The components of a database environment are called its *objects*. The Database window places those objects into categories: Tables, Queries, Forms, Reports, Pages, Macros, and Modules. Since this is not a beginning VBA book, I assume that you are

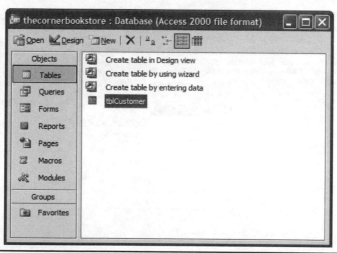

Figure 1-1   *The Database window*

experienced in using many of the features in this window, but we'll take a brief look at the mechanics of using it.

You select the category you want using the column on the left. Once in that category, you should see the list of available objects of that type—for instance, the tables associated with your database. Each category also presents options for creating an object. Many can be created either manually or with the use of a wizard. As an example, if you double-click on Create Table by Using Wizard, you are presented with the screen shown in Figure 1-2.

Here you select the fields you want by examining a number of prebuilt tables for various types of jobs. You can rename the fields to suit your purposes. Once you have selected the fields you want, the Next button takes you to the next step necessary to complete the table. Most wizards work this way.

Returning to the Database window, you can also choose to build the same table by hand by selecting the Create Table in Design View option. You are presented with a grid as shown in Figure 1-3.

Here you can name the field, select a data type, and provide some brief comments about the field. In the Field Properties area in the bottom portion of the window, you can assign default values, data rules, and formatting, for example.

While the mechanics may be slightly different, forms and reports have similar features. You can build them either in Design View or by using the supplied wizard.

In case you have never had an occasion to use it, a Data Access Page, which was first introduced in Access 2000, allows you to display information in a form or report

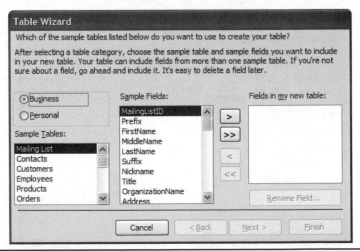

Figure 1-2 *The Table Wizard*

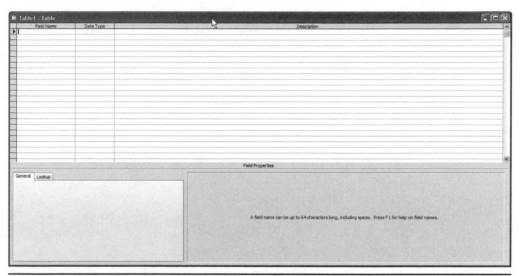

Figure 1-3   *Table in Design View*

on the Web. It converts the form or report to HTML code while binding it to the data it is associated with.

The nice part about this feature is that, even though the form or report is being displayed in a web page, you have all the same tools available as if you were using it within the database environment. You can add, delete, or modify data as well as scroll through it using the buttons of the form or report.

Macros

Macros are simple code that replicates a sequence of steps within Access. Unlike full VBA programming, macros cannot make decisions or loop through a block of code a certain number of times. They do not use variables, nor can you customize their operations through the use of procedures. They simply mimic a sequence of operations that you could perform yourself manually.

When you select the Macros category in the Database window, you will notice that there are no wizards. In some cases, you are going to create macros that are associated with a particular object within your database environment, such as a form or a button on that form. In other cases, you will create a macro for a general scenario within the environment. When we get to Chapters 5 and 6, we will be creating a couple of simple macros and then converting them into full VBA code. For now, if you click on New (located at the top of the Database window in the Macros category), you will see a grid, as shown in Figure 1-4.

Figure 1-4   *The Macro design window*

The window has two sections. The top section allows you to design an action, while the bottom section will be used to set parameters. As an example, suppose you want to write a simple macro to close a form. You would first select Close from the Action list in the top part of the grid (shown in Figure 1-5).

Once you have done that, you need to select what to close. Go to the Action Arguments section of the window and select Form in the Object Type field, as shown here.

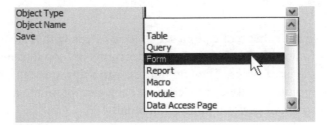

From there on, all you need to do is add the name of the form object you are assigning this action to and save the macro. Simple, but limited in ability!

Modules

Modules are where the VBA code is written and stored. Beginning in Chapter 5, we will be spending the bulk of our time working on our code and learning about the VBA environment. For the time being, let's take a look at the VBA Editor (VBE).

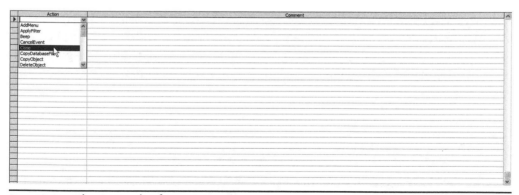

Figure 1-5   *The Action list for macros*

Within the Modules category, select New. You should see the same screen as shown in Figure 1-6.

The main window, taking up most of the screen, is the Code window. The upper-left window is the Project window, and the lower-left window is the Properties window.

Notice the Project window, which is where you will find all the code modules associated with your application. For instance, in sophisticated projects, the VBA

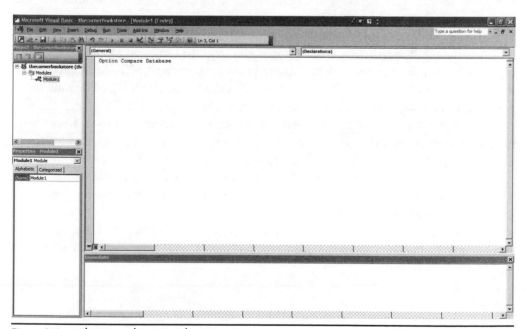

Figure 1-6   *The Visual Basic Editor*

code may be divided up over many modules. The VBA code associated with a particular form or report will go into a dedicated module that holds only the specialized code for that form or report; while code associated with general operations will go into an entirely different module again. We will be looking at this in greater detail beginning in Chapter 5.

The Future of Microsoft Access

Now that we have seen a little of the history of Access, as well as taken a brief tour of its current look, let's gaze into our crystal balls and predict where Microsoft is strongly indicating it is going.

There is no question that the Microsoft Office environment, of which Microsoft Access is a part, serves as the technological backbone for most businesses today. Microsoft has indicated that they will continue to place a great deal of their research and development in the Office environment.

Because of its ease of use, tremendous power, and relatively inexpensive cost, Access is not only serving as a personal database application tool, but is increasingly taking over the enterprise roles of what were, at one time, reserved for more sophisticated packages such as SQL Server and Oracle. There is no better place to see this than the increasing use of Access in building web sites.

Access 2000 took a major step forward with Data Access Pages. This meant that it now had a method to create HTML pages and bind data to them. As stated earlier, 2002 took this even further with the ability to save reports as XML documents. In addition, the ability to save a PivotTable and PivotChart as a web-based document was introduced. Version 2003 then expanded the XML capabilities.

Microsoft has made one thing abundantly clear: it is placing a lot of its future in the development of its new .NET environment. This environment, if it comes to fruition, will allow tighter integration of the components of the Microsoft Office environment with each other as well as the Web. This will allow people to share data with an ease that is not seen now. At the heart of that will be XML and its ability to integrate individual components on the Web.

You will be able to create a document in Microsoft Word, integrate data from Access into it, and then share the document with whomever you need to share it with right on the Web.

Because of this, development will be increasingly focused on web services and the .NET environment, which promises to make the development process increasingly easier and seamless. There are already strong indications that the next version of Microsoft Office will introduce significant changes to the VBA environment. We will probably see the use of Visual Basic .net in order to further integrate Office with web services.

Summary

In this chapter we examined the evolution of Microsoft Access. We traced its growth from a personal database program to a sophisticated tool used in web services. We also looked at some of the tools that make it so easy to use. Finally, we looked at where Access development will most likely be in the future.

Before we get started developing, however, we need to examine the development process. We will spend time in Chapter 2 doing just that. Then, in Chapters 3 and 4, we will examine non-programming techniques that you can use to develop Access applications. Then, beginning in Chapter 5, we turn our attention to VBA development.

Designing an Access Application

In Chapter 1 we saw how Access grew from a personal database package to a sophisticated database development environment that can be used in some enterprise situations. This growth has meant that a more sophisticated approach to the development process is called for. In all but the simplest of applications, you must follow a well-established and systematic approach to development. It is my experience that not following this approach almost guarantees failure.

Many years ago I had the honor of building a close friendship with the famed twentieth-century artist, Pablo Picasso. He never realized it, but he taught me about the software development process through his discussions of art and creativity. He said that as a painter, he needed to stand before the blank canvas and see the finished work as vividly as if it was already painted. He would then need to decide on the tools and techniques necessary to realize his vision.

The process of developing a software application should be exactly like this. We need to "see" the finished work and then decide on the tools necessary to realize it.

I know you are probably anxious to dig into the program and code. That is the fun stuff. However, as a beginner, I want you to learn the process correctly because this is just as important as learning the code itself. For this reason, I ask you to pay close attention to this chapter. In many ways, it may be more important than learning the code itself; without it, the code will have no meaning.

In this chapter we examine the development process. Along the way, you are introduced to the first important topic of VBA development: setting up the database properly. In Chapter 3 we see how to set up the database in detail.

Steps in the Development Process

Nearly any book that discusses the software development process will list the following general phases as necessary for a successful result:

- ▶ Definition of requirements
- ▶ Analysis of requirements
- ▶ Evaluation of requirements
- ▶ Development of the design
- ▶ Implementation and testing
- ▶ Maintenance

These are not clearly delineated steps; in most cases, they overlap, and one phase is not necessarily completed before another begins. Once the project is under way, you could be performing maintenance in one area and evaluating requirements in another. For the sake of discussion, we will look at them in their logical sequence as you begin a new project.

Definition and Analysis of Requirements

Let's begin with one basic premise: most of your clients will be notoriously bad at helping you to define the requirements for the project. Not long ago, I had a good friend who wanted to build a website for his business. When I sat down with him, I asked the steps that would be required to complete an online transaction. Weeks later, he still couldn't define them satisfactorily and eventually gave up on the whole idea of the website. There were so many fine points to my friend's business that he found it impossible to lay it out in a step-by-step format.

Many times, failure to communicate the needs is not the only problem. Clients will frequently have inadequate expectations for time and budget. They will fail to realize the steps involved.

Clients are not the only problem. Consultants often fail to do an adequate "needs analysis" or communicate the needs adequately. In the end, they will not produce what the client was expecting, putting a strain on the client-consultant relationship.

You must begin with a fundamental question:

What problem does the software need to solve?

You and your clients must agree on the problem and the solution. Clients must fully understand the resources that will be needed and what they will get in the end. If the clients' resources are limited, they must understand that finished results may not fully meet all of their expectations. It is most important that these agreements are established early in the process.

As a consultant you must fully communicate what tools you will use, what they will and won't do, how long the project will take, what other people and resources may be needed, and what expectations the client will need to meet.

It has been my experience that putting all of this on paper is a great eye-opener. It not only forces everyone to analyze the project more carefully, but also provides a reference should there be disagreement later.

In the case of large projects, or projects with limited resources, they may need to be implemented in steps. As an example, you might first implement a database project to track inventory, then add a module to process client orders, then develop mailing lists, and so on. Teams of people might need to be hired. You will find that in large projects, most developers cannot be an expert on everything. Each person on the team should contribute a unique solution to a specific problem.

Even if you run a small business and are doing a Microsoft VBA project on your own, put your requirements on paper, analyze your resources, and study what will be required to meet your needs. You will be consultant and client all in one.

Once you have carefully defined the problem to be solved, you'll need to study the requirements and determine the tasks that the software will perform.

Analyzing the Requirements

Needless to say, analyzing the requirements is closely entwined with defining the problem. As you study requirements, you will uncover additional problems. This is the point where you must define exactly what the software needs to do. When I teach software development, I ask my students to perform an exercise. I ask them to study the steps they take in the morning to get ready for work or school and list them. It may come out something like this:

▶ Get out of bed
▶ Shower

► Have breakfast

► Leave for work or school

Next I ask them how they would translate the steps into a computer program. In software development, this is called developing an *algorithm.* An algorithm consists of the steps needed to complete a given task. To develop the algorithm, you use a list of the steps, called *pseudocode*. This is not computer code, but steps that can be easily translated into a computer language.

In your development project, you will need to observe the steps necessary for completing a task. It helps to speak with the people doing the task and even to perform the task, when possible, yourself. You will need to have the parties involved explain what is, or isn't, important. In some cases you may get conflicting opinions that you will need to resolve.

You will then need to decide whether the software can emulate the algorithm the client is presently using or, if it can't, the steps that need to be changed. As stated earlier, budgetary and time requirements may also come into play.

Present your solution to everyone involved in the process. More than likely, there will not be 100 percent agreement, and you will need to make adjustments. One group of people may need the database to do report A, while another group may require the database to do report B. However, the database may require a different structure for A than for B. Sometimes a compromise may need to be established in order to make it work.

Once you have resolved any conflicts, get the parties involved to sign off on the solution before work begins. This could save a lot of conflict later on. Now that you have developed the requirements, and have all parties in agreement (or as close as you can get to agreement), you are ready to evaluate whether the requirements will work or not.

Evaluation of Requirements

If the first two phases have been successfully completed, it is now time to roll up your sleeves and make some hard decisions. In this phase you select the tools needed, build a development team if necessary, reassess the algorithm, and communicate the process to the client.

Since this is a book about developing in the Access environment, we'll assume that it is the tool of choice. Access is easy to use and can be adapted to a large number of situations. However, in many instances (especially with a website or growing company), eventually the project may need to migrate to an enterprise-level database environment such as Microsoft's SQL Server, DB2, or Oracle Corporation's Oracle.

Fortunately, Access can easily migrate to SQL Server. This became especially true with the features introduced in Access 2000. As a matter of fact, the environments are so similar that many SQL Server developers do initial modeling in Access. The difference lies in SQL Server's ability to handle a larger number of tasks at the same time. In an environment such as an Amazon.com, Access would not be able to provide the necessary resources.

In many cases, a team will be needed to do the development. Each member of the team should have his or her responsibilities carefully defined on paper in order to avoid confusion. Also, care should be taken to ensure that there is no redundancy in tasks while other important jobs are left undone.

During this evaluation phase, the first two phases may need to be reexamined. Unexpected scenarios and problems may arise that will require reassessment of the time and resources needed, for example. I have even seen situations, although rarely, where the project had to be abandoned as completely undoable. It is better that any issues are addressed early on, rather than unnecessarily expending further resources. In many cases, only certain aspects of the project may need to be changed or abandoned.

Frank and realistic discussions throughout the process will bring about a solution that will be satisfactory to all involved. Schedules can be adjusted, additional money budgeted, and additional people can sometimes be utilized if needed. Again, I cannot emphasis this enough:

> *Document everything, and make sure the client knows all the details.*

Tell the client what tools you have chosen and why. Make sure the client knows why each member of the team was hired and what, precisely, they will be doing. Let all the parties involved know what, if anything, needs to be changed and why. Finally, if no changes are necessary, let the client know that all is going well and how you are meeting the time and budgetary requirements.

You have now defined the problem, studied the steps, selected the tools and, if necessary, the team. You are ready to start doing the work.

Development of the Design

Let's begin the design phase by revisiting two terms defined in Chapter 1: database and database application. A database is a structure where data is kept. The structure has tools for entering, editing, and retrieving the data. As you will see shortly, it is important that you build this environment properly.

A database application contains the programming that will interact with the database. It should automate the ability to:

▶ Enter and edit data

▶ Retrieve data with the use of queries

▶ Retrieve data with the use of reports

A database application could be a combination of several small applications. Many times, modular construction (better known as "divide and conquer") will help make the whole project more manageable and will facilitate the meeting of conflicting needs.

One team may be developing a database application for the order processing department, while another team may be developing a database application for inventory control. It may be the job of a third team to coordinate and connect the work of the first two teams.

As I stated earlier, the work begins with the algorithm, or steps needed to complete the process. However, you now need to translate this pseudocode into a database and VBA code. Many textbooks on the subject of database design use modeling systems that allow developers to translate the steps into a database application. We will look at the most popular of the models, the entity-relationship model.

Entity-Relationship Model

Sometimes called the object-model relationship, the *entity-relationship (E-R) model* defines four elements and, in many ways, defines the basis for object-oriented programming. The four elements are

▶ Entity, or object

▶ Attribute

▶ Identity

▶ Relationship

Entity, or Object

These are the nouns of the project. For instance, if you design a database application for a bookstore, CUSTOMER will be one entity, BOOKS another, AUTHORS a third, and so forth. Each entity is called a class. Notice that I didn't say that each customer would be an entity, only an entity of type CUSTOMER. That is an important distinction that encompasses all of the customers.

As I have said many times already, it is important to design your database application on paper. At this phase, you should go through the design and pick out the nouns. Each noun will be a class.

Attribute

Class CUSTOMER will have certain characteristics or properties: name, gender, age, reading preferences, and so on. We call these the attributes of the class (in this case the class of customers).

The actual attributes may change from customer to customer. One customer may prefer mysteries, while another may prefer biographies. However, we can agree that all the members of class CUSTOMER will have a reading preference.

Identity

I don't think it would come as a great surprise that each member of class CUSTOMER has a unique identity. That identity could be a name, or a customer number of some sort. How else could we identify each entity, or object, within the class CUSTOMER?

Relationship

All these objects, or classes of entities, do not live in an isolated world. Many times, a relationship needs to be established between them. The three relationships are one-to-one, one-to-many, and many-to-many.

As an example of a one-to-one relationship, let's return to the class CUSTOMER. Now let's define another class called STORE (assuming this is a chain, and they are spread over a wide geographic location). Each CUSTOMER shops in one STORE.

The one-to-many relationship is the most common. As an example, class CUSTOMER will have many of class BOOKS.

The many-to-many relationship is the rarest and most difficult to handle. As an example, there may be cases in which AUTHOR A and AUTHOR B collaborated for BOOK A and BOOK B. This takes a bit of design work, which we will address in Chapter 3.

The E-R model gives us a working framework to construct our design and eventually translate it into code.

Translating the E-R Model into an Access Database

All database programs adhere to the relational database model developed by IBM in 1970. This allows us to give each class its own table (a table is the database component that holds data) and then relate the tables together.

As an example, you could create a table called Customer, as shown in Figure 2-1. The noun is CUSTOMER. Class CUSTOMER has attributes such as a customer number, last name, first name, and so on. The identifier for each customer is the customer number. Since it is the unique identifier, I made that a key field to keep it unique.

You could set up a second table to track the inventory, as shown in Figure 2-2. Noun INVENTORY has the attributes of ISBN number, title, author number, and price. The unique identifier is the ISBN number.

Finally, you could have a table to track a customer's purchase. It might look like the one shown in Figure 2-3.

Here we have a purchase number, customer number, ISBN number, purchase date, and price. Notice that this table employs the customer number from one table and the ISBN number from another table. You can see a graphic representation of these relationships in Figure 2-4.

This is a simple scenario, but it illustrates entities (or objects), with attributes, identities, and relationships. We took those qualities and translated them to tables with fields in Access and then related them with unique fields.

The Purchases table serves as a joining point for the Customer and Inventory tables. Since customers usually make multiple purchases, the relationship between

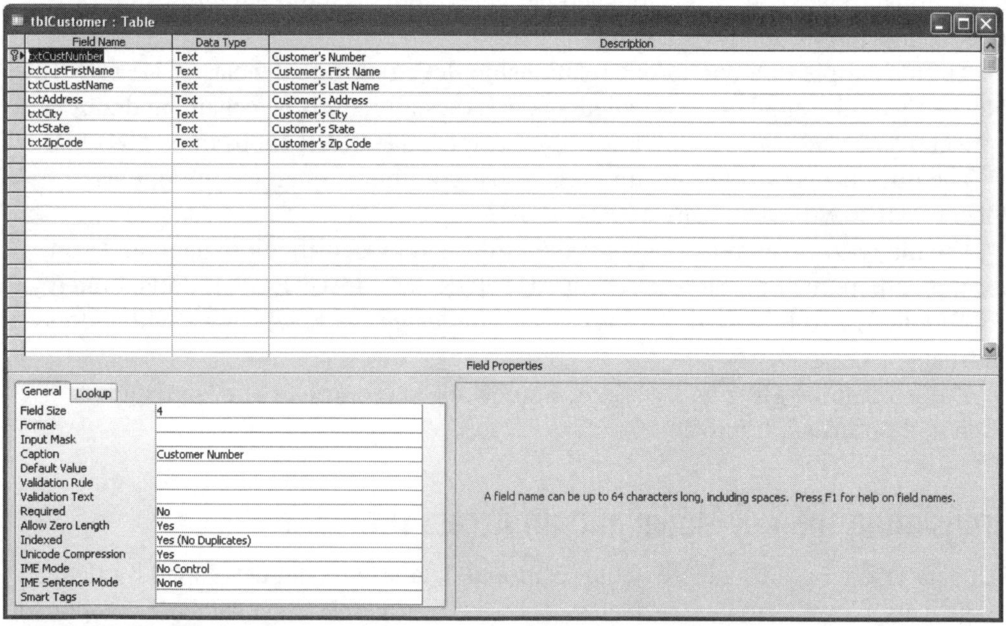

Figure 2-1   *The Customer table in Design View*

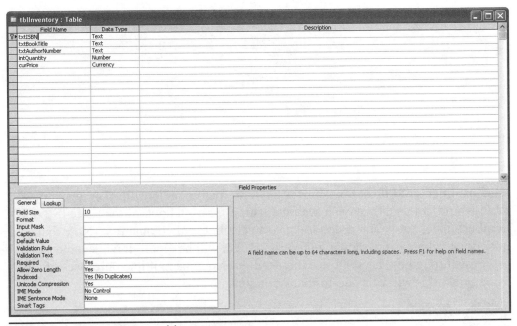

Figure 2-2   *The Inventory table in Design View*

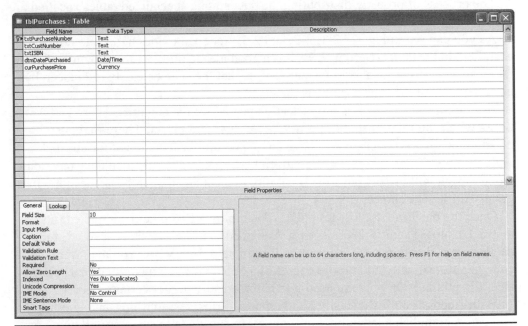

Figure 2-3   *The Purchases table in Design View*

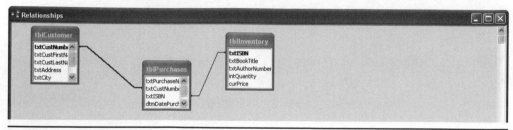

Figure 2-4   *The Relationships window*

the Customer and Purchases tables is a one-to-many relationship. The Inventory table would not usually have a separate listing for each book of the same ISBN number. Instead it would probably have an attribute called quantity. (Note that a quantity attribute is not shown in Figure 2-4. We will be modifying this table as we progress through the book.) Since there will probably be multiple purchases of the same book, this will be a one-to-many relationship also.

NOTE

The example database used here can be downloaded from www.osborne.com.

The process of properly distributing the data among specialized tables is called *normalizing* the data.

As you can see in Figures 2-1, 2-2, and 2-3, Access provides a place to document each field in the table's Design View. It is a good idea to print out the structure of each table, as well as the Relationships window, so that they can be easily referenced by each member of the team as well as the client.

Admittedly, all of this is a simplification geared for the beginner. There will be times when the relationships will not be as clear and direct. There may also be situations when the client will have unique requirements that call for unusual table designs. However, the scenario given here is more the rule than the exception. Good design will usually have the flexibility to meet any demand. Bad design will greatly limit your choices.

Once the database itself is designed, you employ VBA to help complete tasks that the database cannot do on its own. You need to make decisions as to what the database can do on its own and what will need help from VBA. You may want the code to automatically order more copies of a book when the quantity drops below a certain number. Or you may need it to automatically trigger certain reports.

With Access's ability to easily build reports, forms, relationships, and queries, you can accomplish a lot without programming. Needless to say, this will help you complete the project quickly with a minimum of bugs.

As you will see as we progress through the book, your designs must take into account errors that could prevent the normal flow of the process. You should try to anticipate what errors can occur and, if they do, how to handle them.

Another factor in design is security. Security encompasses not only malicious attacks by outside hackers, but also who has authorization to see or edit what information.

During this design phase, you must be careful of "feature creep." It is not unusual for a client to say, "If it can do *this*, can we get it to do *that* now?" Again, good documentation and client signatures can prevent a lot of this from happening.

We will be spending the rest of this book just discussing design issues. Assuming this phase is finished, you are now ready for implementation and subsequent testing.

Implementation and Testing

Once the database application is finished, you begin implementation and testing. This is the phase where you start the nip-and-tuck process. While many of the people involved will find it annoying, parallel testing is recommended. This means that the new system is tested while the existing system is being used.

Of course, the goal is to have the same result at the end but done with greater efficiency. This so-called beta testing process can quickly uncover flaws in the flow and logic of the database application. The bottom line: you should try to intentionally "break" the application and find a way to recover gracefully.

Data should be added using the input forms or by transferring existing data electronically. Without the "live data," you can never test for performance issues such as the speed of data retrieval.

The person who designed and built the application (or the team) is not the best one to test it. Potentially, the designers could be less than objective in their testing procedures and protocols. There are companies that provide professional testing services. These people, who should have no stake in the project itself, should employ everything possible to make the software fail. Why?

Because you want these flaws to be discovered early on, when they will have no effect on the actual process; not long after it has been implemented when you won't be able to recover from an unexpected disaster.

One side effect of testing is that fixing one problem may cause others to occur. Sometimes, these new and unexpected errors may occur in places that were seemingly unrelated to the original error. That is why, after fixing an error, it is important to start testing from the beginning again. In software parlance, we call this *regression testing*. While this may sound time consuming and tedious, the alternative could miss important and costly bugs.

Remember, in your testing, that end users will *not* follow directions. In most cases, when designing software, developers assume that end users will do exactly what they are supposed to do and follow all directions. You, or your testers, should examine every possible scenario in order to provide graceful solutions should they be needed.

Once all the testing is done, the next phase is to formally document the software for the end user.

Documentation

In the development process, the documentation phase, sadly, often gets the least attention. In today's environment, documentation frequently takes the form of online help. I am especially fond of online help because it can be tested and adjusted easily without reprinting and redistributing. Hyperlinks containing cross-references that guide the user to related topics can be easily inserted.

Online help offers another advantage. Software simulation programs, such as RoboDemo, allow you to create an online demonstration of the steps needed to complete a task. It is my experience that this greatly increases the user's understanding and, as a result, averts many potential problems down the road.

Any discussion of documentation must also include a discussion of training. While training provides the ongoing support, it is, for many, the first introduction to the database application. Today's technology allows for two approaches in training: stand-up "live" training and online computer-based training programs. Each offers advantages and disadvantages.

Stand-up, or instructor-led, training allows students to ask questions and get clarification of issues. In addition, a qualified instructor will know how to spot recurring problems and advise their liaisons on the development team. The downside of instructor-led training is cost. Classroom space must be reserved, training manuals must be developed and printed, an instructor must be paid, and an administrator must handle the scheduling of students. It also requires that students be away from work for the duration of the training.

Online computer-based training (CBT) is considerably less expensive to deliver than instructor-led training. All that students need is an Internet connection. They can take the training anytime they want, stop and start as time permits, and review lessons they may be confused about. Programs such as RoboDemo allow software simulation to be developed. This means that students can use the software as if it was the actual system.

However, if they make a mistake, they will be corrected and shown the correct techniques. In addition, online testing can measure students' skills and report the scores to a central administrator. The downside of this method of training is that the student cannot ask questions. In addition, students need to be frequently reminded that they need to complete the training.

In most situations, you will need a combination of training and ongoing documentation in order to have successful use of the database application.

Assuming everything is done and the system is now "live," you will need to consider ongoing maintenance of the system.

Maintenance

A database application is rarely, if ever, completely finished. Foreseeing every potential scenario that may arise is nearly impossible, and as a result, bugs that did not come out during the testing phase may surface from time to time and will need to be fixed. Even the most arduous testing will not reveal 100 percent of the bugs that may be present. I have seen bugs surface weeks, months, and in some cases years, after the main work is completed. You may remember the infamous Y2K bug that took decades to discover.

Since members of the development team know the code structure best, they will most likely be the ones called upon to fix it. This also highlights the need for good documentation. Imagine going back to code months or years after the fact. Without adequate documentation, even within the code, a relatively easy fix could take a great deal of time.

An application is rarely a static endeavor. In addition to fixing bugs that may arise, you will be adding enhancements related to your clients' needs and new technology. Many times a client's needs may evolve over a period of time and, with it, the requirements of the application. New tasks may need to be performed, while existing tasks may need to be deleted or modified. I always tell students that once you have developed a database application, chances are that you will be living with it for the rest of your career.

Whatever the reason, resources for ongoing maintenance should be allocated at the beginning of the project and reviewed periodically.

Summary

In this chapter we examined the development process, or cycle. The steps are not always clearly delimited; however, following a set procedure will give orderliness to the process of defining the specifications, designing the code, writing the code, implementing the application, testing, and providing documentation and training.

In addition, you must consider the resources needed to establish an ongoing maintenance program to fix bugs and periodically update the system.

As I said at the outset, VBA is used to help Access accomplish what the database cannot do on its own. That statement implies that you should maximize the database before you start to develop your VBA code. In Chapter 3, we will be doing just that. We will be looking for ways to minimize VBA code and maximize the database's resources.

Access Development Without VBA

Why would a book whose subject is programming with VBA have a chapter about not programming with VBA? Isn't that a contradiction in terms? Before you go running to get your money back, you will quickly discover that I have a method to my madness (although my publisher will probably feel that there is madness to my method).

In the past six years or so, there has been a trend away from programming with more powerful programming languages. I am speaking about object-oriented programming environments in which the developer takes prebuilt programming modules, each of which does a specialized task, and plugs them into an existing system. For example, let's say you need to format your numbers to currency format. You would not write the code to do it each time you needed it. Instead, you would take a prebuilt and tested module, called a Class file, and plug it into the system.

Writing code can be a costly and time-consuming process. The code must be designed, written, and debugged. If the project has limited resources or a short timeline, this can present a serious problem. Because much of the code is prebuilt and tested, object-oriented environments can reduce the cost and time of a project considerably.

Microsoft Access is not an OOP environment, but you can use the same concepts. By understanding the environment, you can greatly reduce the amount of code and subsequent debugging. Once you have pushed the database environment to its fullest abilities, you can then call in VBA to fill in the jobs that still need to be done.

In this chapter we are going to explore the relational database environment. We touch on file servers and the client-server system. From there, we examine the parts of a database application. We will continue our discussion, from Chapter 2, of relationships and modeling.

We are also going to continue with a subject that will be important when we begin to code in VBA: events. Finally, we explore prebuilt tools that we already have available in Access. Many of the concepts you will learn will be needed when we start to code in Chapter 5.

System Architecture

Chapters 1 and 2 described how Access has grown from a personal database management system (DBMS), to one that is nearly adequate for an enterprise, but here, I want to get more specific about what "personal" versus "enterprise" means. In a *personal* DBMS, the database, VBA code, and user interfaces reside on a single computer and are normally used by one person at a time. This concept gets expanded a bit when speaking about a DBMS in a workgroup environment. In this case, one computer serves as the host to hold the DBMS; however, that DBMS can be accessed by multiple people on different workstations. Access can very easily serve both these roles.

Enterprise environments, such as SQL Server, Oracle, and DB2, distribute data to a vast number of users quickly and efficiently. As an example, if you were building a website, you would need an enterprise system to handle the thousands of requests it could receive each day. While Access has gotten very powerful, it still cannot handle that sort of demand.

In many cases, Access runs on a computer called a *file server*. Early file servers were slow and unreliable and often did not have the capability of knowing what information to send and not to send. So, for example, if you just needed a couple of records from the database, it would send you the whole database file. Fortunately, this inefficient system evolved into a more powerful *client-server model* in which the database system can accept a request for records, process that request, and send only the required information back.

With the growth of the Internet, we've seen the growth of web servers in which you can type a request in a web form that has been downloaded to your web browser. The request is sent to, say, Amazon.com's web server. Their web server reads the request and hands it over to the database server, such as SQL Server. The database application sends it back to the web server that then sends it to a dynamic application server (such as ASP, ColdFusion, ASP.NET, JSP, or PHP), which then converts it to HTML code. The HTML packet is then sent back to the web server, which puts a return address on it and sends it back to your web browser. Your browser reads the HTML and displays the results on your screen. And all of this happens in a matter of seconds.

If you are in a low-demand situation, Access can handle many of these functions. But if you have high-volume demands, you will need to move up to an enterprise system. In some cases, you can take advantage of the easy-to-use tools in Access to build a nice front end to the enterprise-level SQL Server. That way, you have the best of all worlds.

Understanding a Database Application

We have already established that a database is a structured container that holds data. We use SQL (Structured Query Language) within the VBA code to retrieve and sort the data we want to work on. You may want to use the stored data to perform calculations and make logical decisions. But before any of this can happen with any degree of efficiency, the application must be structured properly.

Most database applications, even at an enterprise level, have three main components:

▶ User interface
▶ Business logic
▶ Database

This is sometimes called a three-tier system. Each part has a specialized function. At one end, the user has the ability to interact with the database, which is located at the other end of the system. The business logic is the VBA code that decides how the user interacts with the data. Figure 3-1 shows the interaction.

The user interface consists of the input forms. We will be creating them using text fields, buttons, menu options, and dialog boxes. The user interface must be designed well to avoid confusion and to ensure that data is input properly. During design, it is helpful if you get feedback from the people who will be working with the system.

On the other end of the system is the *database engine*—called the Jet engine in Access. This is the part of Access that does the work. If you are using SQL Server, it is called the SQL Server engine. As I have already stated, Access is compatible with both the Jet and SQL Server engines. You would use the latter in large enterprise applications.

Connecting the user interface and database engine is the business logic. This is where VBA comes into play. This part of the application decides how the

Figure 3-1   *Block diagram of a three-tier system*

database engine will be accessed and what procedures will be followed in handling the data.

Now for the bad news! In addition to learning VBA, you are going to need to look at two other languages: ADO and SQL. VBA, on its own, has nothing to do with Access or its Jet engine. It has no capability of looking at, or manipulating, data. It just serves as a vehicle to a library of programs that can connect with the data. This library is known as ADO (ActiveX Data Objects).

ADO was introduced with Access 2000 as a library of programs capable of connecting with a data source. It is meant to replace an older library called DAO (Data Access Object). As a matter of fact, by the end of 2005, Microsoft has indicated that it will stop supporting DAO. As of this writing, ADO is evolving into ADO.NET. We will be discussing ADO in greater detail in Chapter 15. However, since it is being phased out, we will not be treating DAO in this book.

VBA can perform the basic programming operations of executing a sequence of commands, using loops to execute a task for a certain number of times, and making decisions with If...Else structures. However, ADO has no such capability. Because of that, the two languages work together, with ADO riding the programming structures of VBA.

If all of that does not seem like enough, don't forget the third player, SQL. Please do not get this confused with SQL Server, which is a database engine. SQL is an easy-to-use language that is used to ask the database questions or queries.

In the course of this book, we will first be learning VBA, then SQL, then ADO. You will need all three skills to program in Access, and together, they make up the business logic component.

But the main purpose of this chapter is to see what we can do *before* we need to call in the programming.

Working Without VBA

Throughout this book, we will be working on a simple database called TheCornerBookstore. You can download it from www.osborne.com. I purposely kept it very simple so that the concepts would be easy to understand. In addition, we will be building on it as we go along.

At this stage, the little database does only three things:

▶ Keeps track of inventory

▶ Keeps track of customers

▶ Keeps track of customers' purchases

Of course, you don't particularly need a lot of programming code to accomplish that. However, we will be doing some development to increase its capabilities.

First let's look at our three tables. Figure 3-2 shows the structure of tblCustomer. Here the entity is the customer, and the attributes are listed in the table. We gave the customer a number for a unique identity and marked that identity by making that field a *key field*.

Not all tables have to have a key field (sometimes called a *primary key*), but it is a good idea to assign one. By doing that, you give the field three characteristics:

▶ The value in the field cannot be duplicated.

▶ The field must contain a value in order to save the record.

▶ The table will be sorted on that field.

Figures 3-3 and 3-4 show the structure of the Inventory table and Purchases table.

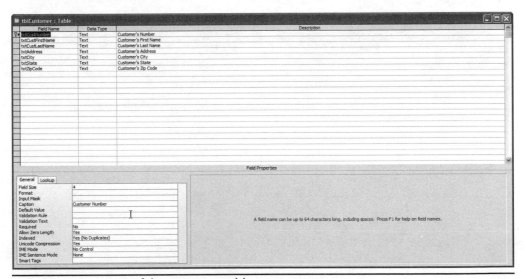

Figure 3-2   *Structure of the Customer table*

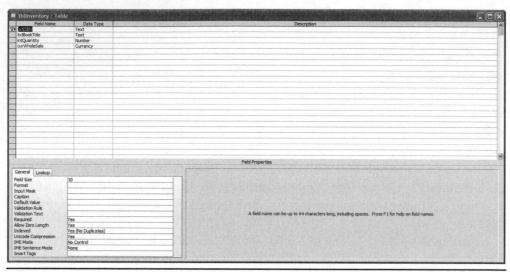

Figure 3-3 *Structure of the Inventory table*

Relationships

As you learned in Chapter 2, there are three basic types of relationships in a database: one-to-one, one-to-many, and many-to-many. We are going to dive into them with a bit more detail.

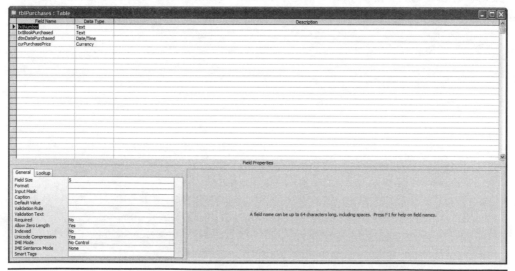

Figure 3-4 *Structure of the Purchases table*

One-to-One

In a one-to-one relationship, an entity of one type can have only one entity relationship with another type. As an example, suppose that to facilitate your mail-order customers, you have a table containing their customer number, credit card number, and expiration date. Obviously, multiple customers would not hold the same credit card number. (A customer could have multiple credit cards, but, for our purposes, we will assume they use one credit card to pay for their books.) Since one instance of CUSTOMER holds only one instance of CREDIT CARD, this is a one-to-one relationship.

If you were to set this up in Access's relationship tool, you would see a 1 on each end of the line.

One-to-Many

The relationship for the vast majority of situations is one-to-many. A customer will make multiple purchases. In this case, one instance of entity CUSTOMER will have multiple relations with multiple instances of entity PURCHASES.

When you have this sort of relationship, you will see a 1 on the one side, and an infinity mark on the multiple side.

Many-to-Many

The many-to-many relationship is very rare. We won't be using it in our little database. However, an instance of entity CUSTOMER can purchase multiple instances of entity BOOK; and entity BOOK can be purchased by multiple instances of entity CUSTOMER.

Many database designers feel that this should be avoided as much as possible because it confuses the role of keys too much. As an example, the primary key in tblCustomer would have to be included in tblBook, and the primary key in tblBook would have to be included in tblCustomer. It is tough to decide what is fully included where.

To overcome this problem, many designers use a *junction table*. This table handles the many side of the one-to-many relationship of each table. Adding this table has the potential of reducing a lot of complexity.

In our case, the junction table could handle the multiple books purchased by a customer, and the multiple customers who bought a book. Neither would be a primary key in the new table.

Using Access's ability to easily define relationships, you won't need to design programming to accomplish this.

Events

Most programming environments are *event-driven systems*. You roll the mouse pointer over a button and click the left mouse button. The clicking of the mouse button is an event. Another block of programming code listens for the event. We call this block the *event listener*. The event listener then sends a message to the block of code that is supposed to work when the event happens. This block is called the *event handler*.

The mouse click may not be the only event. As you will see shortly, things like opening a form, closing a form, selecting an item from a list, and so on can all be events.

Microsoft Windows already has the code to handle routine events built right into it. Because VBA and Access are so closely tied to the Windows environment, a lot of routine functions will be handled without your writing a drop of programming code. All you need to do is tell Access what action you want to occur.

Once you assign the action, Access writes an *event procedure*. This is a small block of VBA code that is written for you. Let's give it a try.

Create a Macro

Open the Forms category in the Database window for TheCornerBookstore. Open the frmCustomer form. It should look like Figure 3-5.

Try clicking the buttons. You will notice that they don't do anything right now. That is because we have not selected an event listener or an event handler. Let's take a look at the steps to do this.

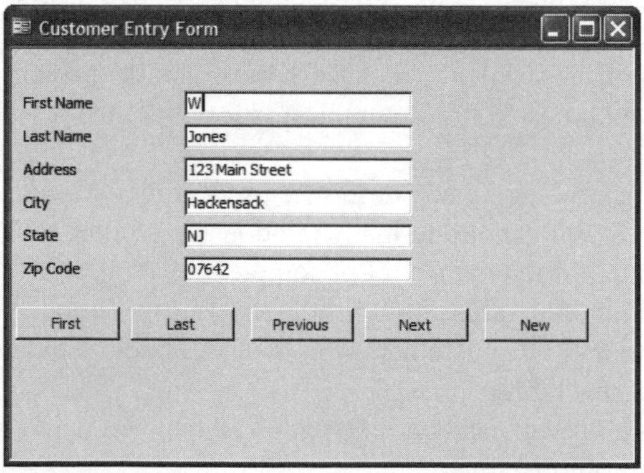

Figure 3-5   *Customer entry form*

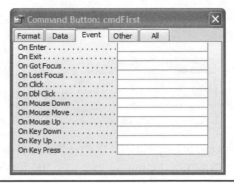

Figure 3-6   *Events for the First button*

Right-click on the First button and select Properties. Once you are in the dialog window, select Events. You should see something like Figure 3-6.

Notice that there are 12 potential events for just one button. They also all begin with the word "On." The most common is the On Click item. Click inside that field and select the button, located on the right, with the ellipses inside it. When you do, you will be asked to choose your builder, as shown in Figure 3-7.

The Expression Builder allows you to set up expressions that perform mathematical operations, compare values in other fields, and employ some limited decision-making capability.

The Code Builder takes you into the VBA Editor. We will talk more about that beginning in Chapter 5.

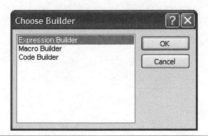

Figure 3-7   *The Choose Builder dialog box*

Select the Macro Builder. You will see something like this, prompting you to give the macro a name:

After clicking OK you are brought to the dialog box shown in Figure 3-8. (Note that, for clarity, Figure 3-8 shows the dialog box with the fields filled in.) Notice that this window is divided into two distinct areas, the Action area at the top and the Action Arguments area at the bottom.

In this example, GoToRecord is selected as the action. Then, for the argument, we selected First as the record we want to go to.

All you need to do now is click on the save icon and close this dialog box. That's it! Your macro is finished.

As a little exercise, if you are sitting at a computer, why don't you follow the same procedure for the other command buttons? The only thing that will change will be the argument or record you will be choosing. The arguments will be Last, Previous, Next, and New. Not one drop of code was written. You can test it now.

There is one thing worth noting here. If you once again select Properties, and go to the All tab, you will notice that the button is named cmdFirst, as shown in Figure 3-9.

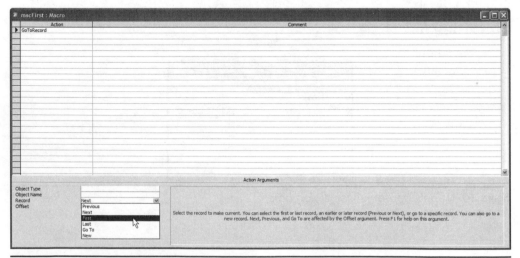

Figure 3-8   *The Macro Builder dialog box*

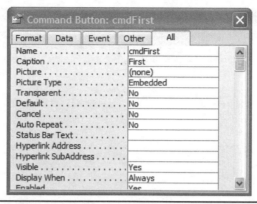

Figure 3-9 *The name field in the properties box*

That was named for you in this downloaded database. However, if you were doing the developing, you would need to name it yourself. If you are going to do VBA programming, you must give each object in your application a unique name. If you don't, VBA won't know what you are talking about. For instance, let's say you wanted to attach an action to a button. VBA would ask you what button you are talking about.

Macros are very limited in what they can do for you. You can't incorporate them directly into a standard VBA programming environment, but you can convert them into VBA code.

Converting Macros into VBA Code

Let's convert our button macros into VBA code. Start by opening the frmCustomer form in Design View and selecting Tools | Macro | Convert Form's Macros to Visual Basic. You will be prompted as to whether you want to add error-handling capabilities and comments:

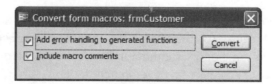

We will be discussing these options as we get more into VBA code. For the time being, just select Convert. You should be prompted when the conversion is finished. Just click OK, and then select Tools | Macro | VBA Editor. You should see a window similar to the one in Figure 3-10.

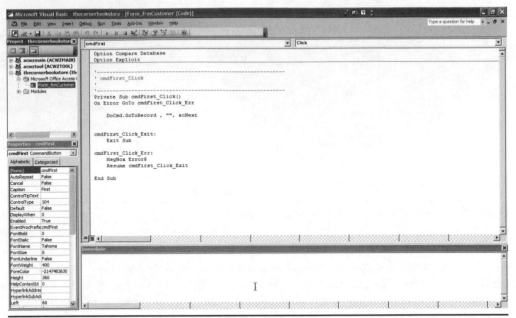

Figure 3-10   *VBA Editor with the converted macros*

You should see the converted code. Without getting into detail yet, you will see a VBA sub procedure, which begins with:

```
Private Sub cmdFirst_Click()
```

This means that it is a VBA sub procedure, which will handle a Click event for the cmdFirst button.

Within this sub procedure, you should see the following line of code:

```
DoCmd.GoToRecord , "", acNext
```

This is essentially the code produced by the macro that tells VBA to instruct the form to go to the first record. (Remember, VBA cannot access records directly.)

While we generated some code, we did not do any coding on our own. Again, you can see the power of Access as a development tool.

Naming Conventions

VBA is *not* a case-sensitive language. However, in the real world, it is going to need to interact with case-sensitive languages. For that reason, naming standards have been adopted by the programming community to minimize the possible problems with the interaction. They are easy to remember:

▶ Everything in lowercase

▶ Midword capitalization

▶ No spaces

In programming terms, any name you assign to something (such as objects, variables, and so on) is called an *identifier*. Let's say you want to use My Address Book as an identifier. Using the programming conventions, you would spell it like this: myAddressBook.

To help identify the type of object something is, you begin the object name with a three-letter prefix. Table 3-1 lists the prefixes used for Access objects.

As an example, suppose you want to make myAddressBook a table. The naming convention would be tblMyAddressBook.

We will be working with these conventions all through the book.

Object	Prefix
Container	con
Document	doc
Field	fld
Form	frm
Group	grp
Index	idx
Macro	mac
Module	mod
Page	pag
Property	pty
Query	qry
Report	rpt
Table	tbl
User	usr

Table 3-1   *Object-Identifying Prefixes*

Predefined Templates

You may be surprised to discover that, in many cases, your database needs will not be as unique as you think. Or maybe parts of your database are common and other parts are unique. Why reinvent the wheel if you don't have to?

Beginning with Access 2003, there are database templates available. If you select File | New, you will see the following pane open on the right side of the window:

Select Templates on Office Online. Your browser will open to the web page shown in Figure 3-11. Here you can select a number of templates for various Office

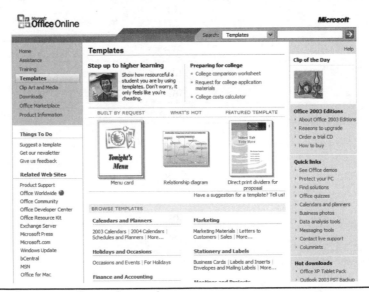

Figure 3-11   *The Microsoft template web page*

applications, including Access. Many times, you may want to use the template as a starting point and then customize from there.

There is one other tool we should discuss to help you set up your application without doing a lot of programming—Switchboard Manager.

Switchboard Manager

Up to this point we have talked about forms interacting with our data. However, do you want your end users to go into the code to run it? I would suspect not.

You can easily build a form to serve as the "front end" of this system. This will contain a menu to show users their options. For this example, I am going to keep it simple and just put one item on it. After seeing how it is done, you should be able to easily add more items as they are needed.

Go to the Database window and select Tools | Database Utility | Switchboard Manager. If this is your first time using the manager, you may get a prompt asking if you want Access to create a default form for you. If you get that, just go ahead and click OK.

Once you have the manager open, it should look something like Figure 3-12.

The default form can be a bit quirky to work with sometimes. For that reason, I like to create one from scratch by clicking New.

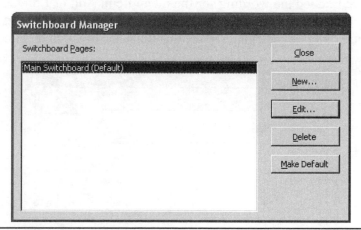

Figure 3-12   *Switchboard Manager dialog box*

Once you select New, you will be prompted to give the form a name. This name will appear as the page title also. For that reason I like to lay it out exactly as I want it to look, for example:

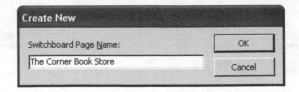

Once you select OK, the name will appear in the Switchboard Manager window. You should then click on it and select Edit. This brings you to the Edit Switchboard Page dialog box that will permit you to add or edit the menu items you want. It should look like Figure 3-13.

To add a new menu item, just click on New. Here is an example of the filled-out Edit Switchboard Item dialog box.

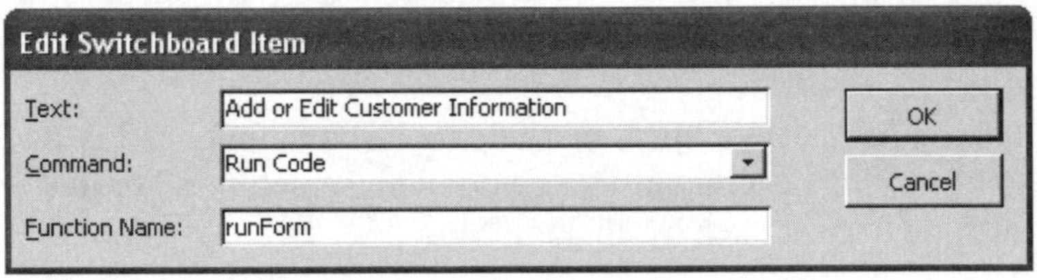

In this case I added the wording for the menu item: Add or Edit Customer Information. For the Command, I selected Run Code. Finally, I specified that I want to run the runForm procedure. (Note that the name of the field, Function Name,

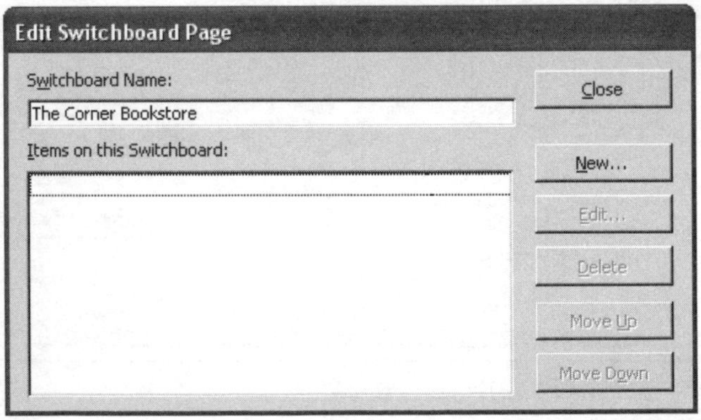

Figure 3-13   *Edit Switchboard Page*

is unfortunate; it implies, falsely, that you can only run functions.) I could have specified any arguments I wanted passed to the procedure also. We will talk about the implications of that in a few moments. However, for now, click OK.

You should now be back on the Edit Switchboard Page dialog box. Just select Close from there.

I find it is a little easier to work if you make your front-end form the default one. You can do this by clicking on it—in this case The Corner Bookstore—and then clicking the Make Default button. You should now see the word "Default" next to The Corner Bookstore.

If you switch to Forms in the Database window, you should have a form listed called Switchboard, as shown in Figure 3-14. If you open it, it should look something like Figure 3-15.

Go ahead and click on its only item, and the runForm procedure will run to open frmCustomer.

Of course, you can edit this form using the same methods you would use with any other form. You can change colors, add graphics, change fonts, and so on.

In many design situations, I create separate menu items for browsing and editing records. Then, when I build the procedure call from the menu, as we just did, I build a program to put in a parameter that the procedure can accept, such as runForm 1, or runForm 2. Next, in the procedure code, I build a decision structure that will turn the CursorType and CursorLocation objects on and off as needed. That way, a single form can handle multiple duties.

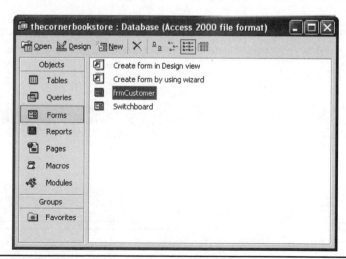

Figure 3-14   *Your Switchboard form in the Database window*

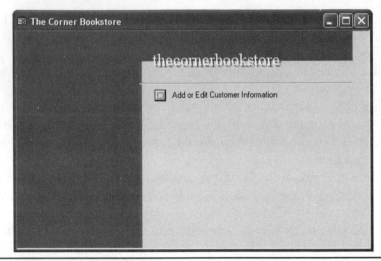

Figure 3-15   *The new Switchboard form*

I find that it is easiest to add and delete items from the Switchboard form by using the manager as we have done. However, interestingly, if you look at the list of tables, Access created a new table called Switchboard that handles all the functioning of the board. If you open it, it should look something like Figure 3-16.

This form shows that we have two switchboards, with the one we created as number 2 set as the default. It also shows that we have one item, and the argument is runForm.

You can take Switchboard one step further by forcing it to open as soon as the database opens. To set this, go to Tools | Startup. Figure 3-17 shows the dialog box filled out.

SwitchboardID	ItemNumber	ItemText	Command	Argument
1	0	Main Switchboard		
2	0	The Corner Bookstore	0	Default
2	1	Add or Edit Customer Information	8	runForm
	0			

Record: 3 of 3

Figure 3-16   *Switchboard form table*

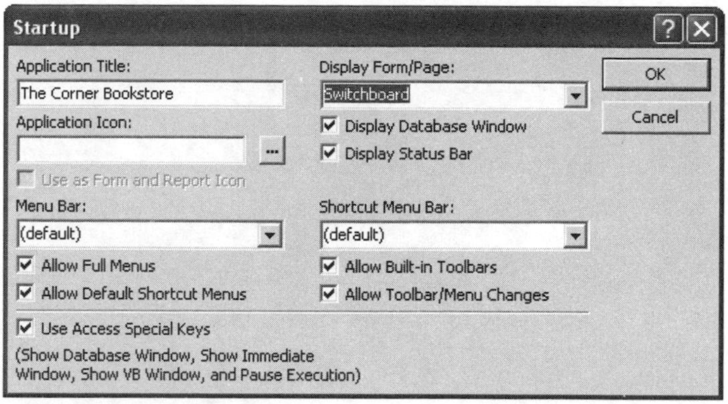

Figure 3-17   *The Startup dialog box*

This is, in some ways, the first step to security. You can give your application a title and set the Switchboard, or any other form you want, to open as soon as the database opens.

In addition, you can prevent the Database window from opening. This will add greatly to security in that it prevents end users from getting behind the scenes.

Interestingly, you can also add an icon for the desktop. That way, there is no reason for the end user to go directly into Access.

Summary

Do you need programming? It depends on what you are doing. In this chapter, we examined how to do a lot of things without the use of programming. We got a small taste of building a database application. We examined the database architecture and where VBA fits in with all the other components.

In addition, you got your first look at some simple VBA coding by building a simple macro and converting it to VBA code. While discussing that code, you learned about the role of events. You saw how naming conventions can assist in the consistency of your code.

Finally, we examined two additional time-saving tools—prebuilt templates and Switchboard Manager.

The next chapter covers how to customize Access's toolbars and menus; again, all without programming.

Customizing the Access Environment

As stated in Chapter 3, it is a good idea to do as much as possible in Microsoft Access without programming. This will greatly reduce potential problems and bugs. In Chapter 3, we examined a few techniques that will help you achieve that end.

In this chapter, we are going to focus on some customization techniques that you can use in Access. We will look at the command bars and how to manipulate and customize them, and I'll show you how to create customized ones. We will be doing many of the same things to shortcut menus: building and manipulating these menus. Most importantly, you will learn a lot of the terminology that will be necessary for you to use VBA to accomplish the same tasks.

Interacting with Access

As a user, you interact with most programs through the use of menus and toolbars. Both menu bars and toolbars come under the broad category of *command bars*. Figure 4-1 shows a typical Access menu.

Each item on the menu, such as Spelling, Relationships, and so on, is a *menu command*. When necessary, the menu command will branch into a *submenu*. These are indicated by the right-pointing arrows next to some menu commands.

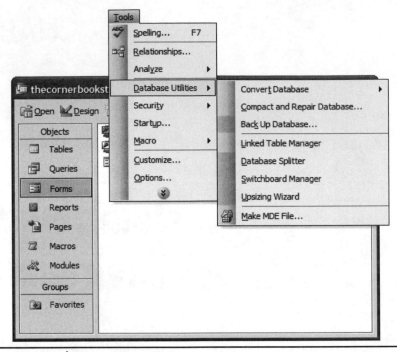

Figure 4-1 *A typical Access menu*

In some cases, Microsoft Office products have *shortcut menus* that can be activated when you right-click over a certain part of the screen. These shortcut menus are context sensitive depending on what task is going on and where you right-click on the screen.

Another important command bar is the toolbar. Toolbars are icon representations of many of the menu commands. For example, the toolbar that opens when you start the program is called the Database toolbar. This has icon representations of the commands File | New, File | Open, File | Save, and so on. You can see the other toolbars by selecting View | Toolbars.

The toolbars that are available on the menu will vary depending on what tasks you are performing. If you are in the Database window, the Database toolbar will be available, as shown here.

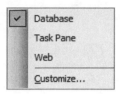

However, in a form, you will have access to the Form View toolbar and the Formatting (Form/Report) toolbar, as shown here.

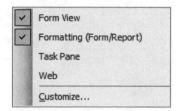

You can use the View | Toolbars menu to switch toolbars on and off. It is worth spending some time examining the toolbars that are available for each task that you do.

Most of the time, you leave the command bars *docked*. This means they are in a fixed position on the screen (usually along the top). On the left side of the toolbar, you usually have a *move handle* to reposition the toolbar wherever it is needed.

The following illustration shows a command bar moved with the mouse pointer over the move handle. The command bar can be easily redocked by double-clicking on its title bar. Using these techniques, you can place the command bars where you want them on the screen.

Two toolbars are always available, no matter what task you are performing. One is the the Task pane, shown here.

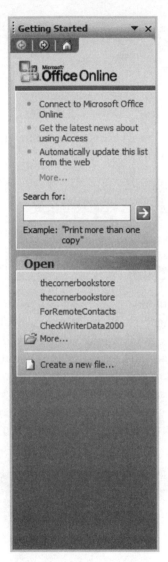

The other is the Web toolbar, shown here.

Customizing a Command Bar

You can see a complete list of all the toolbars available by selecting View | Toolbars | Customize, as seen in Figure 4-2.

Here you can customize a toolbar, delete a customized toolbar, or reset an existing toolbar to its default settings. The toolbars with a check to the left are being displayed at the moment.

While you are in the Customize dialog box, you can select a button on a displayed toolbar and remove it from the toolbar by simply dragging it off. If you want to put a new button on the toolbar, you first select the Commands tab in the Customize dialog box, as shown in Figure 4-3.

Select the general type of command button you want in the Categories list on the left, and then drag the specific command button from the list on the right onto the toolbar. If there is no corresponding icon, the command bar will just hold the text.

You may have noticed that in most of the Office programs, the menus come up in a partial format. Microsoft is taking a guess as to what you want to do. As your mouse has the menu open, it expands after a few seconds to show all the menu options.

Some people do not like that option. If you want to shut it off, go to the Options tab in the Customize dialog box and check the Always Show Full Menus option, as shown in Figure 4-4.

You can also customize a toolbar by selecting the down arrow located at the right end of the bar. If you're working with the Database toolbar, for example, you can

Figure 4-2   *You can customize your toolbars.*

Figure 4-3   *Adding a button to a toolbar*

click the arrow and then select Add or Remove Buttons | Database. You should see the button list shown in Figure 4-5.

To change the properties of the buttons themselves, you must use the Customize dialog box. You can change the icon, colors, name, and many other properties. As an

Figure 4-4   *Customizing your options*

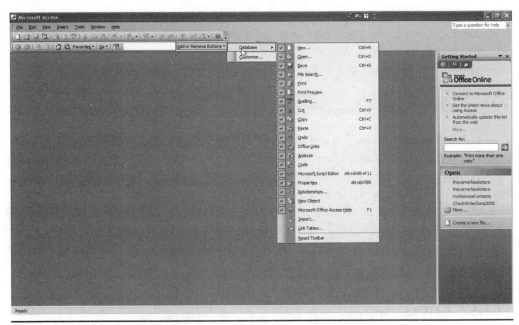

Figure 4-5 *Add or Remove Buttons*

interesting example, with the Customize box open, right-click on the Paste icon on the Database toolbar. You should see the following menu:

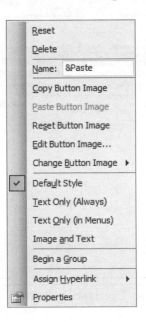

Notice that you can change the name associated with a button. For instance, &Paste means the name Paste with the P underscored. (Note that the underscore appears anywhere there is the "&" symbol.)

If you select the Text Only (Always) option, the icon will appear as text:

Go ahead and turn it back to an icon by selecting the Default Style option.

You can also set the button image and colors. It is worth your time to explore some of the options available. Of particular interest is the Assign Hyperlink option, which opens the dialog box shown in Figure 4-6. Here you can assign the button a link to a file, web page, or even an email address. This will come in handy when you build a customized toolbar.

Creating a Customized Toolbar

To create a new toolbar, with the Customize dialog box open and the Toolbars tab selected, select New. Here you can name your new toolbar:

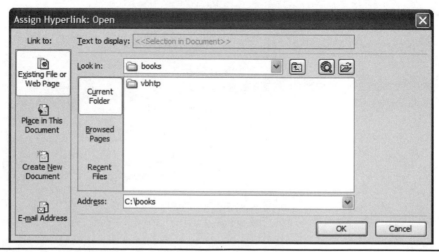

Figure 4-6   *The Assign Hyperlink: Open dialog box*

Once you select OK, you get an empty toolbar. You can then switch to the Commands tab and drag the buttons that you want onto the bar. Once that is done, you can use all of the options discussed throughout this chapter to do any sort of customization you want.

You can delete the customized toolbar by selecting it in the Customize dialog box and selecting the Delete button on the right side of the box.

Customizing Shortcut Menus

Changing shortcut menus can be a little tricky at first. Let's begin by opening the Customize dialog box again and using the Toolbars tab to activate the Shortcut Menus command bar. Doing this will show all the available shortcut menus. Assuming you are in the Database window, you should see the shortcut menus shown here.

If you click on one of the menus, you will see the command menus that are available. For instance, if you click on Query, you will see the options shown in Figure 4-7.

Here you can add or delete items by clicking and dragging the command in question in much the same way as you clicked and dragged buttons off the toolbar. If there is

Figure 4-7   *Command options for the Query shortcut*

another level of submenu, you can expand that and, if necessary, add or delete commands also.

Creating Menus

You can create a new menu and then add submenus to it by using the Customize dialog box. Start by creating a new toolbar as we did above. Just give it a name and it should appear on your screen. In the Customize dialog box, select the Commands tab and then the New Menu category. It should look like Figure 4-8.

Drag the new menu item to the customized toolbar you just created. Right-click on it and change the Name property to (for purposes of illustration here) &File. The menu item should now show the word File with an underscore under the F.

If you click on the new File menu item, it should create a blank box below it as shown here.

Drag the Open command (found in the File category) into the new box. You can now select another command, say the New command (also found in the File category), and drop that below the Open command you just placed.

Let's assume we want to add a new submenu to our little menu now. In the Customize dialog box, select the New Menu category again, and drop it right below the New command you just put in. As before, you can change the text of the item. In this case, let's call it My Sub.

You can select the command that you want (for example, the Cut command in the Edit category) and drop it over the right-pointing arrow so that it now looks like this:

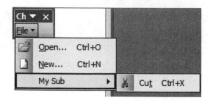

Figure 4-8   *Creating menus and submenus*

Likewise, you can then add menu commands under the new submenu item.

This makes the whole process very easy to work with. You simply drag and drop additional menu items as you need them.

Attaching Code to a Custom Menu Item

We have yet to write any VBA code. However, once we start, we will probably want to have end users access the code via menus and buttons in the application. Up to this point, all we have done is create a few simple macros. We are going to put one of the macros we created on our little menu bar and then, in Chapter 13, use exactly the same technique to attach VBA code to a command bar.

For our example, let's add a New Menu item as we just did in the previous steps. Rename this new menu item My Macros. The custom menu should look like this:

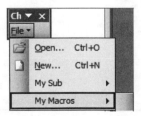

If you now select the All Macros category in the Customize dialog box, you should see a list of any macros you have created to this point. For the sake of simplicity, Figure 4-9 just shows the macFirst macro.

You simply drag the macro's icon and place it as a submenu item as you did with the previous menu item.

Let's take a look at a menu feature we have not had a chance to look at yet by right-clicking on the new macro menu command we just put on the menu bar. A menu should come up, and when you select Properties, you should see the same dialog box shown in Figure 4-10.

Here you can exercise some fine control over your menus as follows:

▶ The Caption allows you to control the menu's text. As you did earlier, you can place an & before any letter you want to contain the underscore.

▶ In the Shortcut Text, you can specify what key combination will be used to trigger this menu item. You must be careful not to use one already used elsewhere. For instance, Ctrl + C is the combination for the Copy command.

▶ The ScreenTip is the helping text that pops up when the mouse rolls over the menu item.

▶ On Action is the important option. This is where you select the name of the macro or VBA code you want associated with the menu command. You can

Figure 4-9   *The All Macros category*

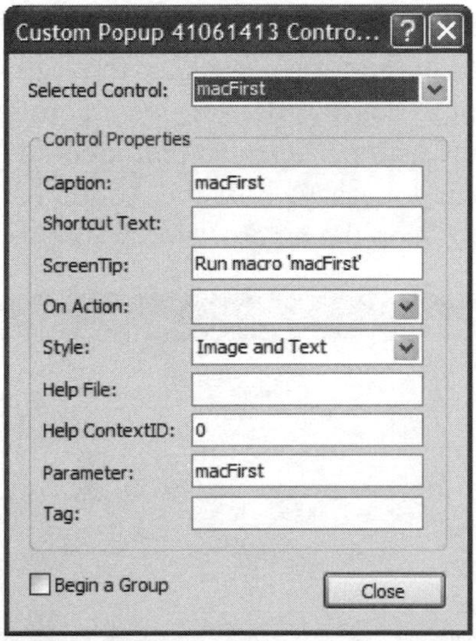

Figure 4-10   *Menu Control Properties dialog box*

also enter simple function procedures into the field, such as iif, by beginning them with an = sign (similar to entering functions in Microsoft Excel).

▶ The Style option allows you to select either text, buttons, or a combination of both in your menu display.

▶ The next two option items, Help File and Help ContextID, allow you to associate a help file with this menu item. The first identifies the help file to open when you select the What's This? button. The second identifies the place in the file that contains help on this item.

▶ The Parameter button allows you to send any parameters, should it be necessary, to the VBA code or macro named in the On Action box.

▶ Tag allows you to give the menu command a unique name so that, if you need to, you can refer to it in the VBA code.

Note that if you now close the Customize dialog box and go to run this last macro, you will probably end up with the error message shown here.

This macro is associated with a form that we worked on earlier (its purpose is to take us to the first record in the form). Because the form is not open, the macro simply does not know what to do. In order for this macro to function properly, you would need to have the frmCustomer open so that it could go to the first record.

If you select OK in the first message box, the Action Failed message box, shown next, opens, allowing you to stop the macro.

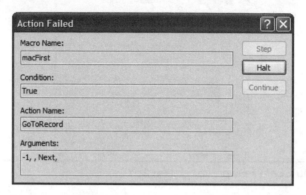

Select Halt to shut down the macro.

In order for this macro to function properly, we would need to have the frmCustomer open so that it could go to the first record.

Summary

In this chapter, you discovered how to create and edit customized toolbars and menus. You even learned to attach a macro (and potentially VBA code) to a menu item. These will be useful tools when creating a VBA project. They will allow the end user easier interaction with your VBA code.

This chapter completes this part of the book. Now that you understand the importance of using the built-in features of Access, we can turn to the job at hand: creating VBA code. Part II is going to serve as an introduction to VBA. Once you understand these basics, we will then examine how to use VBA to create better user interaction by returning to the topics of Part I within a VBA context.

PART II

Understanding the Visual Basic for Applications Environment

Introducing the VBA
Programming Environment

In Part I we examined how not to program. We took a look at Access's built-in tools that save us from the need to program. For example, in Chapter 4, we edited existing command bars and created customized ones.

Eventually, however, we reach a limit to what Access can do on its own. At that point, we need to call in VBA in order to give Access additional instructions.

In this chapter, we begin with a discussion of the history of VBA. From there we will have an overview of the components of VBA, including objects, procedures, attributes, and modules. We will be discussing a lot of the terminology associated with these components.

The chapter ends with an introduction to the place where you will be doing your VBA programming: the VBA Editor.

Introduction to VBA

Visual Basic for Applications is a programming language that contains elements of object-oriented programming (OOP). Despite other writings to the contrary, it is not a full-fledged OOP environment. While it is beyond the scope of this book to get into all the details of an OOP environment, VBA is lacking in several important components.

VBA is a language that is closely tied to the Microsoft Windows environment and the programming backbone of the Microsoft Office environment. Like many other programming languages, it is event driven (the concept of an event was introduced in Chapter 3). In other words, it is waiting for something to happen. The event could be a mouse click, a keypress, a form opening, and so on. When an event happens, VBA calls upon Windows' ability to handle it. As we will be seeing, this has the potential of saving the programmer a lot of work.

History of VBA

Visual Basic, which is the basis for VBA, evolved from a language called BASIC, which stands for Beginner's All-Purpose Symbolic Instruction Code. In many ways, it was an answer to FORTRAN and COBOL, which were very difficult to use and required a great deal of training.

Many members of the academic community felt that something simpler was needed for students to get a grip on programming. Also, BASIC could be run on a computer without huge resources.

All this happened in the 1960s. If we fast-forward to 1982, we see the release of the personal computer (PC) by IBM. The operating system behind this new technology was DOS (Disk Operating System). BASIC was shipped as part of it (actually, it was a version called GW-BASIC). It was not overly popular and had limited use.

Several years later, Microsoft elevated the language with the release of Microsoft Visual Basic. This allowed developers to program visually by using a lot of drag-and-drop techniques as well as selecting options from a property sheet.

A short time later, Microsoft introduced a special version of Visual Basic called VBA (Visual Basic for Applications). This version had a lot of tools that allowed it to work in the Microsoft Office environment. However, it did not have a lot of the GUI tools and controls found in the full version of Visual Basic.

The VBA Model

Before you can start to program, you must understand the VBA model. In order to do that, you need to learn the hierarchy of structures. As you progress through the book, you will be drilling down to greater detail. However, we'll start with an overview so you can get a better picture of how the pieces fit together. We begin with an overview of modules.

Modules

The module is the place where VBA code is written and stored. You can think of modules as drawers in a filing cabinet. You can keep related sections of code in separate modules, which facilitates the ability to organize your code efficiently.

Modules are divided into several types:

▶   The form and report modules hold code associated with a particular report or form. As a matter of fact, if that form or report is moved to another database, the module holding the code usually moves with it.

▶   The standard module holds code that has no association with a particular database object. Most of your coding will be in a standard module.

Procedures

The code within the module is divided into blocks called *procedures*. Most procedures should only perform one specialized job. Procedures fall into two categories: sub procedures and functions.

Sub Procedures

A sub procedure just carries out a job without returning a value to whomever called it. Most procedures you write will fall into this category. An example of what a sub procedure looks like is as follows:

```
Sub Concat()
    Dim strFirstname As String
    Dim strLastName As String
    Dim strFullName As String

    strFirstname = "John"
    strLastName = "Smith"

    strFullName = strFirstname & " " & strLastName
    Debug.Print strFullName
End Sub
```

Don't worry about all the particulars of this sub procedure right now. The procedure opens with the line:

```
Sub Concat()
```

This defines the name of the sub procedure. Of course, you can call it whatever you want, but this is how a sub procedure opens.

The sub procedure ends with the line:

```
End Sub
```

All the code between these two lines is called the sub procedure implementation code.

NOTE

Programmers commonly refer to the sub procedure as a "sub."

Functions

A *function* returns a value to whomever called it. We can recast the previous sub into a function as follows:

```
Function concat() As String
    Dim strFirstname As String
    Dim strLastName As String
    Dim strFullName As String

    strFirstname = "John"
    strLastName = "Smith"

    strFullName = strFirstname & " " & strLastName
    concat = strFullName
End Function
```

Notice that this code opens with the line:

```
Function concat() As String
```

This states that the code is a function, and the value it will be returning is a string. The closing line is

```
End Function
```

Again, don't be concerned about what is going on in between yet.

The Concept of Objects

Even someone who had only a peripheral relationship with computers would probably hear one word over and over again—that word is "objects." There are many definitions for "object." In my definition, I like to say that an object is a prebuilt component that can be plugged into an existing application.

Whenever I teach OOP courses, I always use the analogy of a small object that can format numbers to the currency format. Now, for example, let's assume that it takes 100 lines of code for that object to achieve the currency format. Wouldn't it be time consuming to have to reenter the 100 lines of code each time you want to format a number to currency? However, you can just plug in the object, feed the number into one end, and get the reformatted number out the other end. This makes the whole job easier because you don't need to program and debug.

Access is built on the concept of objects. As discussed in Chapter 1, components like tables, reports, and forms are all called objects in Access. As a matter of fact, these objects are part of a larger hierarchy that includes the *Application object*. The objects associated with your application are part of the *CurrentProject object*. That is why, when using VBA, you might call a report as follows:

```
Application.CurrentProject.Report("myReport")
```

You might want to read this from right to left. You are calling the report object "myReport." That report object is part of the CurrentProject object which, in turn, is part of the Application object. In this light, it is easy to see the hierarchy. You use a dot (period) to separate members of the hierarchy.

All objects can have two basic components: attributes and methods. The *attributes* of an object are, essentially, its fields. For instance, the object may have an attribute to hold the last name and another to hold the first name. If the value of any of those attributes changes (such as a different last name), we say the *state* of the object has changed.

 NOTE

As we progress through the book, the words attribute and properties are interchangeable.

Using the example of an Access form object, some of the attributes might be the sort order, the background color of the form, or the tab stop order. As you will see, VBA has code to set an object's attributes on-the-fly.

The *methods* are the actions the object can perform. For example, if you had an object called BankAccount, two possible methods, or behaviors, could be debit and credit.

Again using the form object as an example, some of the methods might be to move to a record, save a record, delete a record, and filter records.

Many objects contain collections of other objects. As an example, a command bar object will usually have button objects on it. It could also contain combo box objects and pop-up objects.

VBA has the ability to interact with Access to help create and edit objects. As an example:

```
Sub createMenu()
    Dim myBar As CommandBar
    Set myBar = CommandBars.Add("My Command Bar")
End Sub
```

NOTE

This code may not run in your version of Access without some setup that we have not discussed yet.

In the preceding code, we created a sub procedure to create a command bar object called myBar. It will be listed in the View | Toolbars menu of VBA as My Command Bar. If you were to run this sub, and then go to View | Toolbars in the Database window, you would see something like this:

Let's take a brief look at the three main libraries of objects that we will be working with: ADO, VBA, and Access. For the time being, we will only look at one or two essential objects in each so that we can move forward in this book. Of course, as we progress, you will be learning many more.

ADO Objects

Recall that I defined objects earlier as prebuilt programs that can be plugged in as needed. VBA, by itself, has limited interaction with Access. Remember, VBA is not really part of the Access program. Instead, it is a separate program bundled with the Microsoft Office environment to help extend the capabilities of Office.

In order for VBA to interact with the data, a lot of code is needed to make the connection. This could result in extraordinarily long and complicated programs. To address this issue, versions of Access before Access 2000 used a library of objects called Data Access Objects (DAO) to help VBA make a connection with a database's data. This saved a lot of code writing.

It was decided that DAO did not meet the increasing demands made upon databases, and to address that issue, Access 2000 introduced a new library of objects called ActiveX Data Objects (ADO). We will be discussing this in greater detail in Chapter 15, but since we need to reference it from time to time before then, we'll turn it on now. If you do not have it open already, open the VBA Editor by selecting Tools | Macro | Visual Basic Editor.

Once in it, select Tools | References. You should see the dialog box shown in Figure 5-1.

Scroll down and click on the object libraries as shown in Figure 5-1. If your version of ADO does not go up to version 2.7, as shown in the figure, don't worry about it. Just click on the highest number version that you have. Do the same for the Microsoft Office 11.0 Object Library.

Select OK, and those libraries are now available to VBA to help save a lot of coding. Using the command bar example in the previous section, VBA simply had

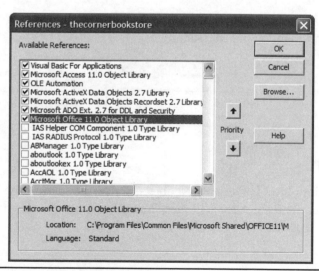

Figure 5-1   *References dialog box*

to say, "create a command bar, call it myBar, and give it the title My Command Bar." The objects in the libraries knew what to do from there.

Don't worry if you don't understand all the details for now. This is just an overview, and we will cover them as we go along.

VBA Objects

So far, we have taken a brief look at ADO, but VBA has a number of objects built into it. As we progress through this book, you will see many of these objects, but again, we are just going to take a cursory look for the time being.

The VBA library contains an object called Interaction. Interaction has two of the most popular methods used: MsgBox and Inputbox. The following code shows a simple example using the MsgBox method.

NOTE

For the time being, I will use the words "method" and "function" interchangeably. As we progress, we will refine our use of these terms.

```
Sub message()
    MsgBox "Welcome to VBA programming!"
End Sub
```

This results in the following Message Box:

Access Objects

Another important object is the DoCmd object. This is not part of the VBA library, but it is connected with the Access library. We will use this object with many of the objects in other libraries. For example:

```
DoCmd.GoToRecord , "", acNext
```

The DoCmd object carries out actions in Access. What the code says is that the DoCmd object has a method called GoToRecord. You distinguish between the object and its method with a dot. The subsequent commas separate the arguments needed for the method to do its job.

The VBA Editor

If you are going to create VBA code, you are going to spend most of your time in the VBA Editor. We will take a quick tour here and then look at what the various tools do in greater detail throughout the book.

If the editor is not open already, select Tools | Macro | Visual Basic Editor. The editor will look something like Figure 5-2. It is divided into distinct windows to help you handle various aspects of your project. The upper-left-hand corner is the Project window. This window helps you maneuver to the various code modules associated with your project. One of the main uses of this window is to find and open the various modules that hold your code.

The VBA Editor is divided into distinct windows to help us handle various aspects of our project.

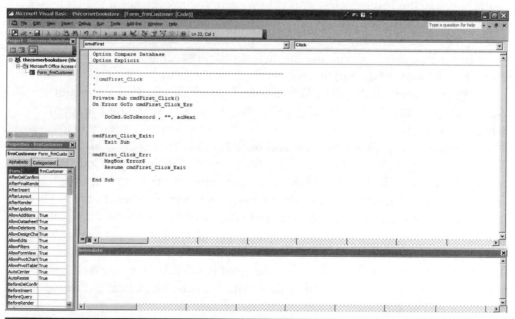

Figure 5-2   *The VBA Editor*

In the upper-left-hand corner is the Project window, as shown in the following illustration.

This window helps us maneuver to the various files associated with our project. One of the main uses of this window is to find out and open the various modules which hold our code.

Right below the Project window is the Properties window, shown in Figure 5-3. In the example, this shows the various properties that can be set for frmCustomer. Setting them in a menu saves a lot of coding. Along the bottom of the VBA Editor is the Immediate window. You use this to test your code. In the course of this book, we will spend a lot of time in this window.

Along the bottom of the VBA Editor is the Immediate Window. We would use this to test our code. In the course of this book, we will be spending a lot of time using this window.

The large center area is where the real work is done. This is the Code window, where you will type your procedures and functions. Right above the Code window are two list boxes. The example shows a form module (we created it in Chapter 3 and have not created any standard modules yet) for the frmCustomer object. The list box on the left displays the objects associated with frmCustomer and is shown in Figure 5-4.

The list box on the right (see Figure 5-5) displays the procedures associated with this form. Here you see the objects we discussed in the previous chapters. Notice that the form's procedures coincide with events, for example, Click, Exit, Enter, KeyPress, and so on.

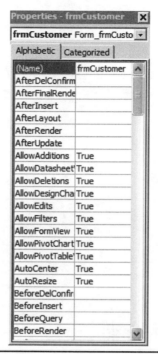

Figure 5-3   *The Properties window*

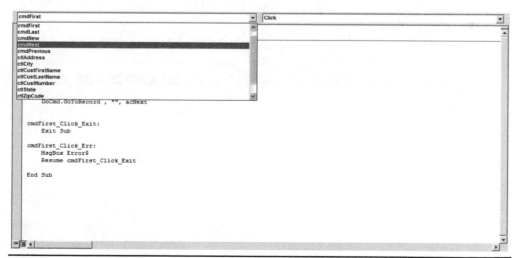

Figure 5-4   *The Objects list box*

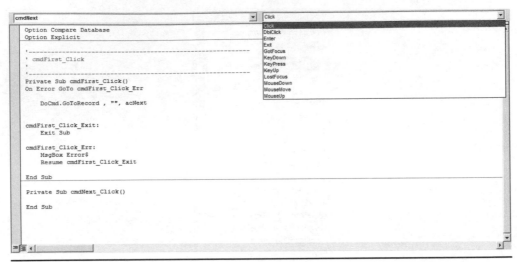

Figure 5-5 *The Procedures list box*

Putting the VBA Editor to Work

Up to this point, the only module in our VBA Editor is a form module that was created when we converted a macro to VBA code in Chapter 3. For the moment, let's imagine that the form module is there with absolutely no code on it, and that you want to create a click procedure for the cmdFirst button. How would you do it? Let's walk through the process.

First, you select the cmdFirst object from the left list box, as shown here.

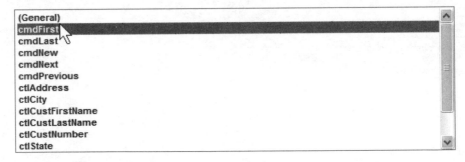

Once you select it, the VBA Editor automatically sets up the sub procedure (remember, it is not returning anything) in the Code window as follows:

```
Private Sub cmdFirst_Click()

End Sub
```

The procedure now has the opening and closing lines. Notice that VBA assumed that you wanted it to be a Click event. This is the *default event* for a command button. You could have selected a different event in the right list box, and the editor would have changed it to whatever event you chose.

All you need to do is add the implementation between the opening and closing lines of the sub. Click between the two lines. As a matter of programming style, I like to indent the code within the sub for clarity. To do this, I press SPACEBAR three times.

Using all lowercase letters (you will see why in a second), type **docmd** and then a period (the dot). Notice that the VBA Editor gives you a list of available methods for the DoCmd object, as shown here.

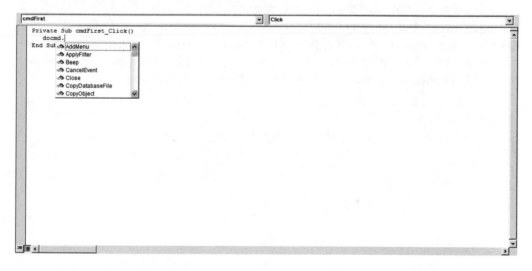

You want the GoToRecord method. You can get to that by pressing G on your keyboard, which should bring you to the GoToControl method. Just click the down arrow until you get to GoToRecord, and then press the SPACEBAR. (Do *not* press ENTER!)

Once you press the SPACEBAR to select GoToRecord, your Code window should look like this:

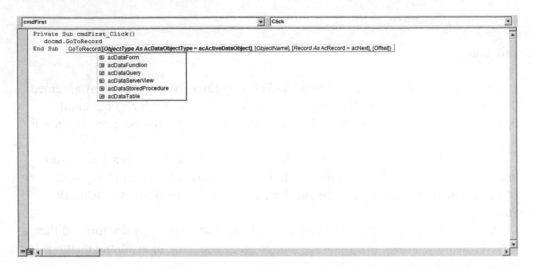

Notice that it is now showing the next argument, ObjectType, as well as a list of possible choices. For the time being, I have to ask you to take me on faith. If I were to explain the meaning of each option at this point, we would get terribly off track.

You don't need an object type at this point. Just press the comma on your keyboard. The bolded option should change from ObjectType to ObjectName:

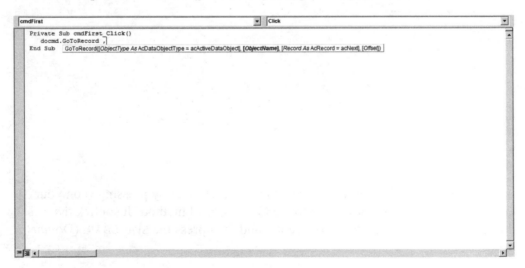

For now, put " " there as an empty name. Once you have put the empty quotes in, press comma again.

You should now have a list of possible values:

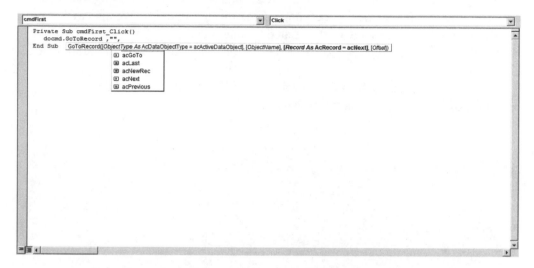

Note that these are not methods. There is a different icon to the left. It is a good idea to become familiar with these icons. Scroll up and select acFirst from the list and press the SPACEBAR.

You are finished building the statement. Using your mouse or arrow key, move off the line you just created. Notice that the docmd changed to DoCmd. Even though VBA is not a case-sensitive language, the VBA Editor examines the line to make sure all the syntax is correct and, if it is, converts the case to programming standards automatically.

Your finished code should look as follows:

```
Private Sub cmdFirst_Click()
   DoCmd.GoToRecord , "", acFirst
End Sub
```

The editor did much of the work for you.

There are a lot more options and features available in the VBA Editor; so many, in fact, that Chapter 7 is devoted to a discussion of the editor. In subsequent chapters you will see additional features as your coding becomes more sophisticated.

Summary

We just got our first small taste of VBA. We spent a lot of time examining the history and structure of VBA, as well as defining some of its terminology. We also took a very brief look at objects and some of the related terminology.

Finally, we took a brief look at the VBA Editor and put it to work in building a simple procedure.

In the next chapter, we turn to the structures of the VBA code and get our first real taste of VBA as a programming language.

Programming Fundamentals Using VBA

In Chapter 5 you learned about the VBA environment by looking at its structure, concepts, and editor. In this chapter, we are going to study the fundamentals of all programming while, at the same time, examine the specific syntax of the VBA language. We are going to review concepts from Chapter 5 and study them in greater detail, beginning with a review of the places where the code is stored and the types of blocks it is stored in. While discussing that, we will visit the subject of variables in greater detail. It is difficult to talk about variables without discussing a special type of variable called an array.

We are also going to look at some of the built-in tools that VBA gives you to make your job easier. We will conclude our discussion by looking at the various types of programming structures and how they are used in a VBA environment.

Programming Fundamentals

As stated in Chapter 5, VBA code is written and stored within modules. Recall that there are two basic types of modules: those associated with forms or reports, and a general module for holding procedures that is applicable to the whole project.

There is one other type, called a *class module*, which contains code associated with an object. We have discussed modules already in the previous chapters and will be referring to them throughout the rest of the book.

Before you can write VBA code, you need to be able to create the module. Since form or report modules are created through their respective forms and reports, we will focus on creating standard modules here.

Creating Standard Modules

There are a couple of different ways of creating a standard module. The easiest way is to use the Modules category of objects right in the Database window, as shown in Figure 6-1. All you need to do is click on New and you are taken to the VBA Editor with a module created, as shown in Figure 6-2.

VBA assigned your new module a temporary name of Module1. You will probably want to give it a more descriptive name. This can be done from the Properties window of the VBA Editor or directly in the Database window.

As an example, in the VBA Editor, highlight the name Module1 in the Properties window, as shown in Figure 6-3, and rename it. You can call it myFirstModule. Once you have changed it in the Properties window, the name is changed in the Project window as well as in the Database window in Access (under the Modules category).

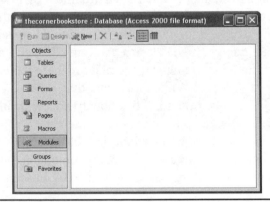

Figure 6-1   *The Modules category selected in the Database window*

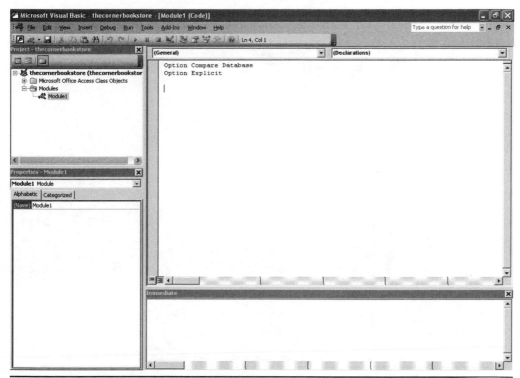

Figure 6-2   *The VBA Editor with a module open*

In addition, you should click on the Save icon in the toolbar. You will be prompted to confirm the name, as shown here:

Now you can confirm that the name has been changed in the Project window (Figure 6-4) and the Database window Figure 6-5).

Figure 6-3   *The Name property*

Figure 6-4   *Project window after renaming the module*

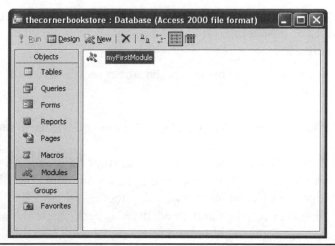

Figure 6-5   *Database window after renaming the module*

NOTE
You can also change the name in the Database window by right-clicking it and selecting the Rename menu command.

Creating Procedures

You will recall from Chapter 5 that most VBA code is contained in blocks called procedures. Further, these procedures are divided into two categories: sub procedures (sometimes called subs) or function procedures. A sub just performs a task but does not return a value, while a function does return a value.

Most of the time, you will see the following two lines of code at the top of the module:

```
Option Compare Database
Option Explicit
```

These are called the *general declarations* of the module. Any code put into this section will affect all the procedures in the module.

The Option Compare line has three possible settings for sorting strings of characters within the code:

▶ **Option Compare Database**   This uses the same sort order as the database itself and is the most common setting.

▶ **Option Compare Binary**   This sorts a string of characters based upon the binary values of the characters. Thus, uppercase letters would be recognized before lowercase.

▶ **Option Compare Text**   This makes the sort case sensitive with regard to the local language.

Throughout this text, we will keep the Option Compare Database setting, which is the default.

The Option Explicit line is, in my opinion, an important one. As you shall see momentarily, that line can keep you from making a lot of coding mistakes by forcing you to formally declare all variables before using them.

If this option does not come on automatically when you create the module, force it to do so by selecting Tools | Options and selecting Require Variable Declaration on the Editor tab, as shown in Figure 6-6.

Think of a procedure as a miniprogram to do one specialized job. For instance, a procedure may be used to add two numbers together. Every time those numbers need to be added, you can just call this prewritten procedure. Without the procedure, you might need to write redundant code every time you needed to do that particular job.

Within the procedure, you declare variables, have loops and If statements, and even call other procedures. Let's build a simple procedure that adds two numbers together. We will discuss each step along the way.

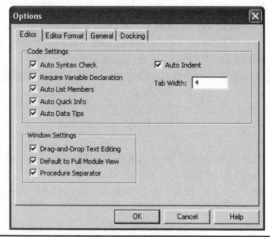

Figure 6-6   *The Require Variable Declaration option*

A procedure is first declared with the following syntax. Of course, the name is anything that you choose it to be.

```
Sub addNumbers()
End Sub
```

Notice that the VBA Editor draws a horizontal line between the general declaration area and the new procedure. This is to help delineate the procedures. It has no bearing on how the procedure works.

When you declare a procedure, it is important that you begin it with the word Sub and complete the declaration with the parenthesis. I say it is important because it is worthwhile to use proper syntax from the beginning. If you don't put the parenthesis in, the VBA Editor will put it in for you as soon as you press ENTER.

Normally you would place any arguments the procedure would be expecting to receive within the parenthesis. Even if no arguments are expected, you need to have the empty parentheses.

As soon as you press ENTER, the VBA Editor adds the End Sub line to close the procedure. All of your code will go between the opening and closing statements.

As we move through this book, I will relate what I feel are good programming habits, or practices. While these are certainly not rules, they are accepted by many programmers and are industry standards.

The first such practice is to name your procedures with a name that reflects its job, for instance, addNumbers. Any other programmers looking at it would easily discern what it does. In addition, even though VBA is not case sensitive, it will sometimes need to interact with programs that are. A common naming convention, as mentioned in Chapter 4, is to use lowercase letters, with the exception of midword capitalization, no spaces, and to begin with a letter rather than a number. In the case of beginning with a letter rather than a number, this is more than just a naming convention; for many programs, including VBA, it is a rule.

The second practice is to indent the code in the procedure. That way, it is easy to spot where the procedure begins and ends. I usually just press the SPACEBAR three times. The VBA Editor will preserve the indenting for subsequent lines.

The third practice is to carefully comment your code. You can easily do that by using the single quote before a line. If you do that, VBA will ignore that line as a comment.

The following example shows the indent and comment:

```
Sub addNumbers()
   'Declare the variables
End Sub
```

Notice the color the VBA Editor uses to indicate the comment. Understanding the color coding in the VBA Editor can help you track what is going on with the code. As an example, code colored red indicates a syntax error.

You can see what the various colors denote by selecting Tools | Options. Once you are in the Options dialogue box, the Editor Format tab will show you what the various colors mean and, in addition, allow you to change the scheme.

Declaring Variables

Within a procedure, you will find two basic components: variables and methods. Quite simply, a *variable* is a piece of information stored somewhere in the computer's memory. It could be a number, a letter, or an entire sentence. The location where it is stored in memory is known by the variable name. As an example, let's say that you have a line of code like this:

```
number = 23
```

From that point on, every time the code refers to the variable name **number**, 23 will be put in its place. Of course, later on, you could assign a different value to the variable name of **number**. This example is a simplification.

In order for the variable to function properly, you should also declare what type of information is going to be kept by the variable. (The reasons for this will become obvious as we progress.) Table 6-1 lists variable types and how they are used.

To declare a variable, you use the keyword Dim. As an example:

```
Dim number As Integer
```

This declares that the variable name **number** will hold only data of type Integer. You will notice that we have not assigned a value yet (and in fact the editor will not allow us to do so). We only declared the name and type. At some future point in the code, we would have a line like this:

```
number = 32
```

NOTE

*Remember that VBA is not case sensitive. The variable names **number**, **Number**, and **numBer** would all be recognized as the same name.*

Variable Type	Description
Boolean	A Boolean type returns True or False. You could also frame it in terms of the numbers, with 0 = False and −1 = True.
Byte	This is one of the least used of the variable types. It can only hold a single value between 0 and 255.
Currency	This does just what it says. It holds a currency value with four decimal places, from −922,337,203,685,477.5808 to 922,337,203,685,477.5807.
Date	This stores both dates and time. Interestingly, the years range from 100 to 9999.
Double	This is one of the two variable types that use decimal points. The other is Single. Doubles are for *very* large numbers. The range runs from −4.940656458411247 * 10^{-324} to 4.94065645841247 * 10^{-324}.
Integer	This is one of the two nondecimal variable types. The other is Long. Integer handles the range of numbers −32,768 to 32,767.
Long	Long is the other of the two nondecimal variable types, with Integer being the first. Long handles the number range −2,147,483,648 to 2,147,483,657.
Object	You can store an object as a variable for later use.
Single	This is the second decimal point type, the other being Double.
String	This is the most common variable type. A String variable can hold up to 2 billion characters.

Table 6-1   *Types of Variables*

There are a couple of things you should be aware of when assigning values to a variable. First of all, a variable of type String *must* have its value enclosed in quotation marks. For instance, this would be a proper assignment:

```
Dim lastName as String
lastName = "Smith"
```

The second thing you must be aware of is that variables of type Date must have their values enclosed in # signs. A proper assignment would be as follows:

```
Dim thisDate as Date
thisDate = #10/08/03#
```

Chapter 5 discussed naming conventions in conjunction with the objects of your database. The same rules apply to variables. Remember, these are not requirements, but conventions adopted by most programmers. The prefixes associated with variables are listed in Table 6-2.

It is a good idea when naming objects of any kind to use descriptive names. This will have the benefit of making the code self-documenting. Using the date example, the proper way of declaring the variable would be as follows:

```
Dim datThisDate as Date
```

Getting back to the original procedure, addNumbers, let's go ahead and add three variables as shown here:

```
Sub addNumbers()
    'Declare the variables
    Dim intNumber1 As Integer
    Dim intNumber2 As Integer
    Dim intSum As Integer
End Sub
```

You should be able to see where this is going. There will be two numbers entered and stored in variables intNumber1 and intNumber2. They will be added and stored in intSum.

Variable Type	Prefix
Boolean	bln
Byte	byt
Currency	cur
Date	dat
Double	dbl
Integer	int
Long	lng
Object	obj
Single	sng
String	str

Table 6-2   *Variable Prefixes*

Variant

There is one other variable type that hasn't been discussed yet: the Variant. Depending on which programmer you talk to, it is either a powerful programming tool or an excuse for sloppy programming.

A *Variant* allows VBA to make its own decision as to what type of data it is holding. It is the default variable type and is used automatically if you leave the "as type" clause off the variable's declaration. It uses the prefix of var.

As an example, let's say we declare a variable as follows:

```
Dim varMyData
```

Because we left out the "as type" parameter, this defaults to the type Variant and will be the same as if you typed:

```
Dim varMyData as Variant
```

Let's say you assign it as follows:

```
varMyData = "This is a Variant"
```

VBA will convert varMyData into a String type. If, later on, you assign the following:

```
varMyData = 12
```

VBA will now convert varMyData into type Integer.

As we progress, you will see situations where a variant could end up being a type other than what was wanted or, even worse, could result in an error. Many programmers also argue that too many variants take up too much memory "overhead" and slow the code down. So before you make the decision to work with variants, you want to carefully weigh the pros and cons.

As a beginner, it is best to approach variants with great caution and stay with one of the standard type declarations.

Constants

Many times you may want to declare a value that will not change. This type is called a *Constant* and is declared using the keyword Const in place of the normal declaration using Dim.

As an example:

```
Const conNumber1 As Integer
Const conDate As Date = #03/02/04#
```

Notice that you preface the variable's name with con instead of the normal type. Also, when declaring a constant, you must assign it an initial value, or you will get a syntax error message when you leave the line.

Input and Output

You now know how to save data with the use of variables. But how do you get the information into a variable? Or read the information that is stored in them? In many ways, that will be what we spend the rest of this book examining. However, let's begin by looking at a couple of simple techniques for testing our code.

One of the simplest techniques for getting information from the user into a variable is to use a built-in function called InputBox. This will give you a simple dialog box with a prompt.

To code this in our small example, you would enter the shaded lines shown here:

```
Sub addNumbers()
    'Declare the variables
    Dim intNumber1 As Integer
    Dim intNumber2 As Integer
    Dim intSum As Integer
    'Create InputBoxes to enter numbers
    intNumber1 = InputBox("Enter the first number")
    intNumber2 = InputBox("Enter the second number")
End Sub
```

Notice that for clarity's sake, I also added a comment to indicate what I am doing.

The entry intNumber1 = InputBox is called an *assignment statement*, and it assigns the value the user enters to the variable. In this case two assignments have been created: one for intNumber1 and the other for intNumber2.

You can execute the code by selecting the Run button:

That brings up a dialog box like the one shown here for the first entry (a second one will appear for the second entry).

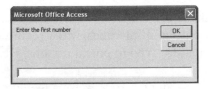

If you followed the preceding steps, the code will run and the variables will be set. However, there is no means of outputting the results. There are two ways to create an output for now. The first way is to add the code, shown with shading, here:

```
Sub addNumbers()
    'Declare the variables
    Dim intNumber1 As Integer
    Dim intNumber2 As Integer
    Dim intSum As Integer

    'Create InputBoxes to enter numbers
    intNumber1 = InputBox("Enter the first number")
    intNumber2 = InputBox("Enter the second number")
    'Add numbers
    intSum=intNumber1 + intNumber 2
' Create an output
    Debug.Print "The numbers entered were " & intNumber1 & " and " & _
intNumber2
End Sub
```

If you run the code now, you will once again get the two dialog boxes. Notice that the output will appear in the Immediate window, located at the bottom of the editor environment:

This window is used as a temporary testing place for our code and will come in handy initially.

There are several issues worth discussing here. First of all, the line:

```
Debug.Print "The numbers entered were " & intNumber1 & " and " & _
intNumber2
```

This is called a *concatenation* because it brings various components together. The literal text is enclosed in quotation marks, and the variables are not. The two types are separated by the ampersand.

Also, notice that the line is broken with a space and then an underscore. When you break up a statement onto multiple lines, VBA requires this. Throughout this book, we may need to do that for typographical reasons. However, you can keep the code on one line.

Another way of formatting an output is to use a technique you first saw in Chapter 4. You could use a message box by replacing the output line with the following line of code:

```
MsgBox "The numbers entered were " & intNumber1 & " and " & intNumber2
```

This will produce output similar to the following:

You now have your first VBA program running.

Control Structures

Computer code only runs in a sequence. It first executes a statement and, if there is no error, moves on to the next statement. We call this a *sequence structure*. However, what happens if you want the next step in the sequence not to be the next line of code? You may need to transfer control of the program to a different block of code if a certain situation occurs. Or you may need a block of code to repeat until a situation occurs (or for a predefined number of times).

We call the mechanisms to accomplish this *control structures*. These structures can be divided into two very broad categories: decision structures and repetition structures. As you will see shortly, a *decision structure* allows the program to make decisions. The most common of them is the If…Then structure. However, VBA provides other possibilities: If…Then…Else, ElseIf, Select Case, and IIF.

A *repetition structure* goes through a block of code either a predefined number of times, or until something occurs to cause the program to break out of the loop.

VBA provides two broad repetition structures: For…Next and Do…Loop. Within those two structures, there are a number of variations.

Decision-Making Structures

Let's consider the pseudocode for a morning routine. You may have one point where you write the following:

> **If** it is raining,
> **Then** I will take an umbrella.
> **Else** I will just go to my car.

The words in boldface are the VBA keywords necessary to make a decision.

You start a decision-making structure by doing a comparison of two entities. Is entity A equal to entity B? Is entity A greater than entity B? Is entity B true? These are called *conditional expressions*. The symbols used for them are listed in the following table.

=	Is equal to
<>	Is not equal to
>	Is greater than
<	Is less than
>=	Is greater than or equal to
<=	Is less than or equal to

Let's take a look at a simple decision-making structure in a subroutine:

```
Sub ifTest()
    Dim intNum As Integer
    Dim strMessage As String

    intNum = 12

    If intNum > 10 Then
        strMessage = "The number is " & intNum
    End If

    Debug.Print strMessage

End Sub
```

There are a couple of things to notice in the code. The line that contains the conditional expression begins with If and ends with Then. Also, like other structures in VBA, the conditional If structure must end with an End statement, in this case End If.

If you run the preceding example in the Immediate window, you should see the results shown here:

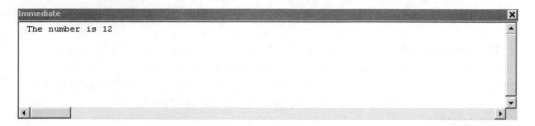

There are a couple of problems here. The code works fine. But what happens if the number is not greater than 10? More importantly, since the number is "hard-coded" to the variable, it will *always* be greater than 10. Let's take a closer look at these problems.

Within an If structure, you can have an alternative path by using an Else statement. Let's modify the code we just used slightly:

```
Sub ifTest()
    Dim intNum As Integer
    Dim strMessage As String

    intNum = 9

    If intNum > 10 Then
        strMessage = "The number is greater than 10"
    Else
        strMessage = "The number is less than 10"
    End If

    Debug.Print strMessage

End Sub
```

Notice that in the preceding code, we assigned new values to the variable intNum and then added an Else statement. Since the Else statement is part of the If statement, it does not need a separate End.

When you run it now, since intNum is less than 10, the Else statement will be triggered, giving you the results shown here:

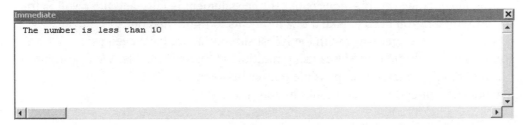

Of course, as we did earlier, you could have used the input box to enter the number and the message box to output it.

AND, OR, NOT

In some cases, you may want to test multiple conditions. Is intNum < 1 OR intNum >= 10? The keywords AND, OR, and NOT are called *logical operators* and will help you to evaluate multiple conditions.

In the case of an AND logical operator, both conditional expressions must be true in order for the If statement to be true.

The following table shows the possible logical outcomes using an AND logical operator.

First Conditional Statement	Second Conditional Statement	Result
True	True	True
True	False	False
False	True	False
False	False	False

With an OR connector, only one of the statements needs to be true for the If statement to be true. The following table shows the logical outcomes of an OR logical operator.

First Conditional Statement	Second Conditional Statement	Result
True	True	True
True	False	True
False	True	True
False	False	False

Finally, the NOT logical operator returns the opposite of what you expect. If the conditional statement is true (A is NOT equal to B), Not (A is NOT equal to B) returns false. However, if A does equal B, the statement is false and the result is true. (Don't worry if you need to take a few moments to figure that out.)

We are going to get fancy with the ifTest subroutine we have been using. We are going to use multiple procedures using multiple If/Else statements. We also want to restrict the user to a range of possible entries between 1 and 15.

Change your code so that it looks as follows:

```
Option Compare Database
Option Explicit
Private intNum As Integer
----------------------------

Sub ifTest()
    Dim strMessage As String

    intNum = InputBox("Enter a number between 1 and 15", _
             "Testing the If structure")

    If intNum >= 1 And intNum <= 15 Then
        iftest2
    Else
        MsgBox "Sorry, the number must be between 1 and 15"
    End If

End Sub
----------------------------------
Sub iftest2()
    If intNum > 10 Then
        MsgBox intNum & " is greater than 10"
    Else
        MsgBox intNum & " is less than 10"
    End If
End Sub
```

Notice that you have to redefine intNum as a global variable. We have not discussed this yet. However, recall from the beginning of the chapter that anything placed in the general declarations area will affect the whole module.

Subroutine ifTest tests intNum to see if it is between 1 and 15. If it is, it calls ifTest2, which contains the code we used earlier. However, if it does not, it returns a message to the user. The call to another procedure is known as a *procedure call*.

Go ahead and run the code a few times. If the number is between 1 and 15, you should get back the less-than or greater-than message, depending on the value you choose. If the number is not between 1 and 15, you should get the following message:

The ElseIf Structure

You can combine several If structures using ElseIf. As an example:

```
Sub ifTest()
     Dim intNum as Integer
     intNum = 12
     If intNum = 1 Then
          Debug.Print "This is the lowest number"
     ElseIf intNum = 15 Then
          Debug.Print "This is the highest number"
     Else
          Debug.Print "The number is between 1 and 15"
     End If
End Sub
```

You can use as many ElseIf statements as necessary to perform as many conditional tests as necessary.

Select Case Structure

If you find yourself using a lot of ElseIf structures, you may want to consider the Select Case structure. It will result in easier-to-read code. Using the ElseIf example in the previous section, you would use Select Case as follows:

```
Sub ifTest()
     Dim intNum as Integer
     intNum = 2
     Select Case intNum
     Case 1
          Debug.Print "This is the lowest number"
     Case 15
          Debug.Print "This is the highest number"
     Case Else
```

```
            Debug.Print "The number is between 1 and 15"
        End Select
End Sub
```

Of course you could add a case to match any situation. VBA will keep going through the structure until it finds a match with the value of intNum and then carry out the instructions. If it can't make a match, it defaults to Case Else. The Case Else statement is optional, but I strongly recommend that you always use it to have all your bases covered.

If you have multiple cases in which you want to carry out the same set of instructions, you can use the syntax:

```
Case 1, 2, 3…
```

Or you could use

```
Case 1 To 4
```

IIF

There is one other structure that we will take a quick look at: IIF. This is referred to as the Immediate If. This is handy if you want to assign the final value to a variable because its syntax is self-contained. The correct syntax is

```
IIF(conditional test, value for True, value for False)
```

So, working code might look something like this:

```
strMessage = IIF(intNum > 10, "Number is greater than 10", _
"Number is less than 10")
```

The performance of the IIF structure is somewhat slow and rarely used by programmers in a larger programming project.

Now let's turn our attention to the second type of control structure—looping.

Loops

You use loops when you need to have a block of code repeated a certain number of times or until an event of some sort happens. The number of times the code repeats can be controlled by a counter. This is called *counter-controlled repetition*. The second type is called *sentinel-controlled repetition*. We will look at both types.

For...Next Loop

The For...Next loop is an example of a counter-controlled repetition. Using either actual numbers, or variables, you can set the following components for the loop:

▶ **Counter**   This is the heart of the loop. It tracks the number of times the loop has repeated.

▶ **Start**   This is the starting number for the counter. It is rare, if ever, to set this to anything else but 1. (Occasionally you may use a different start number for mathematical calculations.)

▶ **End**   This number marks the end of the loop, where you want the counter to stop.

▶ **Step**   You can specify a number for the counter to increment with each loop. This part is optional.

Here is an example of the syntax for a For...Next loop:

```
Dim intCounter As Integer
For intCounter = 1 To 25
       ....... .
Next
```

To repeat, either the start or end numbers can be variables. Notice that the final line of the loop, unlike previous structures we have worked with, is not End, but Next. This instructs the counter to advance to the next number.

We also could have used the following syntax to declare the loop:

```
For intCounter = 1 To 25 Step 5
```

This forces the counter, in this case intCounter, to increment by five on every loop. As a result, the For loop will run five times.

It is not unusual to include If...Then structures within a loop. Let's try the one that follows:

```
Sub forTest()
Dim intCounter As Integer

For intCounter = 1 To 10
    If (intCounter Mod 2) = 0 Then
        Debug.Print intCounter & " is an even number"
```

```
    Else
        Debug.Print intCounter & " is an odd number"
    End If
Next
End Sub
```

All right! I can hear my editor yelling at me that I snuck a couple of extra things in here. Let's take a closer look at a few things in this code.

Here we see a For...Next loop that is instructed to make 10 passes. Within that, I wanted to test to see if a particular iteration was odd or even. I used an If...Then...Else structure to do that. Think about this: we have an If...Then...Else structure within a For...Next structure. When you have one structure within another, it is called a *nested structure*, which is very common in programming.

However, I asked the conditional statement to perform a calculation—specifically, division. I used the keyword Mod, which is short for modulus. Mod returns the remainder of the division (what is to the right of the decimal place). If you divide an even number by 2, the remainder is 0. So, if the counter is divided by 2 and there is a 0 remainder, it triggers the If condition. If the remainder is other than 0, the Else condition is triggered.

The Next just increments the counter.

If you run this subroutine in the Immediate window, you should see the result shown here:

```
Immediate                                                                    ☒
 1 is an odd number                                                          ▲
 2 is an even number
 3 is an odd number
 4 is an even number
 5 is an odd number
 6 is an even number
 7 is an odd number
 8 is an even number
 9 is an odd number
 10 is an even number
 |
                                                                             ▼
◄                                                                           ►
```

Let's now turn our attention to the other type of loop.

Do Loop

You use the Do loop as the sentinel-controlled loop. In other words, it will continue until a specific condition occurs (something equals something, or is greater than something, for example).

There are two variations of the Do loop—the Do While and the Do Until. We will look at each one.

Do While   The Do While loop tests to see if a condition is true. If it is true, the statements in the loop execute. For instance, let's look at the following subroutine:

```
Sub doTest()
    Dim intCounter As Integer
    Dim intTest As Integer

    intTest = 1
    intCounter = 1

    Do While intTest = 1
        Debug.Print "This is loop number " & intCounter

        If intCounter >= 5 Then
            intTest = 0
        End If

        intCounter = intCounter + 1
    Loop
End Sub
```

You will notice that the Do While loop is not as self-contained as the For...Next loop discussed earlier. In this case, you have to set up two variables, one for the counter and one for the conditional test. In this particular subroutine, I wanted the loop to end after the fifth pass.

Unlike the For loop from before, we are not running this based on a counter but, instead, until intTest changes to a value other than 1. I then nested an If...Then structure within the loop and tested the counter value. As soon as that value is equal to 5, the If structure will change the intTest value to 0 and will prevent the loop from running again.

Since it is testing for a condition rather than the number of iterations, you would not normally use a counter in a Do loop. In this case, I forced one with a second variable and incremented it as the last line of the loop. There are a variety of ways to do this.

Notice that this structure ends with the word Loop. Remember, we are not required to work with a counter here.

If you try running the Do While code, your Immediate window gives you these results:

```
Immediate                                                              [×]
This is loop number 1
This is loop number 2
This is loop number 3
This is loop number 4
This is loop number 5



◄                                                                      ►
```

However, here is a question: what happens if, for some reason, intTest never gets a value of 1? Will this Do loop ever run? (All right! Two questions!) The answer is no, it won't. However, what happens if you need the loop to run at least once?

```
Sub ifTest()
    Dim strMessage As String

    intNum = InputBox("Enter a number between 1 and 15", _
                      "Testing the If structure")

    If intNum >= 1 And intNum <= 15 Then
        iftest2
    Else
        MsgBox "Sorry, the number must be between 1 and 15"
    End If

End Sub
----------------------------
Sub iftest2()
    If intNum > 10 Then
        MsgBox intNum & " is greater than 10"
    Else
        MsgBox intNum & " is less than 10"
    End If
End Sub
```

Notice, in the ifTest subroutine, there is a test to see if the user has entered a number between 1 and 15. However, if the user enters a number out of bounds, the program just stops, and you need to start it up again. We want to keep prompting the user until he or she enters a number in the correct range.

Change ifTest to look as follows:

```
Sub ifTest()
    Dim strMessage As String
    Dim intTest As Integer

    intTest = 1

    Do

        intNum = InputBox("Enter a number between 1 and 15",_
                          "Testing the If structure")

        If intNum >= 1 And intNum <= 15 Then
            intTest = 0
            iftest2
        Else
         MsgBox "Sorry, the number must be between 1 and 15"
        End If
    Loop While intTest = 1

End Sub
```

Notice that we are not using a counter of any sort here. Instead, what we are doing is testing for intTest. However, what is interesting here is *where* the test occurs. Unlike the previous example, we are testing at the end of the loop rather than the beginning. This has the effect of forcing the loop to run at least once, which can be very handy in situations such as this.

Do Until   This is a subtle variation of what we just looked at. In a Do While loop, you run the loop *while* a condition is true. However, in a Do Until loop, you run the loop *until* a condition becomes true.

Using the first example of the Do While loop above, with a few changes, you can make it into a Do Until loop:

```
Sub doTest()
    Dim intCounter As Integer
    Dim intTest As Integer

    intTest = 1
```

```
    intCounter = 1

    Do Until intTest <> 1
        Debug.Print "This is loop number " & intCounter

        If intCounter >= 5 Then
            intTest = 0
        End If

        intCounter = intCounter + 1
    Loop
End Sub
```

Notice that here we are saying to run the loop until intTest does *not* equal 1. From that point on, everything else in this example is identical. You should see the same result as with the Do While loop.

Like the Do While loop, you can place the Until condition at the end of the structure after the word Loop. This forces the loop to run at least once.

We will be revisiting loop structures frequently throughout the book. Like variables, they are an integral part of most programming situations today.

Arrays

In many ways, the discussion of arrays is tied closely to variables. An *array* is a variable that contains multiple values. The number of values that the variable will hold must be decided and declared in advance. You are also going to learn how to reference values inside the array.

As I was writing this, my technical editor asked me, "What about dynamic arrays?" Well, as you will learn, the concept of a dynamic array is a slight falsehood. You still need to declare, in advance, the number of values it will hold. The only difference is that you declare them before the array is used, during the runtime of the program (as opposed to when you are writing the code).

You are also going to learn how to allocate memory properly so that your array does not take up too much room.

Components of an Array

Each value in the array is called an *element*. Since an array variable has multiple elements in it, you need a way to pick them out or reference them individually.

You can do that by using a number called an *index*. Most of the time, the first element of an array is index number 0.

If you could look behind the scenes of an array of names, using variable name strName, it might look something like this:

```
strName          (0)  "John Smith"
                 (1)  "Jane Doe"
                 (2)  "Rosemary Brown"
                 (3)  "Anita LaScala"
                 (4)  "Bob Gray"
```

Notice that even though the index numbers only go up to 4, this is a five-element array. Again, the first element usually begins at 0. (Note that as we progress through this chapter, we will see some exceptions.)

If you wanted to select Anita LaScala's name out of the array for printing, you would use

```
Print strName(3)
```

Anita is in index position 3. However, just to confuse things a bit, it is the fourth element of the array. This is the source of many a problem in programming and, a little later on in the chapter, we will examine a way of possibly correcting for that.

VBA gives us two flavors of arrays:

▶ **Static array**   The number of elements in the array, called the length of the array, is decided in advance and remains fixed.

▶ **Dynamic array**   The length of the array is variable and not decided in advance.

Static Arrays

A static array has a predetermined length and does not change. Since this is the simplest of the arrays, we will start here.

Declaring a static array is similar to declaring a variable, with one small exception:

```
Dim intMyScores(10) As Integer
```

You have to be careful how you view this. You are probably thinking that we just declared an array of 10 elements. However, what we really did was declare an array of 11 elements, with the first element being 0, and the last element being index number 10 (sometimes called the *upper bound*). See the difference?

The *lower bound*, or lowest index number, of this array is 0.

You need to do this in order to properly allocate the memory necessary to hold the array.

If you wanted to, you could declare multiple arrays in a procedure as follows:

```
Dim strName(6) As String, intMyScores(10) As Integer
```

By default, the first index value is 0, strings are initialized as empty, and integers are initialized at 0.

Let's set up an example. In this procedure, you are going to create two For...Next loops. The first one will allow you to populate the array, and the second will print the contents of the array back to you. Here is the code:

```
Sub arrayTest()
 Dim i As Integer
 Dim intMyScores(10) As Integer

 For i = 0 To 10
    intMyScores(i) = InputBox("Enter number " & i, "Static Array Test")
 Next

 For i = 0 To 10
    Debug.Print "For array element " & i & " the number is " & _
 intMyScores(i)
Next
End Sub
```

Programmers like to use the lowercase *i* as the variable representing the index of the array. It is just a programming convention. Here we are asking it to serve double duty: it is the counter variable of the For...Next loop, and it is also the representation of the array's index. Notice that you always refer to an array variable by the variable's name followed by the element number, or index, in parentheses. In the example, we are using the loop variable of *i* to help us populate our array.

As a nice little extra, notice that I have a concatenation for the prompt in the input box. This will help you keep track of what element you are entering.

Your input box should look something like this:

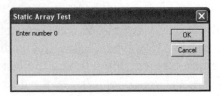

After you enter the elements, the second For loop takes over and should give you the printout in the Immediate window:

```
Immediate                                                    ×
For array element 0 the number is 7
For array element 1 the number is 2
For array element 2 the number is 4
For array element 3 the number is 8
For array element 4 the number is 4
For array element 5 the number is 2
For array element 6 the number is 8
For array element 7 the number is 8
For array element 8 the number is 1
For array element 9 the number is 3
For array element 10 the number is 9
```

With a static array, you declare the size of the array right in the code. In other words, it is done during *design time*.

There is one little problem with the preceding code example. You could somehow end up declaring an incorrect lower or upper bound. This could result in a runtime error. VBA helps you out a bit with two built-in functions: LBound(*array name*) and UBound(*array name*). This returns the bounds of the array.

You could change the syntax of the For loop in the previous code as follows:

```
For i = LBound(intMyScores) To UBound(intMyScores)
    intMScores(i) = InputBox("Enter number " & i, "Static Array Test")
 Next
```

Dynamic Arrays

Many programmers consider the concept of a dynamic array in VBA a slight programming fiction. Essentially, it is still a static array, but you do not declare the size until the program is running. So the only issue is *when* the size is being declared.

You start off by declaring an empty array. For example:

```
Dim intMyScores() As Integer
```

Then you use a keyword, ReDim, to redeclare the size of the array while the program is running and it is known what the size will be.

Let's redo our previous example to demonstrate a dynamic array:

```
Sub arrayTest()
 Dim i As Integer
 Dim intMyScores() As Integer
 Dim intArraySize As Integer
```

```
    intArraySize = InputBox("How many scores are you entering?", "Array Size")

  ReDim intMyScores(intArraySize)

  For i = 1 To intArraySize
      intMyScores(i) = InputBox("Enter number " & i, "Static Array Test")
  Next

  For i = 0 To intArraySize
      Debug.Print "For array element " & i & " the number is " & _
        intMyScores(i)
Next
End Sub
```

You will notice that we first declare intMyScores as an empty array. Then, as shown, we use the ReDim keyword to redefine it as a static array, with the upper bound being controlled by intArraySize, which is entered by the user.

From there on, we just use intArraySize to control the loops.

If you work through this example, you will see a contradiction. If you enter 5 as the number of scores that you want to input, you end up inputting 6 because the index starts at 0. This is a frequent mistake of beginning programmers.

With just a little bit of recoding, you can reassign the first element as 1 instead of 0. This would help keep things a bit more coordinated. Take a look at the following code:

```
Sub arrayTest()
 Dim i As Integer
 Dim intMyScores() As Integer
 Dim intArraySize As Integer

 intArraySize = InputBox("How many scores are you entering?", "Array Size")

 ReDim intMyScores(1 To intArraySize)

 For i = 1 To intArraySize
     intMyScores(i) = InputBox("Enter number " & i, "Static Array Test")
 Next

 For i = 1 To intArraySize
     Debug.Print "For array element " & i & " the number is " & intMyScores(i)
     Next
 End Sub
```

If you run this in the Immediate window, you should see the result shown here:

```
Immediate                                                              [x]
For array element 1 the number is 3
For array element 2 the number is 8
For array element 3 the number is 5
For array element 4 the number is 8
For array element 5 the number is 2
```

Just as intArray is the upper bound of our array, the 1 is now the lower bound of the array. We then have the two For…Next loops starting at 1. (Remember, there is no element 0 now.)

There is another technique for starting the array at index position 1. In the general declarations section, you could type either **Option Base 0** or **Option Base 1**. This will set the default lower bound of the arrays in the module. The only two options are 0 and 1.

Out of Bounds

What happens if you make a programming error and end up trying to access more elements in the array than you declared using either Dim or ReDim?

VBA will not catch this until the program is actually running, not during the coding. This sort of error is called a *runtime error*. If that happens, you will get a message like this:

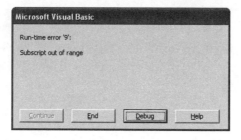

If you click Debug, it will show you where the program thinks the offending line of code is.

Be very careful! The line it brings you to is the point at which the code "crashed." However, many times the crash happens due to things going bad earlier in the program. For instance, you may have set a variable to a wrong size or reference; or perhaps Dim or ReDim declared a wrong value. Finding the problem may require a bit of detective work on your part.

Making the Array Smaller

What happens if you declare an upper bound of 10, but only put four elements in the array?

Remember, the 10 declares the position of the last element of your array. However, unlike trying to use more elements, there is no rule that states you have to use all of the positions. Only using four elements would not cause a problem of any sort. But there is a potential problem in the background.

As a beginner, this is not a huge concern, but a major issue in software design is resource control. A computer has a finite memory capacity. When you declare that your array will have 10 elements, VBA puts a reserve on memory. This means that the rest of the memory is sitting there unused. This is a tremendous waste of resources.

Your first impulse may be to use ReDim to change the size declaration. This causes, however, another rather serious problem. When we used ReDim in the earlier example, the array still had no elements. If you use ReDim with a populated array, it will wipe it out and start anew. Odds are that is not the most desirable solution.

VBA helps us out by combining ReDim with a second keyword as follows:

```
ReDim Preserve intMyScores(4)
```

The Preserve keyword reallocates the memory and retains the elements intact.

Erasing Arrays

You will sometimes have situations in which you want to keep the array declared, but erase the elements within it. You can easily do that with the keyword Erase, as shown here:

```
Erase intMyScores
```

This clears the contents but keeps the declaration.

Depending on the type of array, different things may happen. If it is a numeric array, the elements are set to 0. However, the elements of a string array are set to " ". This is an empty string. If it is a Boolean array, each element is set to False.

IsArray

How do you know if a variable is an array? VBA provides a handy little function to test a variable. Let's take a look at the following code.

```
Sub arrayTest()
   Dim intScores1 As Integer
   Dim intScores2(4) As Integer

   Debug.Print "Is intScores1 an array: " & IsArray(intScores1)
   Debug.Print "Is intScores2 an array: " & IsArray(intScores2)

End Sub
```

This code returns the results shown here:

```
Immediate                                                                    ✕
  Is intScores1 an array: False                                              ▲
  Is intScores2 an array: True
                                                                             ▼
◄                                                                          ► 
```

You can see that IsArray is a Boolean function. It returns a value of either True or False. In the first case above, the result is false because we did not declare it as an array. In the second case, it is true because we did.

Summary

We have covered a lot of territory here. We looked at variables, as well as the various types of structures used in VBA. Yet, even with all of this, our study of the basic VBA structures is far from complete. We will be adding to our discussion as we progress through this book.

In the remaining chapters of this section, we will study the VBA Editor and these structures in even greater detail.

Understanding the Visual Basic Editor

I n Chapters 5 and 6, we took a brief tour of the VBA environment as well as the structure behind the VBA language. In this chapter, as well as subsequent ones, we are going to drill down to greater levels of detail.

We'll start here by revisiting the VBA Editor and the menus and toolbars that you will use with it. We'll look at the different parts of the editor and examine the available options. You will also learn how to use some of the help features available should you need them.

Opening the VBA Editor

A good place to start learning about the editor is to understand the different ways you can access it. You already saw a couple of ways in Chapters 5 and 6, but they are worth reviewing here.

From Microsoft Access, you can access the editor in any of the following ways:

▶ Select Tools | Macro | Visual Basic Editor.

▶ As you may have noticed from looking at the menu, you can also use ALT - F11.

▶ You can create or edit a module from the Modules category of the Database window.

▶   You can create an event property from a form or report. You saw how to do this
     when we looked at forms and events in Chapter 3.

No matter what technique you use to get to the VBA Editor, you should see
something like Figure 7-1 when you open it. The main window, occupying most of
the editor, is the Code window where you do the actual coding. As you will see in
subsequent chapters, the code will vary depending on the object you are looking at.

The Project Explorer window, the window on the upper left side of Figure 7-1,
contains not just the list, but the hierarchy of code objects for the project. The
Properties window, on the lower left side in Figure 7-1, contains a list of properties
associated with an object, such as a form or report, and what their current settings are.

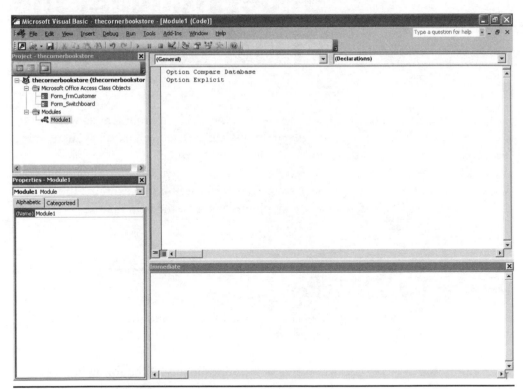

Figure 7-1   *The VBA Editor*

We will look at the interaction of the Properties and Project windows in a bit. However, I want to mention three windows that you will use for testing and debugging: the Immediate window, the Watch window, and the Locals window. These are discussed in greater detail when we look at testing and debugging in Chapter 10.

Each of these windows can be opened, closed, moved, or resized like any other window in the Windows environment. You can also use the View command to assist in this process. As an example, you can close the Properties window by clicking the X in the upper-right corner. To reopen it, select View | Properties Window, or press F4.

Highlights of the Menu System

While many commands are common to all Windows programs, the Edit, View, and Tools menus contain features unique to the VBA Editor that you need to know about to work effectively in the VBA environment.

Edit Menu

Most of the commands in the Edit menu are found in other Windows programs, such as Copy, Cut, and Paste. However, some commands unique to the VBA environment are

▶ List Properties/Methods, which displays a dropdown list box in the Code window that shows the properties and methods available for an object.

▶ List Constants, which displays a dropdown list box in the Code window that lists the constants whose value can be assigned to a property or to a function or sub argument.

▶ Quick Info, which opens a popup in the Code window that provides the syntax for a function, sub, or statement.

▶ Parameter Info, which displays a popup in the Code window that provides information about the parameters of a sub or function.

▶ Complete Word, which completes a word that you are typing in the code window once you've typed enough characters for the editor to successfully identify it.

View Menu

The commands available on the View menu for the most part control which windows are open in the VBA environment and which toolbars are displayed. Among the options available on the View menu are the following:

▶   The Code command displays any code associated with an object if that code is not already showing. (The object it is showing the code for is the object selected in the Project window.)

▶   The Object command switches you to the object in Access.

▶   The Definition command opens the Object Browser, selects the object that is selected in the Code window, and displays its properties, methods, and events.

▶   The Object Browser command also opens the Object Browser, which gives you a list of the objects found in libraries referenced by the project and their respective members (that is, their properties, methods, and events). Unlike the Definition command, the Object Browser command opens the Object Browser for general use, without specifically selecting the object currently selected in the Code window. We will be examining the Object Browser in greater detail later in this chapter.

Tools Menu

The Tools menu allows you to configure the current project as well as the VBA environment as a whole. Options available from the Tools menu include

▶   The References command allows you to open a list of object libraries that are registered in the system registry, such as ADO, and create a reference to them. We will be coming back to this as we progress through this book.

▶   The Macros command simply shows you a list of macros in the current database.

▶   The Options command brings up a dialog box that allows you to change the VBA Editor's environment.

Menu Shortcut

In addition to using the individual menus, you can right-click in the Code window and get a list of commonly used menu items, as shown in Figure 7-2. This is a static menu that offers one-click access to some common menu commands. It is not a dynamic menu whose contents reflect menu items that you've recently selected.

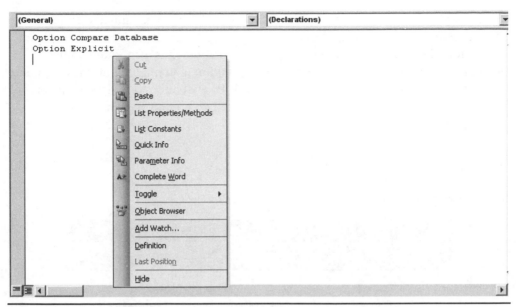

Figure 7-2   *The menu shortcut*

The Debug, Edit, and UserForm Toolbars

In addition to the menu commands, you will be using several toolbars in your work. Besides the Standard toolbar, the Debug, Edit, and UserForm toolbars will be referred to throughout the rest of this book. Let's take a look at them here.

The Debug toolbar, of course, is used in debugging: It contains one-click shortcuts for all of the items on the Run menu, as well as selected items on the Debug and View menus.

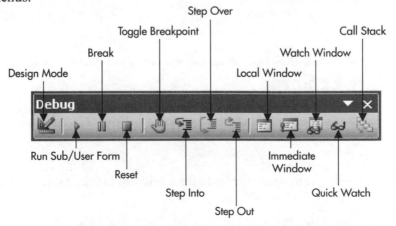

The Edit toolbar provides tools for editing code. Its buttons duplicate options found mostly on the Edit menu, like List Properties/Methods, Indent, and Outdent. In addition, it contains a Toggle Breakpoint button, which is also found on the Debug menu. Finally, it has a Comment Block button to comment out lines of code so that they do not execute, and an Uncomment Block button to remove comments from lines of code so that they do execute. These two buttons have no menu equivalent:

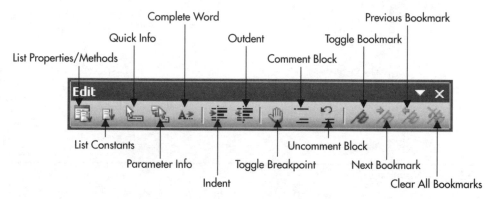

You use the UserForm toolbar to create a GUI object to facilitate the end user's interaction with the system: It contains buttons to order, group, and align objects on user forms.

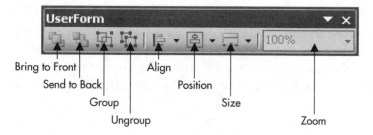

The Project Explorer

You can quickly get to various files and modules in your VBA project using the Project Explorer window. Figure 7-3 shows the Project Explorer window with its buttons.

▶ The View Code button opens the code for a selected object if it isn't already open.

▶ The View Object button opens the selected object in Access.

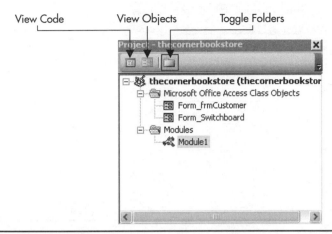

Figure 7-3   *Project Explorer window*

▶   The Toggle Folders button switches the Project Explorer's display between the objects grouped by their classification type and the objects in alphabetical order without regard to their type.

In Folder view (grouped by classification), you can open and close the folders by clicking on the [+] and [-] just to the left of the folder. As stated earlier, you will see all of the files associated with your project; including the modules, documents, forms, and reports.

Managing Modules

There are a variety of ways to manage your modules in the VBA Editor. The following sections cover inserting and deleting, and importing and exporting modules.

Inserting and Deleting a Module

A new module can be created from within the Project Explorer by selecting the project name, which is usually the first item in the hierarchy, and clicking the right mouse button. From the menu that appears, you select Insert and the type of module (Module or Class Module) you want to insert. This is shown in Figure 7-4.

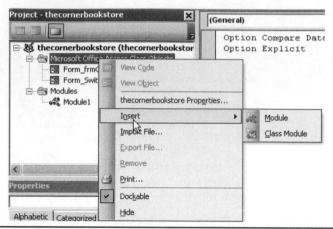

Figure 7-4 *Insert a module*

You can also select the command from the Insert menu or select the second button on the Standard toolbar, as shown here:

If you use the Insert button on the Standard toolbar, you can click on the down arrow immediately to the right of the button to select either a Module or a Class Module.

You delete a module by first selecting it in the Project Explorer and right-clicking. Once in the menu, select Remove (module name):

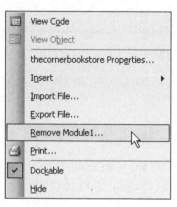

When you select the Remove command, you will have the option of saving, or exporting, the module to an external file:

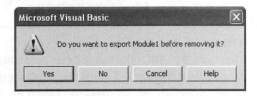

You can also access the deleting and exporting feature by selecting the File menu option.

Importing and Exporting Modules

In computer terminology, the word "persisting" means saving something after the computer is turned off. In a VBA project, you would save a module as part of a project. As a matter of fact, if you make changes to the code in the module and close the VBA Editor, you will not be prompted to save the changes. However, if you then close Access itself, it will prompt you to save whatever module you made the changes to.

Saving the module with the project is certainly handy. However, what happens if you want to use the module in another project? Or if you want to send it to someone else to use?

The VBA Editor gives you the option of exporting or importing the module. You can access this option by either right-clicking on the module name in the Project Explorer, or selecting File | Export File. Class modules are assigned a file extension of .cls, while modules are assigned a file extension of .bas.

NOTE

Exporting the module does not affect the original in the project. It just creates a copy of it in an external text file.

Likewise, we can import a module from an external text file into a project by either selecting File | Import File or right-clicking on the project name in the Project Explorer window. This will make the module from an external location part of the project.

As stated earlier, this feature offers two important benefits:

▶ The ability to back up your work to a remote location

▶ The ability to reuse modules in other projects, thus not having to retype code where needed

Properties Window

Here is the place where you can save a lot of time typing code. As you know, VBA is based on Visual Basic. The "Visual" part of that name means that you don't always need to type code. You can select options from the list in the Properties window. You can open the Properties window by either pressing F4 or selecting View | Properties Window. This window is shown in Figure 7-5 with the Alphabetic tab selected.

Select the Categorized tab to see the items classified by type. This is shown in Figure 7-6. The Categorized view allows you to expand or collapse categories using either the [+] or [-] to the left of each category.

Figure 7-5 *Properties window in alphabetical order*

Figure 7-6   *Properties window in categorized order*

The Object Browser

One of the most important tools you will be working with is the Object Browser. This lets you examine all of the objects available to the project. Notice the word "available." You may or may not use them. Within each object, you will see the properties, methods, and events associated with that object. You will also be able to see a description and other relevant information associated with that object.

It is worth spending a bit of time learning about this tool. While we're at it, you will learn some of the terminology associated with objects.

Open the Object Browser by either selecting View | Object Browser or pressing F2. The Object Browser is shown in Figure 7-7.

Objects are entities in the computer's memory. However, they have to come from somewhere. The source of an object is a *class*, which serves as a kind of template from which an object (which is also called *an instance of a class*) is created. On the left of the browser, you will see an enormous number of classes. (If you don't see a list as extensive as the one shown here, don't worry; you will see why in a bit.) The actual classes and members that are defined in our current project are bolded. Figure 7-7 shows the Form_frmCustomer class selected.

The right side of the browser shows the members of the class. Classes have three main types of members: properties, methods (subs and functions), and events (which are a special kind of sub).

Properties are roughly the equivalent of a field. In true object-oriented programming, a field is sometimes referred to as an *attribute*. Figure 7-8 shows the AllowDeletions attribute selected. Note the icon to the left of the attribute.

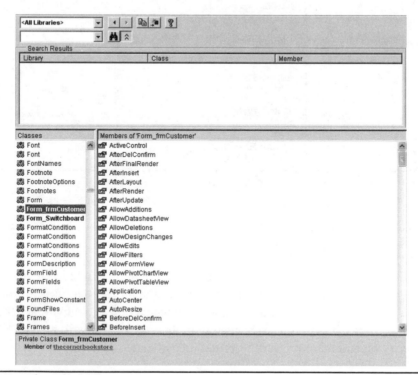

Figure 7-7   *The Object Browser*

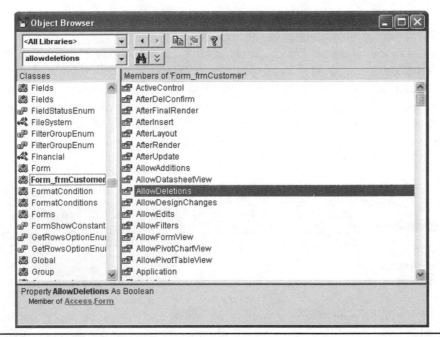

Figure 7-8   *A property in the Object Browser*

Once selected, you can see the description of the property located at the bottom of the browser. Notice that this property returns a Boolean value of either True or False. The form will either allow deletions or not.

A method (which is either a function or a sub), is another type of member. As an example, leave the Form_frmCustomer class selected in the left pane of the Object Browser, then select the GoToPage sub in the right pane. Notice the icon to the left of it and how it is different from the property icon. Also, notice the description at the bottom of the browser, shown here:

```
Sub GoToPage(PageNumber As Long, [Right As Long], [Down As Long])
    Member of Access.Form
```

This is described as a sub. The documentation also shows the parameters the sub will accept, as well as their type and order.

Libraries

These class modules are not just randomly held. Each class module is part of a library of related class modules. In many cases, a class may even access members of other classes. Referring to the previous illustration, you can see the library relationship of the GoToPage sub by clicking on the Member of Access.Form link located at the bottom of the description. Here you can review the other classes in this library.

You can also see the list of available libraries by selecting the library list located at the top of the browser, as shown here:

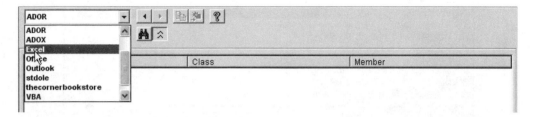

Again, if you do not see the same thing, do not worry; we will be fixing that shortly.

You also have the ability to search the libraries for a particular member. As an example, let's say that we wanted to see which class files have the sub GoToPage. Referring to Figure 7-9, I have selected All Libraries and typed GoToPage in the field below it. I then clicked on the search icon to the right of the field. The results are shown in the Search Results window. In this case, several class files in the Access and Word libraries contain that sub.

Figure 7-9   *A library search*

References

Before a library can be seen in the browser, a reference to it must be created. To do this, you need to open the References dialog box by selecting Tools | References. The dialog box that opens looks something like Figure 7-10.

Here you select the libraries you need to use in your project off of an alphabetical list. In some cases, you will see multiple versions of a library. By selecting multiple versions of the same library, you could sometimes create conflicts. The VBA Editor will usually alert you of potential conflicts.

Once the libraries are selected and you click OK, the selected libraries are moved to the top of the list the next time you open the References box. This makes seeing what you have selected a lot easier.

For the remainder of this book, we will reference the libraries shown in Figure 7-10. If your version of Microsoft Access has earlier versions of these libraries (we are showing examples using Microsoft Access 2003), select them. Since we are working at a beginner level, there should not be a conflict.

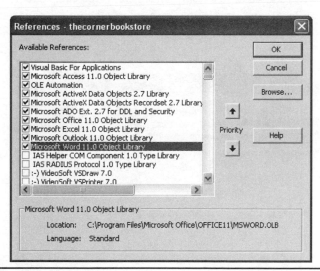

Figure 7-10   *References dialog box*

Using VBA Editor Options

A number of features of the VBA Editor and the VBA programming environment are configurable through the VBA Editor Options dialog box. You access the dialog box by selecting Tools | Options. Figure 7-11 shows the dialog box with the Editor tab selected. In most instances, the default options will work fine. However, let's take a close look at these options and learn about some of the ways you can customize your environment.

Editor Tab

The settings on the Editor tab are the primary options you will be concerned with while working with your code.

Auto Syntax Check

You may have run into the Auto Syntax Check option already. As soon as you leave a line of code (using either the ENTER or arrow keys or the mouse), the checker will examine the line for proper syntax. If it finds anything irregular, it will try to fix it. For instance, it will remove unnecessary spaces, change casing to conform to programming standards, and possibly add missing closing quotation marks and parentheses.

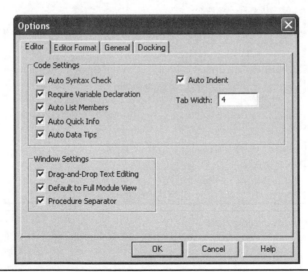

Figure 7-11   *VBA Editor Options with the Editor tab selected*

NOTE

Remember that VBA is not case sensitive, but code is easier to read if you follow accepted programming standards for capitalization.

If the checker cannot make all of the corrections, you will get a message something like the one shown here:

It will give you an indication, which may not always be clear, of what is wrong and how to fix it.

Without this feature turned on, the defective code would be displayed in a different color only.

Require Variable Declaration

We have already seen the Require Variable Declaration option in Chapter 5. It places the statement Option Explicit in the General Declarations area when a new module is open. This requires that you formally declare all variables before you use them. As stated in Chapter 5, I feel that this is important because failure to do so could promote misspellings of variable names, which could lead to all sorts of errors. For instance, you could call a variable myName in one place and, inadvertently, use myNmae in another place. By being forced to declare the variable first, this sort of error can be averted.

Auto List Members

The Auto List Members feature will give you a listing of relevant members when you type the dot after the object name in the Code window. (Remember, members are properties, methods, and events associated with an object.)

The Auto List Members will not come up unless there has been a reference established to the object using the References dialog box discussed earlier. As a very simple example, let's say you type the object **Debug** and click the dot. You will see the list shown in Figure 7-12.

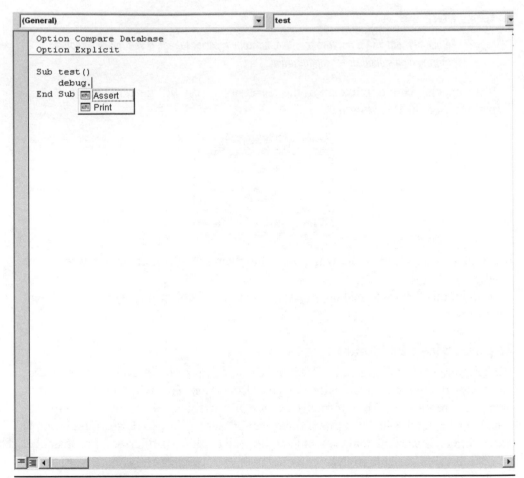

Figure 7-12   *Results from Auto List Members*

As we progress, we will be referring to this feature often.

Auto Quick Info

You can use the Auto Quick Info feature to see the proper syntax for a function. Again, you have probably seen this already when you tried the MsgBox or InputBox functions. In order for this feature to work properly, a reference to the library containing the function must have been added to the project using the References dialog box discussed earlier. Figure 7-13 shows Auto Quick Info for the MsgBox function.

Figure 7-13   *Auto Quick Info for the MsgBox function*

In the process of building the function's syntax, an Auto List Member could pop up where members are required.

Auto Data Tips

The Auto Data Tips option is an invaluable tool for debugging when stepping through a program and for testing. When you roll your mouse over a variable name, the current value assigned to that variable will be displayed.

For instance, as shown in Figure 7-14, if I use the VBA Editor in a debug mode and step through the code past the assignment for intNumber1, then point to intNumber1 in the calculation a couple of lines down, I can take advantage of this feature to be certain that the assignment is being correctly made.

```
(General)                                    ▾    test                                      ▾

    Option Compare Database
    Option Explicit

    Sub test()
        Dim intNumber1 As Integer
        Dim intNumber2 As Integer
        Dim intSum As Integer

        intNumber1 = 3
⇨   |   intNumber2 = 7

        intSum = intNumber1 + intNumber2
                    intNumber1 = 3
    End Sub
```

Figure 7-14   *Using Auto Data Tip*

Auto Indent/Tab Width

Using Auto Indent, once you indent a line, subsequent lines will retain the indentation. This will make the code a little easier to read. You can use either the SPACEBAR or the TAB key to indent.

The default setting for Tab Width is 4. You can change this in the text box if you wish.

Window Settings

Under Window Settings on the Editor tab, you have three options:

▶   Drag and Drop Text Editing allows you to move code around by highlighting it and dragging it to a new location in much the same way as you would in Microsoft Word.

▶ Default to Full Module View allows all the procedures in a module to be displayed in a scrollable Code window. However, if this is turned off, you will see only one procedure at a time. As you will see, you can toggle between these two modes using a button in the lower left side of the Code window.

▶ Procedure Separator will draw a horizontal line across the Code window to show a clear separation of procedures.

Editor Format Tab

On the Editor Format tab of the Options dialog box, as shown in Figure 7-15, you can set the font, size, and colors displayed in the Code window.

Remember, these features have absolutely no effect on how the code operates. They just help visibility and the ability to spot errors quickly. In most cases, the default settings are more than adequate.

General Tab and Docking Tab

The General tab, shown in Figure 7-16, handles the grid settings for setting up a form in Design View. However, you would use these only if you are creating a user interface for a non-Access database. It is not relevant to Microsoft Access. As a result, you will rarely be concerned about this feature. The General tab does have some features we will be examining when we discuss debugging.

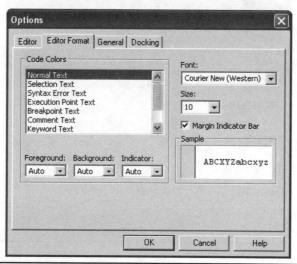

Figure 7-15   *Editor Format tab*

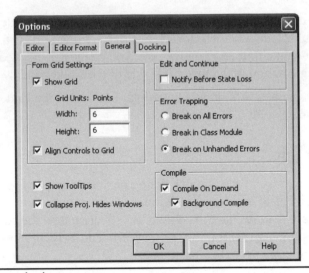

Figure 7-16 *General tab*

The Docking tab, shown in Figure 7-17, allows you decide which windows will be docked, and which will float, when the VBA Editor is open. Leaving these checked will keep your VBA Editor nicely organized.

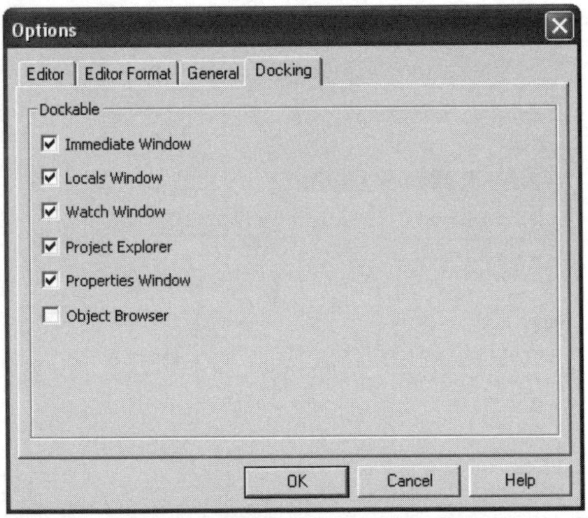

Figure 7-17 *Docking tab*

Getting Help

With each evolution of Microsoft Office, the help feature is becoming increasingly web based. This allows for more extensive and current help than can be normally stored locally. Many times the distinction between what is local and what is web based is seamless.

You can get help by:

▶   Pressing F1

▶   Selecting Help | Microsoft Visual Basic Help from the menu

▶   Selecting the question mark icon from the Standard toolbar

When you select help using one of these techniques, you will be taken to the Table of Contents window shown in Figure 7-18. Once in that window, you can search for a topic.

Figure 7-18   *Table of Contents for Visual Basic Help*

Access 2003 adds an additional search feature. For instance, if you want to find out information about using the Object Browser, type that into the Search field and click on the right arrow button next to it. In Figure 7-19, it returned 63 possible topics.

If you now want to find out information about the ProjectName property, you select that, and a new window opens with a description, as shown in Figure 7-20.

You can treat this new window like any other window by maximizing, minimizing, resizing, closing, and so on. You can even print the contents by clicking on the printer icon located at the top.

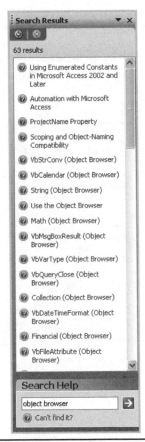

Figure 7-19   *Help for the Object Browser*

Figure 7-20   *Help window for topic*

Starting a New Procedure in the VBA Editor

One of the handiest features of the VBA Editor is the ability to start a new procedure using a dialog box. Up to this point, you have started procedures by typing the keyword Sub followed by the name of the procedure, as follows:

```
Sub addNumbers()
End Sub
```

The VBA Editor adds the End Sub line automatically, as well as the opening and closing parentheses after the procedure name.

There is another way of doing this: by selecting Insert | Procedure. You should see the following dialog box:

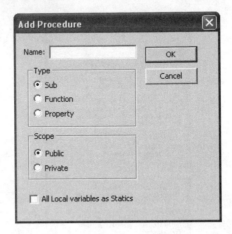

Here you can add the name of the procedure, the type of procedure, and the scope of the variables. If you don't know what that last part is, don't worry! You will find out in the next chapter.

Summary

In this chapter, we looked at the many tools available in the VBA Editor. You saw how it can guide you in the syntax of a function, as well as show what is available in an object. To that end, we also looked at an important tool: the Object Browser. We also examined the various menu and toolbar options that are important in the VBA environment, and saw how to access help if it is needed.

Beginning in the next chapter, we are going to combine the tools discussed here and in Chapter 6 to create the VBA code that we will need. We will finally get a chance to use VBA, and related objects, to perform operations within the database.

VBA Language Components

Teaching a programming language is not a linear process. Many times I need to touch on a topic, move on to the next topic, and then return to the original topic incorporating the second topic. That is what is going on here. We looked at some elements of VBA in Chapter 6, moved on to the VBA Editor in Chapter 7, and now we will bring both together in this chapter. In the process, we will be revisiting topics from both chapters.

We will reexamine objects, events, and variables and take a look at SQL and how to query the database using forms. In between, we will do some actual coding. But first, let's quickly review what you have learned about procedures.

You've seen that a procedure has an opening declaration as well as an ending statement. Between those two lines, you have variables (which could also be arrays), assignment statements, and objects (which contain their own attributes and methods). The procedure can also contain programming structures to make decisions (If…Then…Else) and loops to repeat a block of code a certain number of times, or until a condition is met.

Objects in VBA

Let's take the following line segment of code:

```
DoCmd.GoToRecord …
```

DoCmd is an object. As a matter of fact (recall from Chapter 7), you can look up all its particulars by pressing F2 to open the Object Browser:

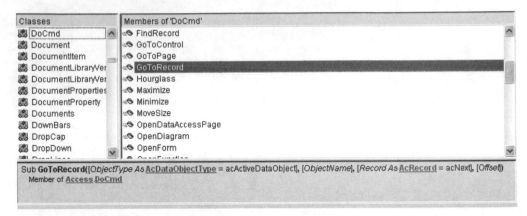

Each component in your project can be represented by an object and accessed programmatically. This includes the tables, forms, reports, and so on. However, as you will see, there are hundreds of objects that are not as obvious to the Access user and will only be used within the VBA environment.

The previous code segment is an *object call*. In essence, you are sending a message to the object, asking it to do its job. However, what job do you want it to do?

After you make the call to the object, you type a dot (or period). As soon as you do, Auto List Members opens, giving you a list of properties and methods available.

All objects have two basic components: properties and methods. (Remember, the words "property," "field," and "attribute" are more or less interchangeable when speaking about objects.) Properties dictate what an object "knows." As an example, let's say you have an object called Car. The attributes might be things like its model, color, number of miles, and so on. Methods are what the object can do with the information located in the attributes. For instance, the car can move, go in reverse, stop, and so on.

From here on, we will be examining all objects in this light.

Intrinsic Constants

Variables and constants both represent particular values. However, a variable's value will change as circumstances dictate, but a constant will always retain the same value. As an example, the value of pi would certainly not change.

You declare a variable with the keyword Dim, and a constant with the keyword Const. There are also constants called *intrinsic constants* that are built into Access, VBA, or the ADO library. The origin of these intrinsic constants can be identified by their prefix. For example:

▶ The prefix vb refers to a Visual Basic constant.

▶ The prefix ac refers to an Access constant.

▶ The prefix ad refers to an ADO constant.

VBA has hundreds of such constants built in. As an example, open the Object Browser and do a search for constants. Then, click on one of the VBA libraries. You will get something resembling Figure 8-1. These constants should work properly anywhere in your code.

Again, if you use the Object Browser and click on one of the Access libraries, you will get something that looks like Figure 8-2. Before version 2000 of Access, these names used the convention of the letter *A* followed by an underscore, for example, A_Next or A_ Record.

We will be exploring ADO constants as we progress further through the book.

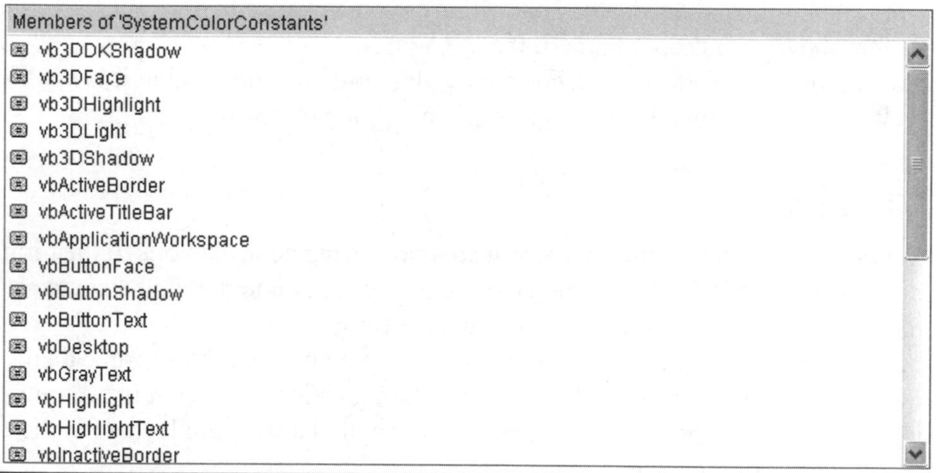

Figure 8-1   *VBA constants*

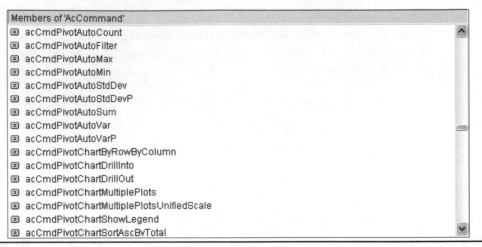

Figure 8-2   *Access constants*

Basic VBA Programs Using Forms

OK, for the past 7 chapters, you have gotten a lot of theory. Now it is time to put some of it to the test and actually do some coding. We are going to begin by setting up some simple form procedures. This will give you a chance to get your toes a bit wet before moving to deeper parts of the VBA pool.

The variations of the following code examples could be endless, but it is my hope that you will have enough examples to experiment on your own.

Setting a Focus

When you set the focus, it means that you are transferring control to one of the form's controls (buttons, text fields, combo boxes, etc.) Let's assume that you want to set the focus to the last name field when you open a form.

Our sample database (available on www.osborne.com) contains a form called frmCustomer. Let's go ahead and open that in Design View, as shown in Figure 8-3. Notice that the mouse pointer is pointing to the small black square located in the upper-left corner of the form.

Right-click on the square, select Properties, and select the Event tab. You want the focus to be set on the last name when the form opens. For that reason, select the OnOpen event and click on the Builder button shown in Figure 8-4.

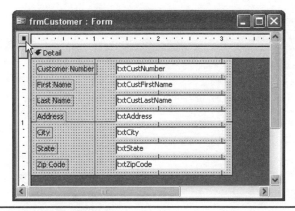

Figure 8-3   *frmCustomer in Design View*

Select the Code Builder option. When you select OK, you will be brought to the VBA Editor with a new form module open and ready to go, as Figure 8-5 shows. Notice the lines:

```
Private Sub Form_Open(Cancel As Integer)
End Sub
```

Figure 8-4   *Event tab and Code Builder button*

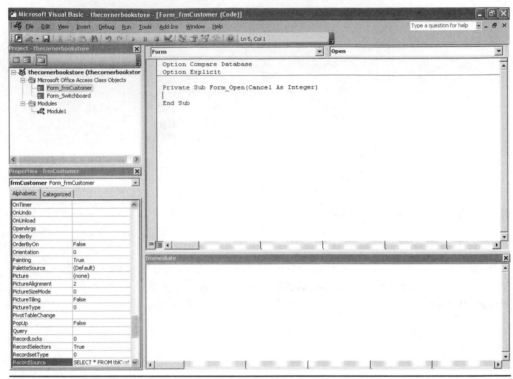

Figure 8-5   *The VBA Editor with the form module open*

This means that the event procedure Form_Open is already set up. In addition, if you look in the Project Explorer, you will see that the module for frmCustomer is already named and listed:

Now click between the opening and closing lines of the procedure and press the SPACEBAR three times (indenting makes for clearer code). Type **docmd** followed by a dot (the period key). Auto List Members should pop up, as shown here:

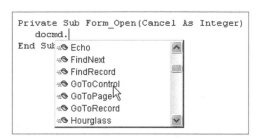

We are going to use the GoToControl method. (You can tell it is a method by the icon to its left in the Auto List Members list.) You can select it by either double-clicking on it or pressing the SPACEBAR.

You now need to add the name of the control that you want to set the focus to. This is done as a string, which means that you have to enclose the argument in quotation marks. If you are new to VBA programming, you might make a beginner's mistake and complete the line as follows:

```
DoCmd.GoToControl "txtCustLastName"
```

When you go to run the form (by opening it), you will end up with the following message:

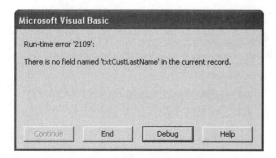

Wait! What's wrong? If you looked at the table structure, you would see that obviously it had a field called txtCustLastname. Now it says it does not exist?

The explanation is easy. A control is an object on the form. In this case, it is a text field that holds the information from the field txtCustLastName. It is not the table field itself, however. As a matter of fact, if you open the form in Design View (if it isn't already), click on the control, and go to its properties, you will see the name of the control at the top, as shown in Figure 8-6.

Figure 8-6 *Properties for ctlCustLastName*

It is traditional to give the control the same name as the field it is associated with. You just change the three-letter prefix to ctl. It is strongly suggested that you go through the form and change the prefixes of the controls to ctl.

Based on that information, the focus will need to be on ctlCustLastName, and the code should be as follows:

```
Private Sub Form_Open(Cancel As Integer)
    DoCmd.GoToControl "ctlCustLastName"
End Sub
```

Save the code by clicking on the save icon in the VBA Editor, and then open the form. If all worked well, it should look like Figure 8-7.

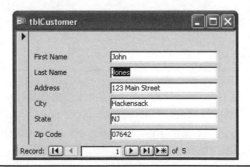

Figure 8-7 *custForm with the focus set on the last name*

There is another way you could have found the control's name. Click on the left-hand drop-down list above the Code window:

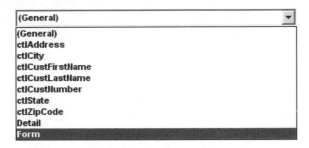

Finding a Record

You have changed the focus to the control for the last name. Let's take this one step further by adding another line to this simple example:

```
Private Sub Form_Open(Cancel As Integer)
   DoCmd.GoToControl "ctlCustLastName"
   DoCmd.FindRecord "Miller"
End Sub
```

If you now go ahead and save and then reopen the form, not only will the focus be placed on ctlLastName, but you are taken to the first record that has a last name of Miller. This is rather simplistic, admittedly, but it serves to illustrate some important concepts.

If you had reversed these two lines and opened the form, you would have received the following error message:

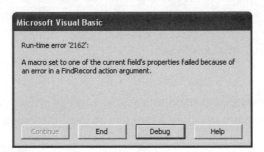

The reason for this is that you have not built the sophistication into the code yet to know where the last name of Miller is unless you first physically put the focus on that field.

Now, this is all good, except, what if you need to find someone with a different last name from Miller? Here is where the concept of variables comes in. Remember, I stated earlier that a variable is something that can change. Keep that in mind as we progress.

You know that the parameter necessary to find the last name is a string. By setting a variable as type String, and then assigning a name to it, you could flow the code as follows.

```
Private Sub Form_Open(Cancel As Integer)
   Dim strLastName As String
   strLastName = "Miller"

   DoCmd.GoToControl "ctlCustLastName"
   DoCmd.FindRecord strLastName
End Sub
```

Notice in this case the string "Miller" is assigned to the string variable strLastName. That variable is then used as the parameter to find the record. Notice that strLastName did not need to be surrounded by quotation marks as the FindRecord argument. You need quotes only when using the string directly.

Now when you save the code and open the form, it has exactly the same effect as before. It takes you to Miller. That does not solve our problem of wanting to find last names other than Miller, though.

In earlier chapters, you used the InputBox function. This would be a good place to employ that again as follows:

```
Private Sub Form_Open(Cancel As Integer)
   Dim strLastName As String
   strLastName = InputBox("Enter a last name")

   DoCmd.GoToControl "ctlCustLastName"
   DoCmd.FindRecord strLastName
End Sub
```

The input from the InputBox is used to assign a value to strLastName. As a result, when you save the code and open the form, you are first presented with the input box:

To summarize the important concepts presented here: First of all, you got to see an event, OnOpen, work. Second, you got to see how variables interact with the code. Third, you saw VBA interact with Access objects. Finally, you interacted with the variables through the use of an input box.

The Me Object

There is one interesting little variation that many programmers like to use to help clarify things a bit: the object Me. Me can be used to refer to whatever object you have open at the moment. For instance, if the frmCustomer object is open, Me will refer to that.

You can change the way you set the focus by adjusting the line:

```
DoCmd.GoToControl "ctlCustLastName"
```

If you delete that line and type **Me** instead, you get the following members:

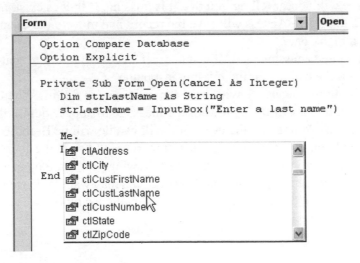

Notice that the controls of the present form are now listed as members. You can select ctlCustLastName and then type a dot again. Now you can select the SetFocus method. The end result should look like the following line of code:

```
Me.ctlCustLastName.SetFocus
```

The end result is exactly the same, and you now know that you are talking about *this* form.

You could also use the Me object to prevent any records from being changed. Add the following line above the SetFocus statement:

```
Me.AllowEdits = False
```

If you now open the form and select a last name, the form will not permit you to make any changes. This could be handy in situations in which you want to give someone access to the records, but not the ability to change them.

Validating a Record

What happens if you want to require a last name? Well, you can certainly set that as a required field in the table, but you can also do it in VBA. Before we look at the code, you must understand a bit about the pseudocode, or sequence of events, which must occur in VBA. First, there will be a test to see if the last name exists. If it does not, a message will appear telling you that it is missing. If it does exist, no message will appear. Either way, Access will save the record and move on to the next record (even if it is a blank one).

If the last name is missing, VBA must instruct Access to return to that record and set the focus on the control for the missing last name.

Understanding that sequence will make the code easy to follow. When you save a record, it is called *updating*. You want the message to appear before the update sequence happens. As a result, the event you will handle will be BeforeUpdate.

As with OnOpen, go through the form's properties, and code the event through the BeforeUpdate property. You should have the following procedure open as a result. (Note that if you are actually trying out this code, you may want to delete the previous OnOpen procedure; it could conflict with the following example.)

```
Private Sub Form_BeforeUpdate(Cancel As Integer)
End Sub
```

You will now use an If...Then statement to test whether txtLastName is null. This will be a good chance to see the If...Then structure at work.

```
Private Sub Form_BeforeUpdate(Cancel As Integer)
    If IsNull(txtCustLastName) Then
        MsgBox "Please enter a last name"
        DoCmd.GoToRecord , , acLast
        Me.ctlCustLastName.SetFocus
    End If
End Sub
```

There are several important points here. First of all, the function IsNull is used to test txtCustLastName to see if it is empty. If it is, the message appears.

Notice the line:

```
DoCmd.GoToRecord , , acLast
```

GoToRecord is a method of the DoCmd object. There is a second optional argument, but you do not need it here. Many times, even though an argument is not used in VBA, you still need to leave a place setting in between the commas. Finally, acLast is an intrinsic constant, which was discussed earlier. The ac prefix means it is an intrinsic constant of Access.

Try saving the code and opening the form. Go to a new record, and enter it without a last name. When you go to move off the record, the preceding code should be triggered and the record should return with the focus set on the last name control.

Connecting with Microsoft Access

Up to this point, you have been coding inside a form module. The module is tied to the form, which is, in turn, tied to Microsoft Access. However, when you program in a standard module, that module may only assume that you are talking about the current database.

Remember, VBA is not really part of Access. The code you write in a standard module could be connected to any database anywhere. For that reason, you usually need to insert information showing what database it should be connected to, even if it is the current database.

If you do not have a standard module, perhaps called Module1, open a new one by right-clicking inside the Project Explorer and selecting Insert | Module. Once there, put the following code into it:

```
Sub openForm()
   DoCmd.openForm "frmCustomer"
End Sub
```

If you go ahead and run this code, using the Run button on the Standard toolbar, it will open the form. Once the form is active, any VBA code in the form module will take over and control the form from there.

This is not great programming, however, since the module assumes you are connected to the current database. It is far better to formally put connection code into it. We will do this as a string and tell the module that the connection will be to the current project.

To use this code, you must first make sure that you have the references shown in Figure 8-8 turned on. You access this dialog by using Tools | References located in the VBA Editor. From here on, you will need to use this code pro forma.

```
Sub openForm()
   Dim con As ADODB.Connection
   Set con = CurrentProject.Connection
   DoCmd.openForm "frmCustomer"
End Sub
```

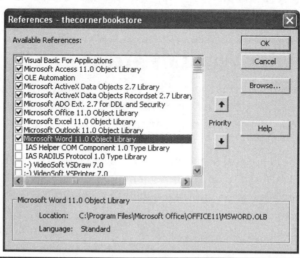

Figure 8-8   *References for Access Programming*

Remember, an object is an entity located somewhere in memory. In order to use it, there must be a pointer, called the *object reference*, to that memory location.

The first line of the preceding code states that the word "con" will be an object reference that will point to the Connection object accessed in the ADODB library. The Set command actually assigns the reference to the object. It is similar to a variable: first you declare it, and then you assign a value to it. You will learn more about this as we progress through the book. The code should run the same as before.

SQL (Structured Query Language)

Before you can move on in your study of VBA, you need to start learning a second language that will work along with VBA.

The power of any database is the ability to ask it questions. This is called *querying* the database. There is a good possibility that you have done this many times without knowing it. If you use an Internet search engine, such as Yahoo! or Google, you have queried a database when you asked it to search for some topic. The language behind the query is called SQL (pronounced "C-Quill").

SQL stands for Structured Query Language, which is the universal syntax for asking database questions. Virtually every database program, with minor variations, uses it. Once you have learned the standard syntax of SQL, which is fairly simple, you can ask a broad range of questions and bring a lot of information together easily.

Covering every aspect of SQL would take a book in itself; instead, we will look at the main points. Let's begin by using SQL in a nonprogramming environment.

SQL — the Basics

If you are an experienced Access user, odds are you have built query objects. Most likely, you have used the graphics tools built into Access to do it. You have dropped the fields you wanted into a grid, selected which fields you wanted the results sorted on, and maybe even added a search criterion. Again, you probably did it all graphically.

What you may not have realized is that Access was writing SQL in the background for you. Let's see an example. Start a new query object in Access, and select the tblCustomer object for the table. If you add some columns, a sort, and a possible search criterion, your screen should look something like Figure 8-9.

Access allows you a peek behind the scenes if you select View | SQL View. You will see the SQL that was written behind the scenes of this query, as shown in Figure 8-10. Let's break the query into sections and discuss them.

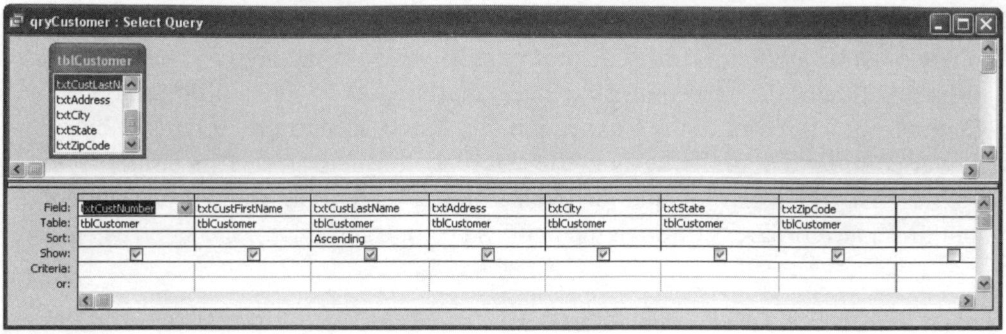

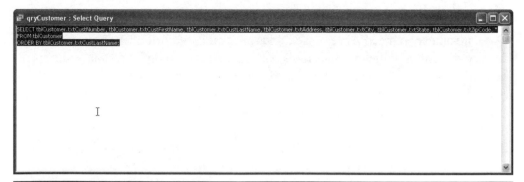

Figure 8-9   *The Query grid*

SELECT

By tradition, programmers usually put SQL keywords in all caps. SQL is not case sensitive, but using uppercase helps SQL keywords stand out better.

The SELECT keyword chooses the columns you wish to use. In the case of multiple columns, they are separated by commas. For example:

```
SELECT txtCustFirstName, txtCustLastName
```

In many cases, you may want to use all of the columns. In this case, you can use an asterisk (*) to indicate all columns:

```
SELECT *
```

Figure 8-10   *The query in SQL View*

But where do the columns come from? Well, the answer is in the question. The SELECT clause needs to be completed with the keyword FROM and the name of the source. You would complete it with:

```
SELECT txtCustFirstName, txtCustLastName FROM tblCustomer
```

If you want to be very correct with your syntax, write the SELECT clause as follows:

```
SELECT tblCustomer.txtCustFirstName, tblCustomer.txtCustLastName,
tblCustomer.txtState
```

When you are using one data source, it is not necessary to precede each field name with a table reference. But in a few moments, this will be important when you work with multiple tables.

This would be considered the mandatory part of the SQL statement. Now you have some options you can add.

WHERE

The WHERE keyword allows you to add search criteria. For instance, you might enter

```
SELECT txtCustFirstName, txtCustLastName FROM tblCustomer WHERE txtState = 'NJ'
```

Notice that because the field txtState is a text field, the search string is surrounded by single quotation marks. This is going to be important when we return to VBA because the search string needs to be differentiated from the SQL string.

In many cases you may have multiple search criteria separated by the logical operators AND or OR. For example:

```
SELECT txtCustFirstName, txtCustLastName FROM tblCustomer WHERE txtState = 'NJ' AND
txtCustLastName = 'Miller'
```

Let's say you want to see all the records in which the last name begins with the letter *M*. You use the operator Like to do pattern matching with an asterisk. For example:

```
SELECT txtCustFirstName, txtCustLastName FROM tblCustomer WHERE txtCustLastName
Like 'M*'
```

You use the asterisk to replace all characters from that point on, or use the question mark to replace one character.

ORDER BY

You use the ORDER BY clause to sort the recordset. This clause can be placed either before or after the WHERE clause. As an example:

```
SELECT txtCustFirstName, txtCustLastName FROM tblCustomer WHERE txtState = 'NJ'
ORDER BY txtCustLastName
```

Let's assume you want to sort by the last name and then the first:

```
SELECT txtCustFirstName, txtCustLastName FROM tblCustomer WHERE txtState = 'NJ'
ORDER BY txtCustLastName, txtCustFirstName
```

By default, the sort is ascending. However, if you want it to be descending, you simply add the keyword DESC, as shown next:

```
SELECT txtCustFirstName, txtCustLastName FROM tblCustomer WHERE txtState = 'NJ'
ORDER BY txtCustLastName DESC, txtCustFirstName
```

INNER JOIN

In many instances, you may want to join two or more tables to bring data from different tables together. This can be a bit tricky because before you can do this, there must be a relationship on a unique value. For instance, two tables could be joined by an employee number. In general, fields such as last name are not a good choice to link because there could be multiple occurrences of the name.

When you do an INNER JOIN, you need to specify the source of the field, as shown earlier with the SELECT clause. The syntax is a bit involved. As an example:

```
SELECT tblCustomer.txtCustNumber, tblCustomer.txtCustLastName,
tblPurchases.txtPurchaseNumber FROM tblCustomer INNER JOIN tblPurchases ON
tblCustomer.txtCustNumber = tblPurchases.txtCustNumber;
```

Beginning with the FROM clause, you name the first table and then add a second table with INNER JOIN. However, you need to specify how the two tables can be linked. In this case, the txtCustNumber field of the tblCustomer table is linked with the txtNumber field of tblPurchases. Notice that the two fields do not have to have the same name. Notice, also, that you had to specify the originating table of the fields.

It is interesting to note that if you use the SQL View of Access to type out a SQL string, the graphic builder will automatically conform to the view. For example, if you typed the preceding SQL statement in SQL View, the graphic builder would look like Figure 8-11.

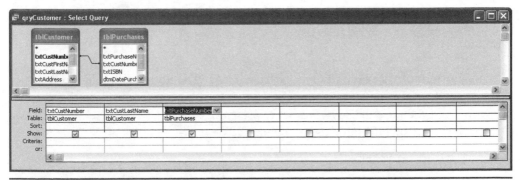

Figure 8-11   *Graphic query builder after typing the statement in SQL View*

In a few moments, you will be adding SQL statements to your VBA code. It is a common practice to set up and test the query using the graphic builder. Then, if it works to your liking, go into SQL View to copy and paste the statement into your VBA code. This saves a lot of typing and helps prevent potential errors.

SQL and VBA

A SQL statement can be plugged into your code as a string and saved in a string variable. We will be creating a Recordset object. A *recordset* is the collection of records that are of specific interest to us. The following code does this:

```
Sub MyFirstConnection()
    Dim con1 As ADODB.Connection
    Dim recSet1 As ADODB.Recordset
    Set con1 = CurrentProject.Connection

    Set recSet1 = New ADODB.Recordset
    recSet1.Open "tblCustomer", con1

    Do Until recSet1.EOF
       Debug.Print recSet1.Fields("txtCustFirstName"), _
                   recSet1.Fields("txtCustLastName")
       recSet1.MoveNext
    Loop
    recSet1.Close
    con1.Close
```

```
      Set con1 = Nothing
      Set recSet1 = Nothing
End Sub
```

This code employs a second object from the ADODB library called Recordset. As with the Connection object, you first declare the object reference—in this case recSet1—and then use the keyword Set to assign it.

You opened a specific table using the line:

```
recSet1.Open "tblCustomer", con1
```

The Recordset object has a method called Open that can be used to open the table containing the data. The con1 reference tells the Open method where the table can be found—in this case, in the current project.

The Recordset object also has a Boolean property called EOF. It can test whether the recordset is on the last record. This can be handy when setting up the loop in the preceding code. It also has a method called MoveNext, which can be used to advance the record pointer to the next record.

When you run the code, you are going to output the first and last names of each record. Again, the Recordset object has a property called Fields, so you can specify the fields from the recordset that you want to include in the output.

If you run the procedure, you will see the result shown here:

Look at the last four lines of the code:

```
recSet1.Close
con1.Close
Set con1 = Nothing
Set recSet1 = Nothing
```

It is good form to use the Close method, in both the Recordset and Connection objects, to close down the connections. Once the connections are closed, you set the object references to Nothing. This will take the objects out of memory.

What if you want to sort the results on the last name? Let's do a little adjustment to the code:

```
Sub MyFirstConnection()
    Dim con1 As ADODB.Connection
    Dim recSet1 As ADODB.Recordset
    Dim strSQL As String

    strSQL = "SELECT * FROM tblCustomer ORDER BY txtCustLastName"

    Set con1 = CurrentProject.Connection

    Set recSet1 = New ADODB.Recordset
    recSet1.Open strSQL, con1

    Do Until recSet1.EOF
       Debug.Print recSet1.Fields("txtCustFirstName"), _
                   recSet1.Fields("txtCustLastName")
       recSet1.MoveNext
    Loop
    recSet1.Close
    con1.Close
    Set con1 = Nothing
    Set recSet1 = Nothing
End Sub
```

Notice that a string variable, strSQL, is declared, and then the SQL statement is assigned to it. Then, rather than having the recordset open the table, the variable containing the SQL statement is used to open the table and produce the recordset. The new results are as follows:

There may be times when you want to select the WHERE criteria at runtime, as opposed to hard-coding it. This is going to require some additional code as follows:

```
Sub MyFirstConnection()
    Dim con1 As ADODB.Connection
    Dim recSet1 As ADODB.Recordset
    Dim strSQL As String
    Dim strSearch As String

    strSearch = InputBox("Enter the last name to find", "Search Criterion")

    strSQL = "SELECT txtCustFirstName, txtCustLastName FROM tblCustomer" & _
            " WHERE txtCustLastName = " & " '" & strSearch & "'"

    Set con1 = CurrentProject.Connection

    Set recSet1 = New ADODB.Recordset
    recSet1.Open strSQL, con1

    Do Until recSet1.EOF
        Debug.Print recSet1.Fields("txtCustFirstName"), _
                    recSet1.Fields("txtCustLastName")
        recSet1.MoveNext
    Loop
    recSet1.Close
    con1.Close
    Set con1 = Nothing
    Set recSet1 = Nothing
End Sub
```

As in the previous example, you set up a string variable and use an input box to obtain a value from the user. However, you need to do a bit of concatenation in the SQL string.

You will recall that the string you are searching for needs to be surrounded by single quotation marks. However, you cannot do that directly to the variable, or it will not be recognized. So you concatenate, as you have before, in the line:

```
strSQL = "SELECT txtCustFirstName, txtCustLastName FROM tblCustomer WHERE
txtCustLastName = " & "'" & strSearch & "'"
```

If you run this code, you should be prompted for the last name that you want, with the results shown in the Immediate window.

Since there is only one record that meets this criteria, the loop encounters the end of the recordset after displaying information from the single record.

Output

You could make the output of the example look a little nicer with just a few simple programming techniques that you have already learned. Right now the output is in columns. By doing a simple concatenation, as follows, you can make it look like a list of names.

```
Sub MyFirstConnection()
    Dim con1 As ADODB.Connection
    Dim recSet1 As ADODB.Recordset
    Dim strSQL As String

    strSQL = "SELECT txtCustFirstName, txtCustLastName FROM tblCustomer"
    Set con1 = CurrentProject.Connection

    Set recSet1 = New ADODB.Recordset
    recSet1.Open strSQL, con1

    Do Until recSet1.EOF
       Debug.Print recSet1.Fields("txtCustFirstName") & " " & _
                   recSet1.Fields("txtCustLastName")
       recSet1.MoveNext
    Loop
    recSet1.Close
    con1.Close
    Set con1 = Nothing
    Set recSet1 = Nothing
End Sub
```

Notice that a simple concatenation is performed, within the loop, of the results of the recordset. As a result, the output now looks like this:

```
Immediate                                                          ×
 John Jones                                                       ▲
 Jane Smith
 Jack Harris
 Susan Miller
 Robert Jones
                                                                 ▼
◄                                                              ►
```

You could send the output to a message box for an even better result. However, if you use the loop as you are using it now, you would end up with a new message box for each record in the recordset. Instead, you need to declare a new string variable and build the output within that variable. Then, you output the entire variable to the message box. Let's take a look at the following code:

```
Sub MyFirstConnection()
    Dim con1 As ADODB.Connection
    Dim recSet1 As ADODB.Recordset
    Dim strSQL As String
    Dim strOutput As String

    strSQL = "SELECT txtCustFirstName, txtCustLastName FROM tblCustomer"

    Set con1 = CurrentProject.Connection

    Set recSet1 = New ADODB.Recordset
    recSet1.Open strSQL, con1

    Do Until recSet1.EOF
        strOutput = strOutput + recSet1.Fields("txtCustFirstName") & " " & _
                                recSet1.Fields("txtCustLastName") & vbCrLf
        recSet1.MoveNext
    Loop
    recSet1.Close
    MsgBox strOutput
    con1.Close
    Set con1 = Nothing
    Set recSet1 = Nothing
End Sub
```

You assign to the variable strOutput whatever was previously in strOutput and then add a concatenation. At the completion of the concatenation, an intrinsic constant, vbCrLf, which represents a new line character, is used.

Now your output looks something like this:

For large quantities of data, this may not be practical. But for quick results involving a relatively small recordset, it does the job quite nicely.

Notice that in all of the preceding examples, using the objects contained in the ADODB library saved a tremendous amount of programming. Both the Connection and Recordset objects contain hundreds of lines of code. If you did not have these objects, you would need to write all of that code just to perform the simplest of tasks.

Chapter 15 contains a more complete discussion of these libraries.

Summary

We really covered a lot of territory here, and you just had your first taste of connecting VBA code to the database. We started with simple form examples and then saw the power of ADODB objects not only to connect to the database, but to save hundreds of lines of programming code. You also saw how to use these objects to help present formatted outputs of the resulting recordsets. In many ways, the rest of this book will explore the power of these objects.

We now turn our attention to building procedures and learning how they can interact with each other.

Sub Procedures

I n the previous chapter we put a lot of pieces together. You learned how to connect the code with the database by getting your first look at ADO. In addition, you got some experience in implementing objects.

Up to this point, we have used procedures. However, we have not taken a close look at the mechanics and options available with procedures. In this chapter we are going to concentrate on the mechanics of building a procedure. You will learn the various ways to declare and run a procedure, the various ways arguments can be passed, and the meaning of the word "scope." You will also learn the differences between sub procedures and functions.

Finally, we will continue to build on the previous chapter by finding various ways to connect with the database.

Declaring a Procedure

The term *procedure* can have two completely different meanings: it can refer to either a sub or a function. A *sub* is simply a block of code that carries out a set of instructions. A *function* returns a value to whatever called it (usually another procedure).

A procedure does its job when it is called by name and given any arguments needed. Procedures usually are not isolated entities; they usually operate in symphony with each other. Imagine this scenario: Procedure A is called. In order for it to complete its job, it needs more specialized information from procedure B. So, in order to get it, it calls B. B, in turn, needs information from procedure C.

Procedure C then sends information back to procedure B, which in turn sends information back to procedure A.

This scenario may sound a bit far-fetched to the beginning programmer, but it is actually common in VBA projects. Each procedure should have a specialized purpose. While you may think that would make the project unmanageable, it actually adds to the ease of manageability. If something is not working right, you can go directly to the procedure in charge of that particular job.

There is another benefit: specialization adds to the reusability of procedures. If you have a procedure, for example, that formats a number to the currency format, you can reuse that procedure in any project that needs that particular job done.

Finally, this method cuts down on code redundancy. If you have a procedure whose only job is to format a number to the currency format, it can be called from anywhere within the project. Thus, you won't need to write the same code over and over.

NOTE

When speaking about concepts that encompass both subs and functions, I will sometimes just use the generic word "procedure."

In its simplest form, a sub is declared as follows:

```
Sub Name_of_Sub_Procedure(Arguments)
```

And a function is declared as follows:

```
Function Name_of_Function(Arguments) As Type
```

In both cases, the name must meet the following rules:

► It must start with a letter (rather than a number or special character like _). However, after that, it can contain any combination of letters and numbers.

► It cannot be more than 255 characters long.

► It cannot contain spaces. In general, try to follow naming conventions discussed in the first three chapters. You can sometimes use an underscore (_) to simulate a space.

► It cannot use a VBA keyword.

► It must use parentheses to accept arguments, even if there are none.

As with variables, it is a good idea to use descriptive names so that the procedure is almost self-documenting.

Declaring a function is a bit more involved. Remember, a function returns a value. However, as with a variable, you have to declare what type of value you are going to be returning. The types that a function can return are the same types that variables use. So, if your function is going to return a string, you would declare it as:

```
Function myFunction() As String
```

You can also declare who has access to the procedure with the keywords Private and Public. See "Design and Scope," later in the chapter, for more on this.

The sub and function constructs also include a statement to indicate where the procedure's code ends. In the case of a sub, it is:

```
End Sub
```

For a function:

```
End Function
```

VBA gives us a handy tool to assist in building procedures and functions. It is called the Add Procedure dialog box and can be found in the Insert menu:

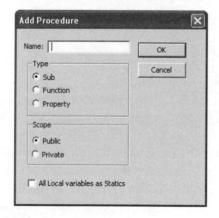

Here you can name the procedure, specify its type, decide whether it will be Public or Private, and even decide how the variables will be treated. If some of these options are unclear to you now, don't worry! We will be treating them as we progress through this chapter.

At any given point, you can either use this dialog box or type the procedure name.

Functions

Since we have already had some experience with sub procedures, let's concentrate for now on functions. Let's assume you either start, or open, an existing module. A simple function might look as follows:

```
Function fullName() As String
    Dim strFirstName As String
    Dim strLastName As String
    Dim strFullName As String

    strFirstName = "John"
    strLastName = "Smith"
    strFullName = strFirstName & " " & strLastName
End Function
```

Seems pretty straightforward! Well, since we are not using a GUI, you will have to use the Immediate window to test it.

Testing a function in the Immediate window is a little different from testing a sub. Remember, you are asking the function to return a value, in this case, a string. You are asking, "What is the full name?" In order to do that, you type the following in the Immediate window:

```
?fullName
```

Then press ENTER.

Whoops! Nothing. Not even an error!

Wait, you were asking the function, fullName, to return a string. You just forgot one little part: what string? Do you want it to return strFirstName, strLastName, or strFullName?

It may be obvious to you that you want it to return strFullName, but it is not so obvious to VBA. (Chapter 3 discussed the importance of using the proper sequence.) Here is how it works: A function is like a variable in that it stores a value to a name that will be returned to whatever is calling that name. However, the value returned by the function must be assigned to a variable with the same name as the function. To illustrate this, let's add one more line of code after the concatenation:

```
fullName = strFullName
```

Go ahead and test it now. It should work fine.

Whatever you assigned to the function name will be the return value of the function. Also remember that if you do not assign a value, nothing will be returned.

Notice that unlike subs, you don't need to place the Debug.Print statement in your code to show an output in the Immediate window because a function is already returning a value that will show in the window.

A little later in this chapter, you will see how to find functions prebuilt within the VBA library.

Parameters

Up to this point, our procedures have been self-contained. For learning purposes, that is very handy. But in reality, this will rarely happen. Usually, the variables within your procedures will need to get their values from an outside source. To do this, you need to set up *parameters* in the parentheses after the procedure's name. In programming terminology, the process of sending information to those variables is called *passing parameters*.

Let's start with a simple illustration. We are going to vary the fullName function as shown below:

```
Function fullName(strFname As String, strLname As String) As String
    Dim strFirstName As String
    Dim strLastName As String
    Dim strFullName As String

    strFirstName = strFname
    strLastName = strLname

    strFullName = strFirstName & " " & strLastName

    fullName = strFullName
End Function
```

Let's take a few minutes to examine what is going on.

Our function now needs the caller to send it two pieces of information before it can do its job: a first name and a last name. It doesn't care what those names are (as long as they are strings), just that it needs them.

Let's go to the Immediate window and type the following:

```
? fullName ("Jane", "Doe")
```

The call sends two arguments. The first one goes to strFName, and the second goes to strLName.

You may find it curious that I made the parameter names different from the variable names inside the function. This is standard programming practice. You never want a caller to access the variables of a procedure directly. The moment you do, you have lost control of that variable. Many times you may create If...Then structures to test the incoming parameters for validity. As an example, you may want to put the following filter in your procedure:

```
If strFName = " " Then
     strFirstName = "(Name not provided)"
Else
     strFirstName = strFName
End If
```

On the caller side, it is important that the arguments are sent in the correct order and with the correct data type. The parameters are separated by a comma.

Just to illustrate a point, try typing

```
?fullName ("Doe", "Jane")
```

The procedure now thinks "Doe" is the first name and "Jane" is the last name. It has no way of distinguishing what you really want from what you sent.

Let's set up our module with a second procedure now:

```
Sub getName()
    Dim strFirstName As String
    Dim strLastName As String
    Dim strFullName As String

    strFirstName = InputBox("Enter the First Name", "First Name")
    strLastName = InputBox("Enter the Last Name", "Last Name")

    strFullName = fullName(strFirstName, strLastName)
    MsgBox strFullName, , "Full Name"
End Sub
```

A lot is going on here that we need to look at.

First of all, notice that the same variable names are declared in each procedure. Aren't they going to clash? These are called *local variables*. They only exist for the procedure they are in, and once the procedure does its job, they disappear. You could have as many procedures as you want with the same variable names, and they will not see each other or clash.

The procedure getName calls the procedure fullName with the two required parameters. fullName then does the job of concatenation and returns the combined string to the caller, getName. What you don't see is that when the value is returned, the call

```
fullName(strFirstName, strLastName)
```

is converted to

```
fullName = "Jane Doe"
```

That is how functions return information. From there on, we used the variable fullName in the message box as we have at other times.

All you need to do is call the sub, getName, from the Immediate window. Remember, because it is not a function, you don't need to preface it with the question mark.

This is all very neat. However, as you are about to see, things can get somewhat complex now.

Optional Parameters

You want your procedures to be as flexible as possible. However, as you just saw, they expect a certain number of arguments, each of a certain type, and in a certain order. That certainly does not sound very flexible.

As an example, suppose that some of the data going to the fullName function contains a middle name, while other data does not. Based on the preceding description, you could not handle that. However, VBA comes to your aid with a unique programming tool. It is called the optional argument. You could declare the function as follows:

```
Function fullName (strName as String, Optional strMName As String,_
Optional strLName As String)
```

The Optional parameters should be the last ones because once one is used, any subsequent parameters must be optional.

You now have four ways of calling this function. You can call it with:

```
fullName(strFirstName, strMiddleName, strLastName)
```

Or you can call it with

```
fullName(strFirstName, , strLastName)
```

Or you can use

```
FullName(strFirstName, strMiddleName)
```

Finally:

```
FullName(strFirstName)
```

Notice the placeholder in place of the second argument in the second function call. (Even though it is not shown here, you would need to adjust the code in the fullName procedure to handle the new parameter and include it in the concatenation.) This adds a lot of flexibility to the procedure.

In many instances, you may want to substitute a default value if an optional parameter is not provided. Let's take a look at the following potential procedure declaration:

```
Sub account (strFirstName As String, strLastName As String, -
Optional intBalance as Integer = 0)
```

Here, intBalance is an optional parameter. However, rather than just leave it null, a default value of 0 will be set if no other value is provided.

Named Parameters

It is easy to see that all these parameters, with assorted options, can get Byzantine in their declarations. For instance, let's say you have a scenario such as this:

```
Function fullname(Optional strFName As String, _
Optional strMName As String, Optional strLName As String)
```

As stated in the preceding section, this procedure can now be called in a variety of ways. Just to name a few:

```
fullName(strFirstName, , )
```

or

```
fullName(, strMiddleName, )
```

or

```
fullName(, , strLastName)
```

or

```
fullName(strFirstName, strMiddleName, strLastName)
```

Let's also add a scenario of different callers possibly calling the procedure with the parameters in different order.

Getting the idea? There is an easier way. By simply using the function's actual parameter names and a colon, many of your problems will be solved.

Again, using the preceding function, you could call it as follows:

```
fullName(strFName: = "John")
```

Isn't that much easier?

As a matter of fact, even without optional parameters, you could have done something like this:

```
fullName(strMName: = "E", strLName: = "Smith", strFName: = "John")
```

You can completely rearrange the arguments as needed. Needless to say, this greatly streamlines the process by allowing for a number of different ways of passing parameters without doing additional coding.

As an interesting note, as you will see in Chapter 12, you can use a named parameter in VBA code as a Goto point. In that setting, it is sometimes referred to as a LineLabel. Again, it is a name followed by a colon.

Design and Scope

As I have stated several times, you can have as many modules in your project as you need. However, is it wise just to throw any procedure on any module without thought? Of course not!

Here is a design point: each procedure should perform one specialized task. For instance, in this chapter, we have used an example of a function whose only job is to concatenate a last name and a first name. It is not unusual to see that. By doing it that way, you end up with code that is easier to manage and debug. It also makes the procedure reusable. For instance, anytime in the project you need to concatenate, you can call the same procedure. While this will not add to memory "overhead," your project could end up with many procedures. In programming parlance, the term *overhead* is the amount of resources something uses.

You have also seen that a procedure rarely exists on its own. As stated at the beginning of this chapter, in most projects, it is not unusual to see procedure A call procedure B, which in turn calls procedure C, and so on.

While there are no hard-and-fast rules, you should try to group procedures in the modules with their dependence in mind. For instance, you may want all the procedures for formatting names in one module, while the procedures to do date calculations are in another module.

In practice, you preface procedures with the keywords Public or Private. Public means that the procedure can be accessed by another procedure in another module. Private means that it can be accessed only by procedures in the same module. Again, deciding which procedures to make public, and which to make private, is a design issue with no hard rules.

Many times you will make only one or two procedures public. In programming terms, these procedures serve as the module's *interface*. In other words, this is the controlled access point to the module from other modules.

Variables have a scope also. The term *scope* means who can see it. As you saw earlier, a variable within a procedure normally can only be seen within that procedure; when the procedure's job ends, the variable and its contents fade into the sunset. We say that its scope is *local* to that procedure.

Again, to summarize, a local procedure has a lifetime of the procedure that it is located in.

Next, I will be talking about two other types of variables whose lifetime is outside of a procedure.

Global and Static Variables

As stated earlier, a variable is only visible within the procedure and will only exist until the procedure completes its job. There are two exceptions—global variables and static variables.

Global Variables

You will recall that the code at the very top of the module is the general declarations area. What goes there affects the whole module. Up to this point, we have only used two lines of code there:

```
Option Compare Database
Option Explicit
```

For the sake of review, Option Compare Database forces VBA to use the Access sort order when comparing strings. You could also set it to Option Compare Binary. This, in essence, will make strings case sensitive when comparing two strings. It would look upon the strings "Test" and "test" as being unequal.

Option Explicit means that a variable must be declared before it can be used. As I have pointed out earlier, it is a good idea to use this. It will make for fewer potential programming errors.

Interestingly, these are not the only things you can do in the declarations area. You can also set a variable there. The variable will be available to all the procedures in the module. As an example, you could set the following *global variable*:

```
Private strFullName As String
```

Notice the example is set as Private. As with procedures, Private means it can only be seen by procedures in the module. Public means it can be accessed by other modules. In my many years of programming, I have never set a global variable as Public. Again, it is strongly recommended that your variables should only be accessed through procedures. By not doing that, anyone can put any value into a variable that they want. That is not a very secure way of doing things.

Static Variables

A *static variable* is one that will stay in memory after the procedure has completed its job. However, it can only be accessed by that procedure.

As an example, the procedure may need to keep a running total of a count. Every time the procedure runs, it may need to add to that total. For that, a static variable does the job quite nicely.

Let's take a quick look at a static variable. Set up a procedure as follows:

```
Sub staticTestProcedure()
    Static intCounter As Integer
    intCounter = intCounter + 1
    Debug.Print intCounter
End Sub
```

Notice that intCounter is declared as being Static. Again, this means that intCounter is still local to this procedure. No other procedure will have access to it. However, when the procedure is finished, intCounter will be retained in memory with the last value assigned to it.

If you run the procedure multiple times from the Immediate window, intCounter will increment to the next number each time.

Neither global nor static variables are used frequently. However, it is a good idea to have them in your collection of tools for special occasions.

Using Procedures to Change a Database Structure

Up to this point, we have been using procedures to look at data. In order to accomplish that, we have used objects from the ADODB library to connect to the database. ADODB is part of a larger library called ADO (ActiveX Database Objects). ADO will be discussed in greater detail in the course of this book. However, in order to accomplish anything, we need to touch on certain aspects of it.

Another part of ADO is the ADOX library. Briefly, objects from this library have the task of handling structural issues of the database. For instance, you would use the ADOX objects to construct and analyze the structure of a table. Let's try a simple example to demonstrate the use of these objects.

Constructing a Table

Within the ADOX library, there are several important objects:

▶ The Catalog object looks at the structures of the objects within the database. An important property of this object is ActiveConnection. This will tell the Catalog object what database structure you are talking about. Think of this object as a giant container that will hold the objects (tables, reports, forms, queries, etc.) of your database. Within this container, you would have a collection of objects for Tables.

▶ The Table object, within the Catalog container, contains the columns, fields, indexes, keys, and so on.

▶ Within the Table object is the Column object, which contains the properties of name, type, attributes, size, and numeric precision.

▶ The Table object also contains the Index and Key objects. The Index object contains the properties of name, indexnull, primarykey, unique, and clustered. The Key object contains the properties of relatedtable, deleterule, updaterule, and type.

Let's build a simple table using the ADOX objects.

```
Sub makeTable()
    Dim currCat As New ADOX.Catalog
    Dim newTable As New ADOX.Table
    Dim newKey As New ADOX.Key

    currCat.ActiveConnection = CurrentProject.Connection

    With newTable
       .Name = "tblTestTable"
       .Columns.Append "custNumber", adInteger
       .Columns("custNumber").ParentCatalog = currCat
       .Columns("custNumber").Properties("AutoIncrement") = True

       newKey.Name = "PrimaryKey"
       newKey.Columns.Append "custNumber"
       .Keys.Append newKey, adKeyPrimary
```

```
        .Columns.Append "custFirstName", adWChar
        .Columns.Append "custLastName", adWChar
    End With

    currCat.Tables.Append newTable

    Set currCat = Nothing
End Sub
```

Notice that in this code you created a new instance of the Catalog object called currcat (the object reference). Then, within that, you created a new instance of the Table object with the reference of newTable. Finally, you created a new instance of the Key object with reference of newKey.

Past that, you use a structure that we have not examined called With. The With structure allows you to reference the object once using the With keyword. From there on, all you need to do is type the dot (the period key) and select the object's member on a line-by-line basis. This has the potential of saving you a lot of typing as well as offering improved performance.

You would use the Name property to give the table a name.

In this little example, there is a key field. The sequence of events is interesting. You must first use the Append property to create the column, give it a name, and indicate the data type.

Since it is going to be a primary key, you need to attach it to the Catalog object using the ParentCatalog property. Finally, you set the Boolean value of the AutoIncrement property to True.

Just making the column an auto-incrementing column does not make it a primary key automatically. You now need to attach the Key object to the column by creating a reference to it and then appending that reference to the column. Finally, you indicate that it is the primary key with the adKeyPrimary constant.

The next two lines add two text columns to the table: custFirstName and custLastName. Notice that they each have a data type of adWChar. If this sounds cryptic, it is an ADO equivalent of the Text data type in Access.

Recall from the previous chapter that these are called intrinsic constants and, as such, have an identifier prefix. Since these are within ADO, their identifier is ad.

Table 9-1 gives you the conversions for these types.

Finally, after the With structure has ended, you need to append the table to the catalog that contains the structure for the database. In other words, this last part actually takes the constructed table and adds it to the database.

Microsoft Access Data Type	ADO Equivalent
Binary	adBinary
Boolean	adBoolean
Byte	adUnsignedTinyInt
Currency	adCurrency
Date	adDate
Numeric	adNumeric
Double	adDouble
Small Integer	adSmallInt
Integer	adInteger
Long Binary	adLongBinary
Memo	adLongVarWChar
Single	adSingle
Text	adWChar

Table 9-1   *ADO Equivalents to Access Data Types*

If you now go to the Database window, you will see the new table listed, as shown in Figure 9-1. If you do not see it, it should appear after you select the Refresh option from the View menu, or press F5.

If you look at the structure, it should be as we defined it, as shown in Figure 9-2.

Figure 9-1   *The new table in the Database window*

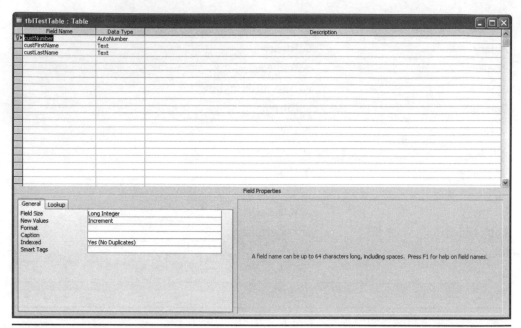

Figure 9-2 *Structure of the new table*

Summary

We now have examined the various ways procedures can be declared and called. You saw how to use optional parameters, as well as parameters that can be called specifically by name. We also distinguished between a sub and a function. Chapter 11 will have more to say about functions.

Finally, you used a procedure that incorporated objects from the ADOX library to create a table.

We are now going to turn our attention to handling errors (none of which are of our making…of course!).

Debugging VBA Code

W hile we certainly have not covered all topics, you now have a good foundation in using VBA programming to access data and objects within the Access environment. In the past few chapters we have looked at programming structures, procedures, and many objects associated with the ADO libraries. We have even used SQL to create recordsets.

In this chapter we examine what happens when you encounter an error. In the process, we will discuss the types of errors that can occur, the tools you have available to fix them, how to step through an error, and how to write code to handle errors.

Basics of Error Handling

If you have tried code examples from this book, you have probably run into something like this:

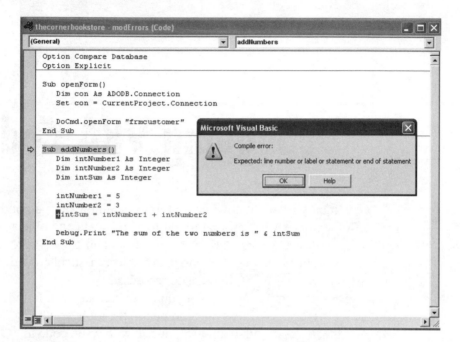

What is going on is that the VBA Editor is trying to help you out a bit.

As you leave a line, the editor looks at the code and tries to spot potential errors. The first thing it does is try to repair the errors without your even knowing about it. If it cannot, however, you will get a message similar to the one shown.

This is a very simple example of a *design-time error*. Examples of design-time errors are undefined variables, missing End statements (such as End If, or End With), and improper syntax. Most of these errors will be easy to fix, and they require little discussion. You simply need to look up the proper syntax or follow the message that the VBA Editor will give you as to the type of error.

The more difficult type of error to solve is the runtime error.

Runtime Errors

Once you have written a program well, nothing ever goes wrong. True or false? I don't think it would come as a surprise to anyone that the answer is false. In fact, a lot can go wrong that has nothing to do with the quality of the coding. As an example, as mentioned in previous chapters, you could open databases in different locations. What would your program do if the database file was missing from the location you indicated? What would happen if the database file was where it should be, but someone modified it, and a table or form being called was missing?

Some errors occur during the design stage, which, as you have just seen, VBA catches as soon as you leave the erroneous line of code (provided it is a syntax error and not an error in logic). Some errors occur when the code actually runs. This type of error—a runtime error—is often an error in logic. For instance, the code may cause an array to go past the upper boundary setting ("out of bounds" error). You have no way of knowing that this is happening until the code runs.

What we are going to be talking about here is known in programming parlance as *exceptions*. An exception is something that causes an interruption to the normal flow of the program. We use the word "exception" because this problem is usually something that will occur infrequently.

As a programmer, you must anticipate the potential problems and provide code to help the program resolve the problem gracefully. Again, in programming parlance, we call this *exception handling*. Since VBA does not distinguish between errors and exceptions, I will use the term "error" to mean exception. As a programmer, you must be able to anticipate what could go wrong and write the necessary code to handle it.

Let's begin with a simple coding example where we will intentionally cause an error to happen:

```
Sub errorTest()
    Dim intNumerator As Integer
    Dim intDenominator As Integer
    Dim intResult As Integer
    intNumerator = InputBox("Please enter a numerator", "Numerator")
    intDenominator = InputBox("Please enter a denominator",_
"Denominator")

    intResult = intNumerator / intDenominator
    MsgBox "The result is " & intResult
End Sub
```

As you can see, this is a pretty simple bit of coding that asks the user to input an integer for the numerator and an integer for the denominator, divides the two numbers, and then outputs the results to a message box.

You can go ahead and give it a try. But I want to break a commandment of mathematics. When you start the code, you should see the first input box. Let's enter the number 11 for the numerator:

After selecting OK, you are presented with the denominator input box:

Notice that 0 is entered as the denominator. Division by zero is a mathematical impossibility, which most programs treat as an error. Once you click OK, you should get the following error box.

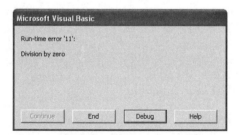

Notice that this gives you an error number (11) and an error description ("Division by zero"). You also have the option of ending the program or, by clicking the Debug button, going to what VBA "thinks" is the offending piece of code. (I don't mean to make the last sentence sound cynical. However, as many programmers will point out, where the error is, and where the program crashes, can sometimes be two different places.) The error box is the point where the program crashed. VBA is assuming everything before it is correct (and, in this case, it is). Note that in some cases, you are also given the option to continue the program. Such is not the case with "division by zero."

Do you really want your end user to see this error box? Wouldn't you like a more graceful way of helping your user to get out of this?

Let's make some modifications to the code as indicated by the gray shading shown here:

```
Sub errorTest()
    Dim intNumerator As Integer
    Dim intDenominator As Integer
    Dim intResult As Integer
    On Error GoTo mytrap
    intNumerator = InputBox("Please enter a numerator", "Numerator")
    intDenominator = InputBox("Please enter a denominator", "Denominator")
    intResult = intNumerator / intDenominator
    MsgBox ("The result is " & intResult)
    Exit Sub

mytrap:
    MsgBox "You cannot divide by zero"
End Sub
```

Before we examine the code, let's once again run it and force the "divide by zero" message. This time, instead of getting the error box shown earlier, you should see this new message box.

Defining what has happened is a much more graceful way of handling the error. You do this by adding the command On Error, which instructs VBA where to go when it encounters an error. In this case, you are telling it to go to the line of code that is labeled MyTrap:

```
myTrap:
    MsgBox "You cannot divide by zero"
End Sub
```

Notice that this line is identified with the label myTrap ending in a colon. This is called a *line label*. (You also could have instructed VBA to go to a line number, but since line numbers can easily change, that is not the best solution.) Line labels can be a handy tool for moving through code nonsequentially. As a little aside, please note that while line labels are used most often in error trapping situations, as is shown here, they could be used in any type of nonsequential programming situation.

In programming parlance, this whole process is called *error handling*, and in this case, myTrap is an *error handler*. It will only run when an error is encountered, and its only job is handling an error.

We have one other problem that we solved with this code. Programming code runs sequentially. Normally, the preceding code would hit the error handler, myTrap, whether the user divided by zero or not. You prevent this from happening by issuing a command to exit the sub procedure, Exit Sub, right after the calculation is completed and the results are shown, and right before the line label and the error-handling code. That way, you assure that the error handler is isolated and will only be called upon if an error occurs.

One other small problem needs to be solved. We have error handling and an error handler, but when we dismiss the error message, the program ends. Wouldn't it be far better to have a way to return the user to the input box to reenter the denominator?

Let's add a couple of lines to our code as follows:

```
Sub errorTest()
    Dim intNumerator As Integer
    Dim intDenominator As Integer
    Dim intResult As Double

    On Error GoTo mytrap
        intNumerator = InputBox("Please enter a numerator", "Numerator")

enterDenominator:
        intDenominator = InputBox("Please enter a denominator", _
                            "Denominator")
        intResult = intNumerator / intDenominator
        MsgBox ("The result is " & intResult)
    Exit Sub
mytrap:
    MsgBox ("You cannot divide by zero")
    Resume enterDenominator

End Sub
```

Notice that in this case, we used the command Resume inside the error-handler code. Normally, Resume will return the user to the line where the error occurred.

This is handy if you have some code inside the error handler that might fix the problem. However, in our case, it would return the user to the calculation. We need to go back an additional line to the point where the denominator is entered. In order to solve that, we put a line label just before the denominator entry point and then, in the error handler, instructed Resume to go back to that line label.

All of this has created a tidy little solution that is fairly easy to follow and understand. But what happens if there are more complicated situations in which multiple errors could occur? To solve that, we need to go behind the scenes a bit more.

The Err Object

You may not have realized it, but when you got the "division by zero" error message, what you were really seeing was the information stored in an object. As soon as an error occurs, VBA generates an object of type Err, which holds details about that error—specifically, the error number and the error description. You may be wondering how that is any different from what you saw in the message box. Let's take a look at the possibilities in coding.

In the first example, we are going to set up an object as we have done in previous chapters, create an error, and then query the object for the error number and description:

```
Sub errorTest()
    Dim intNumerator As Integer
    Dim intDenominator As Integer
    Dim intResult As Double
    On Error GoTo mytrap

        intNumerator = InputBox("Please enter a numerator", "Numerator")

enterDenominator:
        intDenominator = InputBox("Please enter a denominator", _
                            "Denominator")

        intResult = intNumerator / intDenominator
        MsgBox "The result is " & intResult
    Exit Sub
mytrap:
    MsgBox "The number of this error is " & Err.Number
    MsgBox "The description of the error is " & Err.Description
    Resume enterDenominator
End Sub
```

In this code, you queried the object and isolated each piece of information. If you run it and set the denominator to 0, you end up with two message boxes, first showing the returned error number:

then, showing the returned error message:

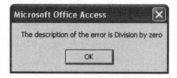

If you are not completely sold as to the programming implications of this, let's take this to the next step by making some changes to the error handler:

```
mytrap:
    If Err.Number = 11 Then
        MsgBox ("The description of the error is " & Err.Description)
    Else
        MsgBox ("Something else is going wrong")
    End If
    Resume enterDenominator
```

Remember at the outset I asked what would happen if there was the possibility of multiple things going wrong. In this simple example, you see that you can handle multiple situations by conditionally testing the Err.Number property.

In essence, this program says that if an error occurs, transfer control of the code to the designated error handler called myTrap. Once in the handler, the handler will determine how to handle the error based on the error number.

The Err object offers a nice feature with the Source property: it tells you what is generating the error. Let's modify the event handler as follows:

```
mytrap:
    If Err.Number = 11 Then
        MsgBox (Err.Source)
    Else
        MsgBox ("Something else is going wrong")
```

```
End If
Resume enterDenominator
```

If you generate the "divide by zero" error now, you end up with this message showing the source of the error:

Since we are in TheCornerBookstore project, Source is showing that as the source of the error.

The Errors Collection

The Err object can handle one error at a time. For many beginning programmers, this object is an easy-to-use solution to error handling. However, as you get into more complex situations, involving use of the ADO libraries, a problem could cause multiple errors to occur. This means multiple error objects being created (programmers use the word "thrown") at once. ADO has a means of collecting these objects and allowing the user to examine all of the errors returned.

The Err object is part of the VBA error-handling system and handles errors generated by VBA. The ADO error-handling system is separate from the VBA system and handles errors generated by the ADO objects. As a result, you must sometimes handle potential errors from both.

Since this is a beginning book, we will just take a brief look at the ADO Errors collection. The actual mechanics of using it are only slightly different from the Err object in the VBA system.

When we used the Err object, we did not need to implicitly declare it. It is built right into VBA. However, when using the Errors collection, you have to declare the object as you have done with any other object to this point.

Let's create a code example in which we try to open a connection that doesn't exist. In this example, we are going to throw an ADO exception that will be trapped and reported in the Immediate window:

```
Public Sub errorTest()

    Dim myConn As ADODB.Connection
```

```
        Dim myErr As ADODB.Error
        Dim strError As String

        On Error GoTo myHandler

        ' Intentionally trigger an error
        Set myConn = New ADODB.Connection
        myConn.Open "nothing"

        Set myConn = Nothing
        Exit Sub

myHandler:

        ' Move through the Errors collection and display
        ' properties of each Error object
        For Each myErr In myConn.Errors
            strError = "Error #" & Err.Number & vbCr & _
                "   " & myErr.Description & vbCr & _
                "   (Source: " & myErr.Source & ")" & vbCr & _
                "   (SQL State: " & myErr.SQLState & ")" & vbCr & _
                "   (NativeError: " & myErr.NativeError & ")" & vbCr
            If myErr.HelpFile = "" Then
                strError = strError & "   No Help file available"
            Else
                strError = strError & _
                    "   (HelpFile: " & myErr.HelpFile & ")" & vbCr & _
                    "   (HelpContext: " & myErr.HelpContext & ")" & _
                    vbCr & vbCr
            End If

            Debug.Print strError
        Next
        Resume Next
End Sub
```

As I said at the outset, this code intentionally causes an error by opening a nonexistent connection. Let's examine what is going on a piece at a time.

In the first few lines, you need to set up a reference to the Error object, as follows:

```
Dim myErr As ADODB.Error
Dim strError As String
```

Here the object reference is myErr, and it is of type Error found in the library ADODB. The String, strError, is going to be used in the event handler to build the error message.

A little farther down, we have the code:

```
Set myConn = New ADODB.Connection
   myConn.Open "nothing"
   Set myConn = Nothing
```

Essentially, this opens the connection to nothing and causes the error to be thrown intentionally for our demonstration. At that point, if all worked well, the sub procedure is exited. However, if an error is thrown (as it intentionally is here), control of the code is transferred to the label myHandler, which is the error handler.

At the beginning of the discussion, I mentioned that the advantage of the Errors collection is that it can collect multiple error objects. In this case, our handler needs to be able to move through those objects and return multiple messages if needed. Since myConn caused the error to happen, it serves as the container to hold the collection. For that reason, in the event handler, we set up the following loop specifications:

```
For Each myErr In myConn.Errors
```

Recall from Chapter 5 that an array is a collection of data referenced by a single variable name. Here, we have a slight variation. We have a collection of objects, located within myConn, referenced by one object reference named myErr. This loop will keep traversing through it until it has queried all the objects.

Once in the loop, we now use our String variable to set up a message string for printing in the Immediate window, as follows:

```
strError = "Error #" & Err.Number & vbCr & _
         "     " & myErr.Description & vbCr & _
         "    (Source: " & myErr.Source & ")" & vbCr & _
         "    (SQL State: " & myErr.SQLState & ")" & vbCr & _
         "    (NativeError: " & myErr.NativeError & ")" & vbCr
```

This string contains each of the properties of the Error object.

We see the properties Number, Description, and Source, which mimic the Err object seen earlier. The SQLState property will contain errors returned by the database server within your SQL string syntax.

The NativeError property returns error codes generated by the providing server.

Although I didn't speak about it before, one feature of both the Err and the Error objects is the ability to access customized help files within the context of the error message number. You could specify the location and name of the help file with the HelpFile and HelpContext properties (in many ways, I treat these as one property). In our example, we are not going to use these properties. We can specify that by using an empty string. As you can see, in the following excerpt from the preceding code, I put it in the context of an If structure:

```
If myErr.HelpFile = "" Then
        strError = strError & "   No Help file available"
    Else
        strError = strError & _
            "   (HelpFile: " & myErr.HelpFile & ")" & vbCr & _
            "   (HelpContext: " & myErr.HelpContext & ")" & _
            vbCr & vbCr
    End If
```

This code example produces an error. As a result, the output in the Immediate window should look like this:

```
Immediate                                                                    ×
 Error #-2147467259
    [Microsoft][ODBC Driver Manager] Data source name not found and no default driver spec
    (Source: Microsoft OLE DB Provider for ODBC Drivers)
    (SQL State: IM002)
    (NativeError: 0)
    (HelpFile: )
    (HelpContext: 0)
```

NOTE

vbCR is an intrinsic constant of Visual Basic (as identified by the vb prefix) and returns a carriage return.

Tools for Debugging Code

As stated earlier, many times the runtime error will be caused by poor programming logic. For instance, code may be out of sequence, or a variable value may not be set before it is called upon. These are sometimes referred to as *logic errors*.

The VBA Editor offers a number of tools to track the sequence of events in your code and detect the value of variables at any given point.

The Immediate Window and Breakpoints

The Immediate window offers a variety of tracing and debugging tools that are quite easy to use. For testing purposes, let's use the following simple code example:

```
Sub addNumbers()
    Dim intNumber1 As Integer
    Dim intNumber2 As Integer
    Dim intSum As Integer

    intNumber1 = 5
    intNumber2 = 3
    intSum = intNumber1 + intNumber2
    Debug.Print "The sum of the two numbers is: " & intSum
End Sub
```

This sets two variables, adds them, and prints the results to the Immediate window.

Up to this point, we have run procedures by clicking on the Run button. However, you can also run the procedure by simply typing its name into the Immediate window, as shown here:

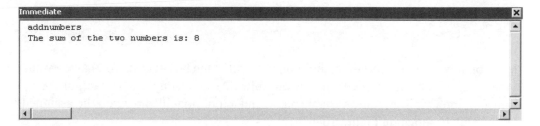

It makes no difference if you run the procedure from the Run button in the toolbar or type the name in the Immediate window. The results are the same.

If this was all the Immediate window could do, its usefulness would be limited. However, let's look at a couple of handy features that can help you trace problems in your code.

You can set a breakpoint in the code. This tool allows you to set a point for the code to halt and wait for you to tell it to resume operation. You can set a breakpoint by clicking in the margin to the left of the line where you want to stop the code.

In this example, let's stop the code where the two variables are added and assigned to the sum. You should see the code highlighted at the breakpoint:

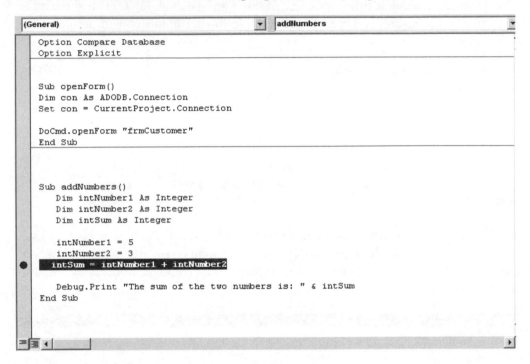

```
(General)                                    addNumbers

    Option Compare Database
    Option Explicit


    Sub openForm()
    Dim con As ADODB.Connection
    Set con = CurrentProject.Connection

    DoCmd.openForm "frmCustomer"
    End Sub



    Sub addNumbers()
        Dim intNumber1 As Integer
        Dim intNumber2 As Integer
        Dim intSum As Integer

        intNumber1 = 5
        intNumber2 = 3
●       intSum = intNumber1 + intNumber2

        Debug.Print "The sum of the two numbers is: " & intSum
    End Sub
```

If you now run the procedure, the code will halt at the breakpoint. You have several ways to check the assignments to the variables. As an example, you can put the mouse pointer right over the variable name and a tool tip will show you the assigned value. This is shown in Figure 10-1.

You could also test the value in the Immediate window by typing a question mark followed by the name of the variable you are testing. You would then press ENTER to get the following result:

```
Immediate                                                        ×
?intNumber1
 5
```

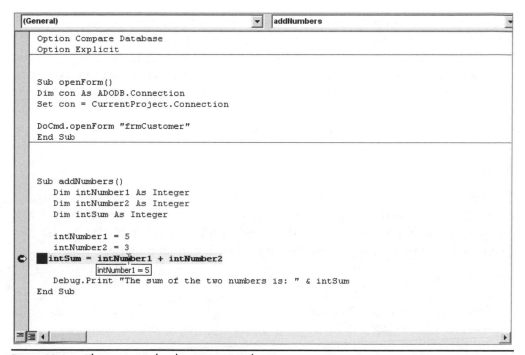

```
(General)                                      ▼  addNumbers                              ▼

   Option Compare Database
   Option Explicit


   Sub openForm()
   Dim con As ADODB.Connection
   Set con = CurrentProject.Connection

   DoCmd.openForm "frmCustomer"
   End Sub



   Sub addNumbers()
      Dim intNumber1 As Integer
      Dim intNumber2 As Integer
      Dim intSum As Integer

      intNumber1 = 5
      intNumber2 = 3
   ● ■ intSum = intNumber1 + intNumber2
              │intNumber1 = 5│
      Debug.Print "The sum of the two numbers is: " & intSum
   End Sub
```

Figure 10-1   *The assigned value to intNumber1*

Once the values are established, you can continue operation of the code by clicking on the Continue button (the same button as the Run button) in the Standard toolbar.

The Immediate window also lets you override the assigned value. While the code is halted at the breakpoint, you can type the name of the variable you want to change and assign a new value. Then press ENTER. Once the code is resumed, the results should reflect the new value, for example:

```
Immediate                                                                    ✕
 intNumber1 = 2
 The sum of the two numbers is: 5
 |
```

The breakpoint can be taken off the code the same way it was put on: by clicking in the margin.

The breakpoint feature offers another advantage. You can reassign the sequence. As an example, suppose you set the breakpoint to be the intNumber1 assignment. Then further suppose you want to bypass the intNumber2 assignment and go directly to the addition. When you run the code and it hits the breakpoint, you can take the margin indicator and drag it to the line where you want to resume the code. Then resume the code.

You can also build a breakpoint directly into the code using the keyword Stop.

Assert

You could also use the Assert member of the Debug object to test the value of an object. In the following code, we are going to ask the Assert method if the value assigned to intNumber1 is 5. We will then ask if intNumber2 is 7. We know in the first case it will return true, and in the second case it will return false.

```
Sub addNumbers()
    Dim intNumber1 As Integer
    Dim intNumber2 As Integer
    Dim intSum As Integer
    intNumber1 = 5
    intNumber2 = 3
    Debug.Assert intNumber1 = 5
    Debug.Assert intNumber2 = 7

    intSum = intNumber1 + intNumber2
    Debug.Print "The sum of the two numbers is: " & intSum
End Sub
```

If you run the procedure now, you get the results shown in Figure 10-2. It skipped over the first Assert because it was true, but flagged the false value of the second assertion.

The Locals Window

With a breakpoint set, the Locals window will show any objects and variables assigned in the procedure, as well as the current values assigned to them. As an example, if you set a breakpoint at the addition point and run the procedure, the

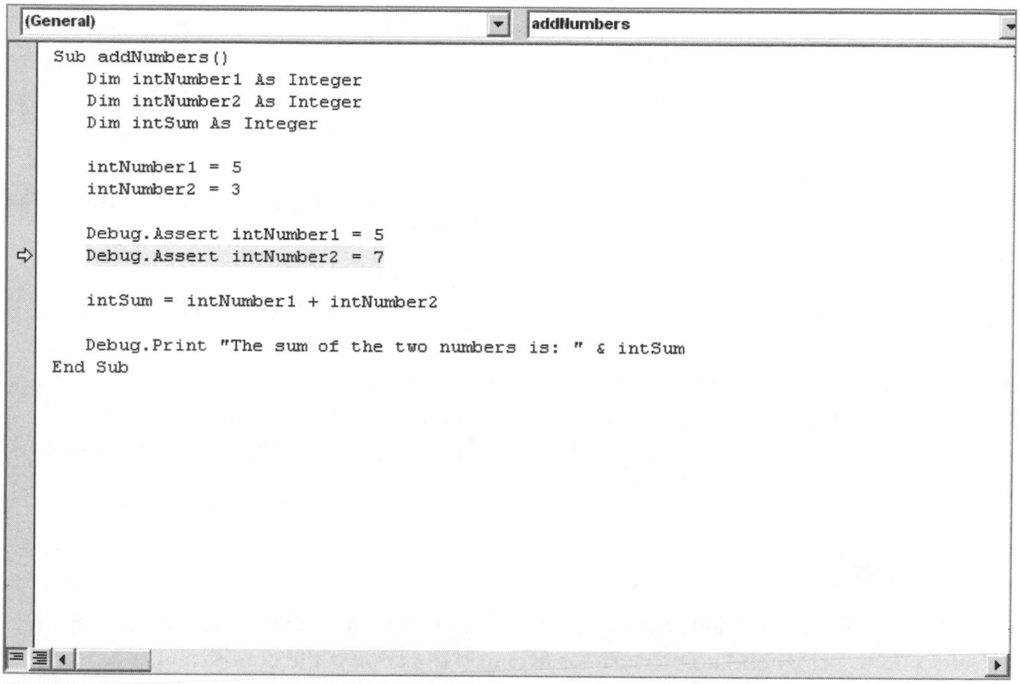

```
(General)                                    ▼   addNumbers                    ▼

    Sub addNumbers()
        Dim intNumber1 As Integer
        Dim intNumber2 As Integer
        Dim intSum As Integer

        intNumber1 = 5
        intNumber2 = 3

        Debug.Assert intNumber1 = 5
⇨       Debug.Assert intNumber2 = 7

        intSum = intNumber1 + intNumber2

        Debug.Print "The sum of the two numbers is: " & intSum
    End Sub
```

Figure 10-2   *The Assert method flagging the false value*

code will halt there. You then select View | Locals Window to open the Locals window, shown in Figure 10-3.

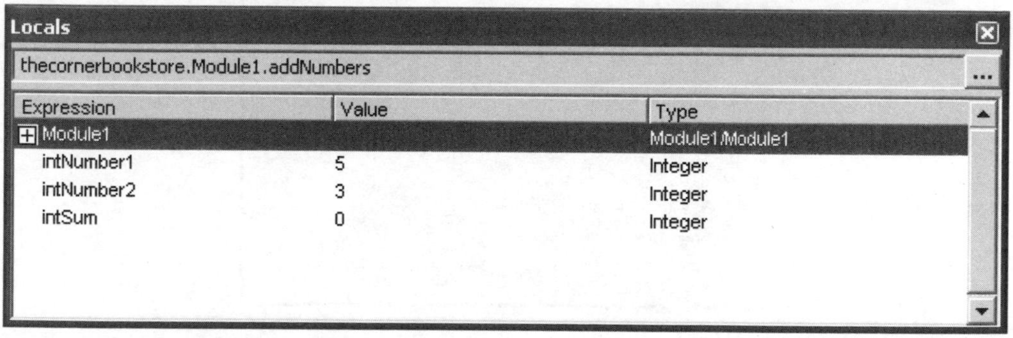

Locals		
thecornerbookstore.Module1.addNumbers		...
Expression	**Value**	**Type**
⊞ Module1		Module1/Module1
intNumber1	5	Integer
intNumber2	3	Integer
intSum	0	Integer

Figure 10-3   *The Locals window*

Here you find the assigned values, at that point, for the two variables. Since the code was halted before the addition took place, intSum is showing a value of 0. You can also click on one of the values, change it, and press ENTER. This will assign a new value to the variable in much the same way that you did in the Immediate window earlier.

The Locals window also allows you a rather unique way to trace your code. Select View | Toolbars | Debug. This opens the Debug toolbar. One of the buttons, Step Into, allows you to walk through the code one line at a time.

You can open the Locals window and then use the Step Into button to walk through the code. As you press the button and advance the code one line at a time, you will see the values of the variables change in the Locals window.

If a variable is an array, it will be shown with a [+] to the left of it. When you click on that [+], the tree will expand to show the values of individual elements of the array.

The Watch Window

The way the Watch window works is similar to the Assert method you saw earlier. It allows you to set a condition to test for and stop the code if the condition is not met.

Let's assume you want to test to see if intNumber2 was assigned a value of 3. Start off by highlighting the statement. Then select Debug | Add Watch. Figure 10-4 shows the dialog box that opens.

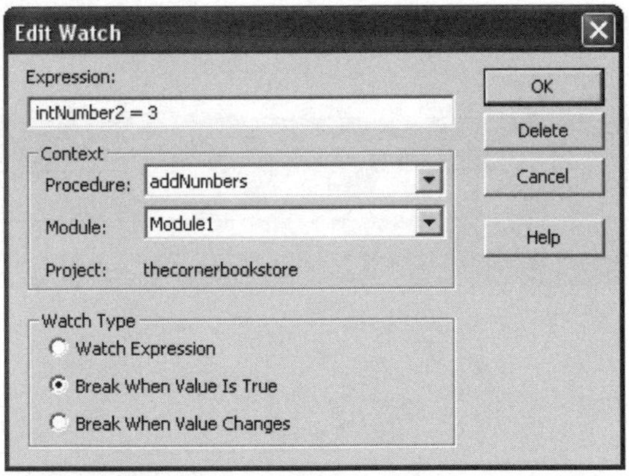

Figure 10-4   *Adding a Watch*

You can then tell it to just watch the expression, break if the expression is true, or break if the value changes. Once you make the decision as to what action to take, the following window opens when you select OK.

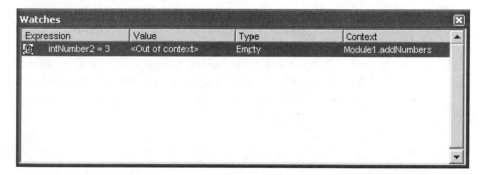

The value will remain "out of context" until the procedure runs. Once it runs, the value will show and the appropriate action will be taken depending on your choices, as Figure 10-5 shows.

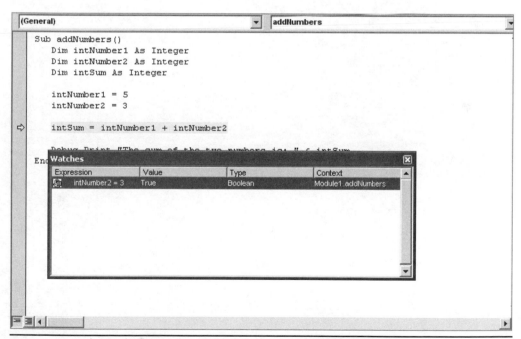

Figure 10-5   *The code flagged and the Watch window showing true*

Summary

You learned an important lesson in this chapter on understanding how to handle errors. This will keep your programs running smoothly no matter what the circumstances are. In actuality, you may need to add more error-handling code to your project as unanticipated problems arise.

You also saw how to use the various tools the VBA Editor gives you to trace the actions of your code. You even had a chance to change and override the values.

We are now going to explore the role of functions within VBA programming.

Function Procedures

U p to this point, when I have spoken about procedures, I talked about subs (I am not including methods found in objects). Subs, as you will recall, are blocks of code that perform a task, but do not return a value to the caller. The syntax for functions is similar to that of subs with only a few differences. Much of what you have learned will be used in a similar fashion. So, for that reason, this chapter will also serve as a review.

In this chapter, you will learn the differences between functions and subs, passing arguments, and examining the built-in functions. Needless to say, this will not be an exhaustive study of these built-in functions. That would require a book in itself. We will look at some commonly used functions, specifically the MsgBox function, as well as the built-in date, time, and payment functions.

Subs vs. Functions

Think, for a moment, about what a sub does. It can

- ▶ Accept parameters from the procedure that is calling it;
- ▶ Take those arguments and carry out a series of instructions.

Like a sub, a function does these two things as well. Unlike a sub, though, a function returns a value to the caller. The data type of that value is defined by the

As *type* clause of the function declaration. To use the example of the fullName function that we developed in Chapter 9, its declaration was:

```
Function fullName(strFname As String, strLname As String) As String
```

The fullName function, then, returns a String value. In the body of the function, the actual value returned by the function is determined by the value assigned to a variable whose name is the same as the function.

If you'd like to review functions and the way in which they differ from subs, see the "Functions" section in Chapter 9.

Typically, you call a function precisely because of the value that it returns. But interestingly, you can call a function as if it were a sub and ignore its return value. For example, you could call the fullName function from Chapter 9 and discard its return value by using the following code:

```
Sub callFullName()
    fullName "John", "Public"
End Sub
```

In this function call, the parentheses surrounding the function arguments have been removed, and the function's return value has not been assigned to a variable or referenced in any other way. We have treated our function and called it as if it were a sub.

In most cases, of course, you wouldn't want to discard a function's return value, since that would make it completely pointless to call the function in the first place. But there are some cases in which you are interested in an operation that the function performs, but you don't care about the value that a function returns. This is particularly true when it returns a Boolean indicating success or failure, and you either don't care about the result of the function call or you're certain it will succeed.

The functions that you code yourself (they're often called user-defined functions) are not the only functions that you'll be using. They may not even be the primary functions that you use. Visual Basic comes with an extensive set of function libraries. These functions, which are called intrinsic functions because they are built into VBA, provide such services as string handling, file input and output, mathematical and numerical operations, date and time manipulation, and handling input and output. Although you've already used some of these intrinsic functions, in the next section we'll look at them in greater detail.

Built-in Functions

You may not have realized it, but you have already used two built-in functions: MsgBox and InputBox.

MsgBox

You have used the MsgBox function a number of times in this book already. Up to this point, it has only been with an OK button to acknowledge receipt of the message. However, other possibilities are available.

Table 11-1 shows the buttons and icons available to the MsgBox function. We will discuss the meaning of the values in a few moments.

Up to this point, the syntax we have used for the MsgBox has been as follows:

```
MsgBox "Welcome to VBA"
```

This will give you the result shown here.

There are two other arguments you can add to the function (actually, there is one more for a compiled help file that we will not be treating here). The second argument is the button or icon you want to use, from the list in Table 11-1, and the third is the title above the box.

If you modify the preceding code as follows:

```
MsgBox "Welcome to VBA", vbYesNoCancel, "VBA Message Box"
```

you will see these results:

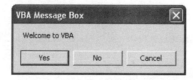

Constant	Value	Description
vbOKOnly	0	Displays OK button only.
vbOKCancel	1	Displays OK and Cancel buttons.
vbAbortRetryIgnore	2	Displays Abort, Retry, and Ignore buttons.
vbYesNoCancel	3	Displays Yes, No, and Cancel buttons.
vbYesNo	4	Displays Yes and No buttons.
vbRetryCancel	5	Displays Retry and Cancel buttons.
vbCritical	16	Displays Critical Message icon.
vbQuestion	32	Displays Warning Query icon.
vbExclamation	48	Displays Warning Message icon.
vbInformation	64	Displays Information Message icon.
vbDefaultButton1	0	First button is default.
vbDefaultButton2	256	Second button is default.
vbDefaultButton3	512	Third button is default.
vbDefaultButton4	768	Fourth button is default.
vbApplicationModal	0	Application modal; the user must respond to the message box before continuing work in the current application.
vbSystemModal	4096	System modal; all applications are suspended until the user responds to the message box.
vbMsgBoxHelpButton	16384	Add Help button to the message box.
VbMsgBoxSetForeground	65536	Specify the message box window as the foreground window.
vbMsgBoxRight	524288	Text is right aligned.
vbMsgBoxRtlReading	1048576	Specify that text should appear as right-to-left reading on Hebrew and Arabic systems.

Table 11-1   *Buttons and Icons in the MsgBox Function*

You could add the Information icon, if you wanted, as follows:

```
MsgBox "Welcome to VBA", vbYesNoCancel + vbInformation, "VBA Message Box"
```

That would result in the MsgBox with the Information icon added:

Why the numeric values in Table 11-1? Those values can be substituted for the constants that indicate the name of the button. For instance, you can substitute the following syntax for the MsgBox:

```
MsgBox "Welcome to VBA", 3 + 64, "VBA Message Box"
```

This will yield the same results as shown in the previous illustration. But it also opens a lot of programming possibilities. Let's look at the following very simple example to see what I mean.

```
Sub messageBoxTest()
 Dim intInput As Integer
 Dim intButtonStyle As Integer
 Dim intIconStyle As Integer
 Dim strMessage As String
 Dim strTitle As String

 strTitle = "MsgBox Example"

 intInput = InputBox("Enter either a 1 or 2")

 If intInput = 1 Then
    strMessage = "Do you want 1?"
    intButtonStyle = 4
    intIconStyle = 32
 Else
    strMessage = "I guess you wanted 2"
    intButtonStyle = 1
    intIconStyle = 64
  End If

  MsgBox strMessage, intButtonStyle + intIconStyle, strTitle
End Sub
```

In this example, the user is asked to enter either 1 or 2 (we have not put any code in to test for the validity of the entry). The If....Then...Else structure will set the integer values of the variables according to the values in Table 11-1. We then substitute the variables for the actual values in the MsgBox syntax.

If the user selects 1, the MsgBox shown here will come up:

But if the user selects 2, this box will be shown:

By using this technique, you can make the MsgBox reflect whatever programming situation has occurred.

We have one small problem here: all the buttons do is dismiss the box. What if you want a specific action associated with a button that has been selected?

Each of the available buttons will produce an integer result. These results are shown in this table.

Constant	Value	Description
vbOK	1	OK
vbCancel	2	Cancel
vbAbort	3	Abort
vbRetry	4	Retry
vbIgnore	5	Ignore
vbYes	6	Yes
vbNo	7	No

Let's look at the following code that determines which button was pressed.

```
Sub messageBoxTest()
 Dim intButtonPressed As Integer
```

```
intButtonPressed = MsgBox("Welcome to VBA", vbYesNo, "Message Box Test")

If intButtonPressed = 6 Then
   MsgBox "Yes was selected"
 Else
    MsgBox "No was selected"
  End If
End Sub
```

Notice in this case, when assigning the value of the MsgBox to a variable, you have to enclose the arguments in parenthesis. When it is serving as just a message box, you do not.

Based on the information in the previous table, you can see that vbYes returns an integer value of 6, and vbNo returns an integer value of 7. You could have used the following syntax to get the same results:

```
If intButtonPressed = vbYes Then
```

If you select "Yes," you should see the response shown here:

Selecting "No" will result in this response:

Remember that all of these buttons are VB constants, which are easily identified because of the vb prefix.

The full syntax for MsgBox is

MsgBox prompt, buttons, title, helpfile, context

The only argument that is required is *prompt*.

InputBox

The InputBox will prompt the user for information. The value that the user enters into the box needs to be assigned to a variable. Once inside that variable, you can manipulate that value any way that you choose.

The syntax for an InputBox is as follows:

InputBox (prompt, title, default, xposition, yposition, helpfile, context)

Of these, only the *prompt* is required. If you do not list a default value, the input box is left empty. The x and y positions will determine the horizontal and vertical positions of the input box on the screen.

Date and Time Functions

Many times, you will need to format a date or time to have a specific appearance. As an example, March 30, 2004 could look like that or:

```
3/30/2004
```

or

```
Tuesday March 30, 2004
```

Of course, there is a whole variety of possibilities. However, in addition to doing formatting, you may also want to calculate the number of days between, say, January 3, 2003 and March 30, 2004.

VBA has a number of built-in Date and Time functions to assist with formatting and date arithmetic. The following program shows the basic functions. Most of the functions you will see are, in my opinion, self-explanatory. I added some explanations where I felt it was needed. I strongly suggest you try the following code examples.

```
Sub dateFunctions()
    Dim strDateString As String

    strDateString = "The present date and time is: " & Now & vbCrLf & _
                    "Today's date is: " & Date & vbCrLf & _
                    "The day of the month is: " & Day(Date) & vbCrLf & _
                    "The day of the week is: " & Weekday(Date) & vbCrLf & _
```

```
             "The name of the week day is: " & WeekdayName(Weekday(Date)) & vbCrLf & _
             "The weekday abbreviated is: " & WeekdayName(Weekday(Date), True) & vbCrLf & _
             "The month is: " & Month(Date) & vbCrLf & _
             "The name of the month is: " & MonthName(Month(Date)) & vbCrLf & _
             "The month abbreviated is: " & MonthName(Month(Date), True) & vbCrLf & _
             "The year is: " & Year(Date)

    MsgBox strDateString
End Sub
```

This will result in the message box shown in Figure 11-1.

Notice that two lines of the previous code have the extra argument of True added. This tells VBA to abbreviate the names of the month and weekday.

You can also break a single date down to its individual components using the DatePart function shown in the following example:

```
Sub dateFunctions()
    Dim strDateString As String

    strDateString = "The year part is: " & DatePart("yyyy", Date) & vbCrLf & _
                    "The quarter part is: " & DatePart("q", Now) & vbCrLf & _
                    "The month part is: " & DatePart("m", Now) & vbCrLf & _
                    "The day part is: " & DatePart("d", Now) & vbCrLf & _
                    "The weekday is: " & DatePart("w", Now) & vbCrLf & _
                    "The week part is: " & DatePart("ww", Now) & vbCrLf & _
                    "The hour part is: " & DatePart("h", Now) & vbCrLf & _
                    "The minute part is: " & DatePart("n", Now) & vbCrLf & _
                    "The second part is: " & DatePart("s", Now)

    MsgBox strDateString
End Sub
```

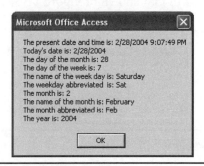

Figure 11-1   *A compendium of date functions*

Figure 11-2 *The DatePart function*

This will give the response shown in Figure11-2.

You could use the DateDiff function to calculate the differential between two dates. This function takes three arguments: the unit of measure, the first date, and the second date.

The following example shows the difference between two dates in days and months:

```
Sub dateFunctions()
   Dim strDateString As String

   strDateString = "The days between 3/15/2000 and today is: " & _
               DateDiff("d", "3/15/2000", Now) & vbCrLf & _
               "The months between 3/15/2000 and today is: " & _
               DateDiff("m", "3/15/2000", Now)

   MsgBox strDateString
End Sub
```

This results in output similar to that shown in Figure 11-3.

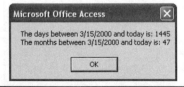

Figure 11-3 *The DateDiff function output*

Note that if you put the later date as the first argument, a negative number will show up in the output.

Notice that Now returns today's date and time.

There are several different ways to approach formatting the date and time. The following code shows the possibilities.

```
Sub dateFunctions()
  Dim strDateString As String

  strDateString = "m/d/yy: " & Format(Now, "m/d/yy") & vbCrLf & _
                  "d-mmm-yy: " & Format(Now, "d-mmm-yy") & vbCrLf & _
                  "d-mmmm-yy: " & Format(Now, "d-mmmm-yy") & vbCrLf & _
                  "mmmm d, yyyy: " & Format(Now, "mmmm d, yyyy") & vbCrLf & _
                  "ddd: " & Format(Now, "ddd") & vbCrLf & _
                  "dddd: " & Format(Now, "dddd") & vbCrLf & _
                  "ddddd: " & Format(Now, "ddddd") & vbCrLf & _
                  "dddddd: " & Format(Now, "dddddd") & vbCrLf & _
                  "Hh:Nn:Ss AM/PM: " & Format(Now, "Hh:Nn:Ss AM/PM") & vbCrLf & _
                  "ttttt: " & Format(Now, "ttttt") & vbCrLf & _
                  "vbShortDate: " & FormatDateTime(Now, vbShortDate) & vbCrLf & _
                  "vbLongDate: " & FormatDateTime(Now, vbLongDate) & vbCrLf & _
                  "vbGeneralDate: " & FormatDateTime(Now, vbGeneralDate)

    MsgBox strDateString
End Sub
```

This would result in the output shown in Figure 11-4.

Figure 11-4   *Possible date formats*

As you can see, there are different ways to format the date by using either the Format function or the FormatDateTime function.

Payment Function

Many times you will need to calculate the resulting payment, given the principal, interest rate, and term of a loan. This can be easily calculated in VBA by using the Pmt() function.

The syntax of this function is as follows:

```
Pmt (interest, term, principal, future value, type)
```

The *future value* and *type* are optional arguments. You would use these if you were calculating the future value of a stream of payments and if you needed to decide whether the payment was at the beginning or end of a period. The default is the beginning of the period.

In the following example, I have hard-coded the values into the procedure. However, most times, these numbers would be retrieved from an outside source, such as an input box or a database.

```
Sub loanPayment()
    Dim dblRate As Double
    Dim intTerm As Integer
    Dim dblPrincipal As Double
    Dim dblPayment As Double

    dblRate = 0.075
    intTerm = 5
    dblPrincipal = 75000

    dblPayment = Pmt(dblRate / 12, intTerm * 12, -dblPrincipal)

    MsgBox "The monthly payment is: " & dblPayment

End Sub
```

Notice that in this example, we had to convert the rate into a monthly rate by dividing by 12, and we had to convert the term to a monthly term by multiplying by 12. In addition, the principal must be entered as a negative number (this is standard mathematical practice).

Here is the result:

Notice that the output is not really formatted in proper currency format. You could fix that by using the Format function and making the following changes to the code:

```
Sub loanPayment()
   Dim dblRate As Double
   Dim intTerm As Integer
   Dim dblPrincipal As Double
   Dim dblPayment As Double
   Dim strFormat As String

   dblRate = 0.075
   intTerm = 5
   dblPrincipal = 75000
   strFormat = "$###.##"

   dblPayment = Pmt(dblRate / 12, intTerm * 12, -dblPrincipal)

   MsgBox "The monthly payment is: " & Format(dblPayment, strFormat)

End Sub
```

The Format function allows you to predefine a format; in this case, the pound symbol in the string that is assigned to the strFormat variable represents a placeholder. Because it is a string, you can also add whatever characters you want. In this case, the dollar sign was added.

You then use the Format function to connect the created format to the number you want to format in the MsgBox line. The Format takes two arguments: the first is the number to be formatted, the second is the variable containing the created format.

Here is the new result:

Notice that the format has the added advantage of rounding the number properly at the second decimal place.

Summary

In this chapter we took a careful look at functions. We saw the differences between a function and sub. Finally, we took a look at built-in functions within VBA. Specifically, we explored the uses of the MsgBox and InputBox functions, as well as date, time, and financial functions.

This completes this section. We are now going to turn our attention to techniques used to have interactivity between the user and the database.

PART

III

Interacting with VBA

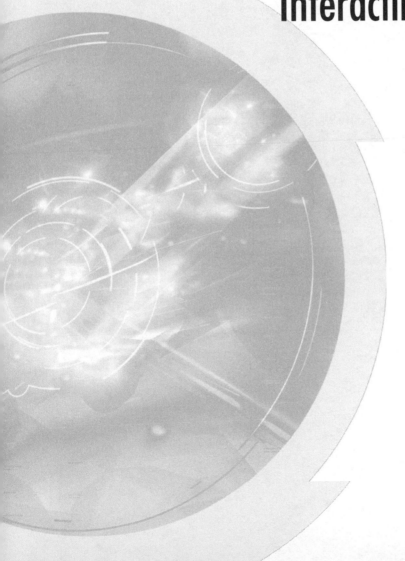

Forms

Most database applications focus around forms, to edit or add data, and reports, for the presentation of the data. The forms serve as the interface between the user and the data. For that reason, a discussion of form design is essential to a discussion of VBA programming in the Microsoft Access environment.

In this chapter we are going to examine forms and their controls. You'll learn how ADO builds the recordsets that the forms use and how forms handle a one-to-many relationship with just a few simple settings in Access. You will also see how VBA can interact with the controls on the forms.

Forms and Data

Building a form in Access has never been a particularly difficult job. You have an AutoForm button and, for fancier forms, a Form Wizard. As a matter of fact, if you click once on the tblCustomer icon, located under table objects in the Database window, and select AutoForm from the toolbar, you will have a form that looks something like Figure 12-1.

As you can see, the form has fields for each of the columns of the tblCustomer table object and a nice set of navigation buttons at the bottom. Since this form is connected to the table object tblCustomer, we say that it is *bound* to the tblCustomer and that each field on the form is bound to the columns in the table.

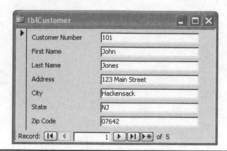

Figure 12-1   *A simple form built with AutoForm*

The fields in the form will also take on the properties of the columns in the table. This offers a certain measure of type safety and data validation. You can, for instance, only input numeric data into controls bound to numeric columns, and data input into controls bound to date fields must contain valid dates.

You can also base a form on a query so that each time you open the form, the query will run. Beginning with Access 2002, if the record source of the form has a one-to-many relationship, AutoForm will automatically build a subform. As an example, if you have Access 2002 or Access 2003, let's use the Database window and go to Tools | Relationships. We will use the tblCustomer and tblPurchases table objects.

Draw a line establishing a relationship between txtCustNumber in tblCustomer and txtNumber in tblPurchases. You should see a dialog box in which you can select Referential Integrity, as shown in Figure 12-2. (I have turned the options on in the figure.)

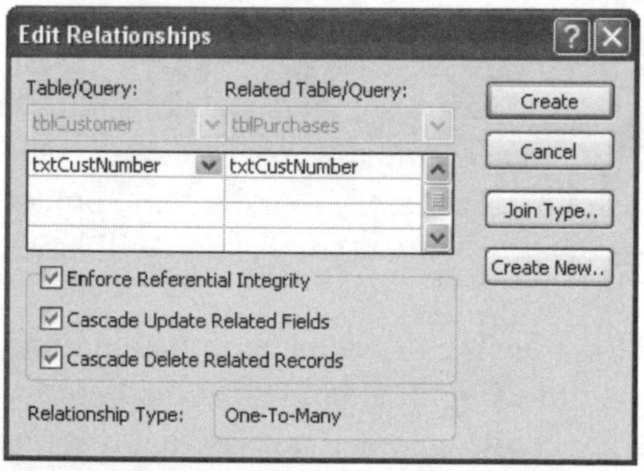

Figure 12-2   *Edit Relationships dialog box*

Referential Integrity assures that you do not have a customer number appearing on the many side, tblPurchases, that was not first entered on the one side, tblCustomer. If you permitted that, you would probably lose the whole purpose behind having a relational database. Without it, the database would probably turn into a useless mess quickly. A record appearing on the many side that does not have a parent record on the one side is called an *orphan*.

You also want to use the two Cascade options that are shown in Figure 12-2. That way, if you change or delete a customer number in tblCustomer, all the records in tblPurchases related to that customer number will subsequently be changed or deleted.

You can select Create, then save and close the Relationships window. If you now click on tblCustomer, and use the AutoForm, it should look like Figure 12-3. The outer form is tblCustomer, and the inner form holds the related records of tblPurchases. Each has its own navigation bars.

NOTE

This feature of AutoForm is available in Access 2002 or 2003. If you have Access 2000, this can also be done, just not automatically.

Access allows you to base forms on either tables or queries. However, beginning with Access 2000, you can build SQL statements and recordsets directly into the

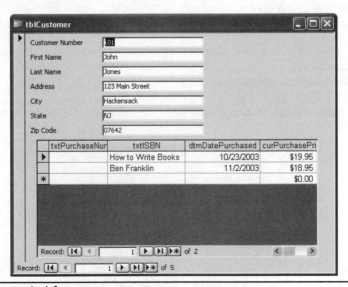

Figure 12-3   *Form/subform using AutoForm*

form structure. As an example, let's switch the form we just created and saw in Figure 12-1 to Design View. Once there, select View | Properties. The resulting dialog box, with the All tab selected, is shown in Figure 12-4. You can see that the Record Source is tblCustomer.

You could easily select a different source from the drop-down list. However, for this example, let's click on the Query Builder button (with the three ellipses) located to the right of the Record Source field. You should get the following message box:

If you select Yes, you are taken to familiar territory: the query grid that you have used so many times already.

Let's assume that you want this form to see only the records for customers who live in New Jersey. As you have done in the past, set it up with all of the fields, and set the criteria for the txtState column to be NJ, as shown in Figure 12-5.

If you then go to close this grid, you are presented with a message box that asks if you want to apply this to the Record Source of the form. After selecting Yes, the Record Source of the form now contains a SQL string, as Figure 12-6 shows. The entire string appears as follows:

```
SELECT tblCustomer.txtCustNumber, tblCustomer.txtCustFirstName,
tblCustomer.txtCustLastName, tblCustomer.txtAddress, tblCustomer.txtCity,
tblCustomer.txtState, tblCustomer.txtZipCode FROM tblCustomer WHERE
(((tblCustomer.txtState)="NJ"));
```

If you now run the form, it should only bring up records for customers in New Jersey.

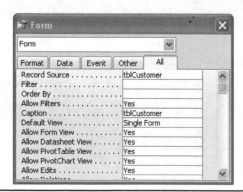

Figure 12-4   *Form properties*

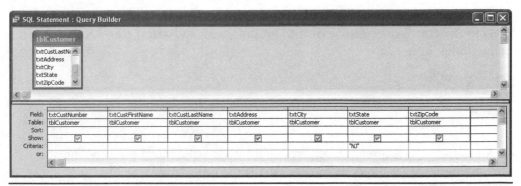

Figure 12-5 *Query Builder grid*

It is this feature, combined with the DoCmd object, that is going to make forms easy to work with in VBA.

Let's assume we saved the example form object as frmCustomer and that our database is now located in C:\BegVBA. You can write the following code in VBA to use the form:

```
Sub runForm()
    Dim con As ADODB.Connection

    Set con = New ADODB.Connection
    con.Open "Provider=Microsoft.Jet.OLEDB.4.0;" & _
        "Data Source=C:\BegVBA\thecornerbookstore.mdb;"

    DoCmd.OpenForm "frmCustomer"
End Sub
```

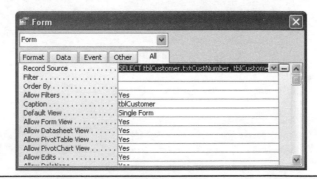

Figure 12-6 *The form's property box with SQL string*

After opening the database connection, as you have done in the previous chapters, you use the OpenForm method of the DoCmd object and specify the string that is the name of the form.

NOTE

When you run this procedure, the form may open in a different window, to which you will need to switch.

All of the SQL is already built into the form's structure, and based on the query that you built earlier, you should only see the records where txtState = "NJ".

You may find it easier, especially if you have a lot of coding and the form's name is longer, to assign the name of the form to a string variable and use that in lieu of the full form name.

Assigning Recordsets Dynamically

You have already seen how to use SQL to build recordsets in the VBA environment. For the sake of review, remember that the recordsets are collected and contained within the Recordset object. (In actuality, the recordset contains a set of pointers to the data required by the Recordset.)

Beginning with Access 2000, you can assign these recordsets dynamically to the form while using VBA. This is a little different from building the SQL code into the form, as you did in the previous section.

Let's assume that you now want your recordset to show only the customers who live in New York. Furthermore, you want your form (the frmCustomer form used in the previous section) to reflect that recordset. Let's look at the following code:

```
Sub runFormNY()
    Dim con As ADODB.Connection
    Dim recSet As Recordset
    Dim strFrmNm As String

    Set recSet = New ADODB.Recordset
    recSet.CursorType = adOpenKeyset
    recSet.LockType = adLockOptimistic

    Set con = New ADODB.Connection
    con.Open "Provider=Microsoft.Jet.OLEDB.4.0;" & _
        "Data Source=C:\BegVBA\thecornerbookstore.mdb;"

    recSet.Open "SELECT * FROM tblCustomer WHERE txtState = 'NY'", con
```

```
        strFrmNm = "frmCustomer"

    DoCmd.OpenForm strFrmNm
    Set Application.Forms(strFrmNm).Recordset = recSet

    recSet.Close
    con.Close
    Set recSet = Nothing
    Set con = Nothing
End Sub
```

We built the recordset as we did in Chapter 9. However, you may have noticed two new lines that we have not examined before:

```
    recSet.CursorType = adOpenKeyset
    recSet.LockType = adLockOptimistic
```

The CursorType property controls how you navigate through the recordset and is mandatory when you use the recordset with forms. Essentially, there are four main types of cursors:

▶ **Dynamic** (adOpenDynamic)   This means that the changes made to the source data are incorporated dynamically into the recordset. So if others change the source data, those changes are available for you to see. You are also free to make any edits necessary to the recordset and to move through it in any direction necessary.

▶ **Keyset** (adOpenKeyset)   This does not allow the recordset to dynamically incorporate changes made to the source data by others. However, you can make any edits to the recordset that you want.

▶ **Static** (adOpenStatic)   This does not allow for any changes to the recordset. You can look through it both forward and backward.

▶ **Forward-only** (adOpenForwardOnly)   This is just as it says. You cannot edit or move backward through the set. You can only move forward.

The preceding list is arranged in order of performance. The more interaction with the recordset, the slower it runs. Dynamic is the slowest and Forward-only the fastest. If you are working with a large amount of data, you may need to make some decisions about which CursorType will work best and still be efficient.

The other new line uses the LockType property. This works with the CursorType property and controls when the record will be locked from use by others. Locking could be used to resolve editing conflicts in a multiuser environment.

The four types of locks are

▶ **adLockReadOnly**   This locks the whole recordset while editing is taking place.

▶ **adLockPessimistic**   This locks others out of that specific record while it is being edited.

▶ **adLockOptimistic**   This prevents conflicts by locking the record while it is being saved. This prevents two people from saving an edited record at the same time.

▶ **adLockBatchOptimistic**   This locks others out while records are being updated in a batch mode.

I have already talked about error handling. An error will occur if the recordset or record cannot be locked. You would receive one of three errors: 3218, 3260, or 3197.

Here is an interesting question you might want to ponder: In this example, we set a location for the database connection. Let's assume we are in database A, which contains a tblCustomer and a frmCustomer. Let's further assume that we set the connection for database B, which also contains a tblCustomer and a frmCustomer. Which tblCustomer and which frmCustomer will we be using when we run the procedure?

Give up?

We will be using the data from the tblCustomer in database B in the frmCustomer of database A. When you establish a connection, you are only establishing it with the data, not all of the objects of the database container. This has enormous implications from a design standpoint. This means that the forms can be in one place and the data in another. Also, you can bring data in from a variety of data sources.

Appending and Editing Data

If you had run the procedure from the previous section (Sub runFormNY()), you would have noticed an interesting problem: you are locked out from appending new data to the database you are connected to. Nor can you edit data. Notice that the New Record button is grayed out in the form:

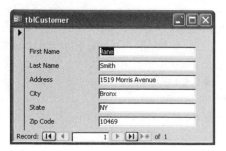

Besides the CursorType property, there is a second "Cursor" property you need to deal with: CursorLocation. This defines the location (client side or server side) of the service that tracks the movement of the record pointer through a dataset. By default, without specifying a CursorLocation, the records open in a read-only mode. You can fix that, however, by adding the following highlighted line:

```
Set recSet = New ADODB.Recordset
    recSet.CursorType = adOpenKeyset
    recSet.LockType = adLockOptimistic
    recSet.CursorLocation = adUseClient
```

As you can see, the New Record button is now available, as is full editing capability:

Controlling Controls in Forms

When writing this book, it was my intention to use techniques that could be applied equally among the various versions of Access. However, Microsoft didn't cooperate. Access 2003 handles some aspects of form controls a little differently than 2000 and 2002. For that reason, the techniques that I show you may not be the most elegant solutions, but they work between versions and are fairly easy to use.

Let's begin with a discussion of forms and controls. A good place to begin is by opening the form frmCustomer in Design View, as shown in Figure 12-7. Each object on the form is called a control. All we have here are label controls and text controls. The text controls are bound to the columns of either tblCustomer or, depending on your coding, the recordset. When a form is automatically generated, as this one is, Access assigns names to those controls automatically.

In the case of the bound text controls, the name is usually the same as the column it is attached to. If you are using Access for day-to-day record keeping, this does not cause a problem; however, if you are going to use it in a VBA environment, it could cause some programming confusion. For that reason, I usually right-click on each of

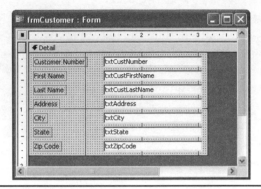

Figure 12-7 *frmCustomer in Design View*

the text boxes and select the Properties option. This opens the Properties window, whose All tab is shown in Figure 12-8.

Notice that in Figure 12-8, I changed the Name property to ctlCustNumber to differentiate the control name from the Control Source of txtCustNumber.

The label controls are usually named Label1, Label2, Label3, and so on. Once again, I usually change them to something like lblCustNumber, lblCustFirstName, and so on. As you will be seeing in a few minutes, this practice will make your life a lot easier in a VBA environment.

You can use the form module to set a control's properties programmatically. As an example, you may want to set the visibility of the control to either true or false. Or you may want to change the control to a read-only mode.

Figure 12-8 *The Properties window for a text box*

As you saw in earlier chapters, in a form module, the name of an event procedure is based upon a form's actions. As an example, let's say we want certain properties set when a form first loads. You would use a Form_Load procedure in a form module.

Don't worry too much about naming conventions; VBA will handle a lot of that for you.

Let's see a quick demonstration.

While in the Design View of frmCustomer, click the form's Properties window, as opposed to the control's, by double-clicking on the square located in the upper-left corner, as shown here:

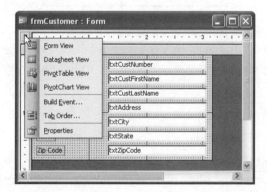

This will open a Properties window like the one shown in Figure 12-9. In the figure, the Event tab is selected, where you can see the various events associated with the form. The most common events are On Load and On Close. The On Load handles actions that will be triggered when the form loads, and On Close triggers before the form closes.

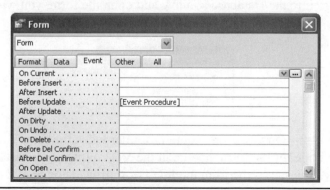

Figure 12-9   *The form's Properties window*

If you click inside the On Load field, you see the Expression Builder button located on the right. Clicking on that will open this dialog box:

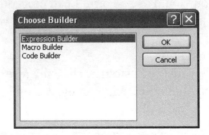

You use the Expression Builder to construct an expression. You saw an example of macros in Chapter 2. However, in VBA, you would choose the Code Builder. Selecting OK then opens a form module with the following procedure:

```
Private Sub Form_Load()

End Sub
```

The actual name of the procedure is Form_Load().

You could go into the procedure and do something simple like add a message box, as follows:

```
Private Sub Form_Load()
  MsgBox "Welcome to the Customer Form", , "Customer Form
Introduction"
End Sub
```

If you now go into the Database window and open the form, you will see the following message box:

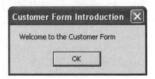

The concept of the On Close procedure is similar when the form closes.

While in the code for the form module in the VBA Editor, you will notice that the Project window now shows the form module Form_frmCustomer and our working VBA module, myTest. This window is shown in Figure 12-10. You can switch back and forth between the two modules from this window.

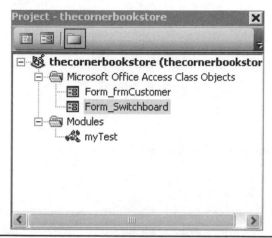

Figure 12-10   *The Project window*

Here is one of the niceties of ADO. You can actually pass code into the form module and through the Form_Load procedure. The result is exactly the same as if you wrote the code in the form module.

Let's take a look at the following block of code.

```
Sub runFormAll()
    Dim con As ADODB.Connection
    Dim recSet As Recordset
    Dim strFrmNm As String

    Set recSet = New ADODB.Recordset
    recSet.CursorType = adOpenKeyset
    recSet.LockType = adLockOptimistic
    recSet.CursorLocation = adUseClient

    Set con = New ADODB.Connection
    con.Open "Provider=Microsoft.Jet.OLEDB.4.0;" & _
        "Data Source=C:\BegVBA\thecornerbookstore.mdb;"

    recSet.Open "SELECT * FROM tblCustomer", con

    strFrmNm = "frmCustomer"

DoCmd.OpenForm strFrmNm
Set Application.Forms(strFrmNm).Recordset = recSet
Form_CustomerForm.ctlCustFirstName.SetFocus
```

```
    Form_frmCustomer.ctlCustNumber.Visible = False

    recSet.Close
    con.Close
    Set recSet = Nothing
    Set con = Nothing
End Sub
```

Let's pay particular attention to the line

```
Form_frmCustomer.ctlCustNumber.Visible = False
```

From within the VBA code you call up the Form_frmCustomer. However, as you're entering code, when you type the period after Form_frmCustomer, VBA displays an interesting prompt, as shown in Figure 12-11. You will see all the controls for the form object that you would normally associate with the form module. From there on, you can set the properties of controls as if you were setting them directly in the form module.

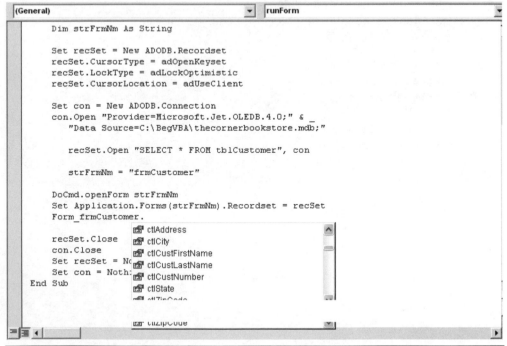

Figure 12-11   *Control prompt for Form_frmCustomer*

In the previous example, the visibility of ctlCustNumber is set to False. If you run the procedure now, the form should look like this:

The ctlCustNumber is hidden. As a variation, you could have changed the property with the two lines as follows:

```
Form_frmCustomer.ctlCustNumber.Visible = True
Form_frmCustomer.ctlCustNumber.Enabled = False
```

Essentially, this makes the ctlCustNumber read only, as can be seen here:

As you can see, every control has a large number of possible properties that you can use as needed. It is not unusual to see an If....Then structure—if condition A occurs, use one set of properties; but if condition B occurs, use a different set of properties.

It is important to note that you can even do conditional formatting. For instance, if a number is negative, you can change its color to red. However, Access 2003 handles this a little differently. Please refer to the Access 2003 documentation to learn how to use this feature.

Summary

Granted, this was a brief excursion into forms and how they interact with ADO in the VBA environment. You saw how to use forms just to browse information, link dynamically into recordsets, and edit information, and how to manipulate the controls using VBA.

The topic of forms could fill an entire book itself. You will want to explore features such as AutoRefresh, separate code for subform controls, and, beginning with Access 2003, conditional formatting.

We are now going to turn our attention to what could be thought of as the opposite of forms: reports. As you will see, however, many of the topics and discussions are similar.

Reports

As stated at the beginning of Chapter 12, the topics of forms and reports have many similarities. You can dynamically attach recordsets, have subforms and subreports, and even use certain controls that assist with the display of data. For many people, the report is the only part of Access that they see. For many companies, major decisions are made based upon the accuracy and quality of the reports.

As you will learn, you can create reports both manually and within VBA. However, Access has powerful report-writing capabilities, and, as you will also learn, harnessing that power can save you a tremendous amount of time when coding and debugging. For that reason, as we did with forms, we will focus on this capability. Then we will look at how to incorporate the finished report within VBA.

We'll begin our discussion by developing an understanding of a report's anatomy and then move into the programmatic issues of reports.

Anatomy of a Report

In Access, most reports are divided into distinct sections. Figure 13-1 shows a simple report in Design View. As you can see, the main data is located in the Detail section. This section repeats for each record in the source data.

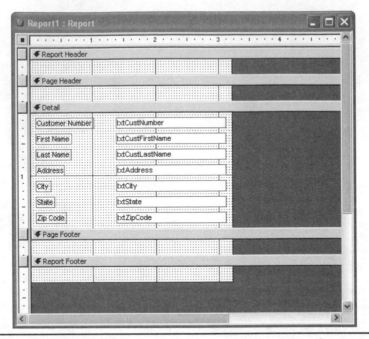

Figure 13-1   *Report in Design View*

As the names imply, the page header and page footer appear at the top and bottom of each page of the report, and the report header and report footer appear at the beginning and end of the report.

Interestingly, the Page and Report sections can be turned off using the View menu option when a report is open in Design View. However, you must be careful here. If you do turn them off, Access is not just hiding them; it is physically deleting them. If you turn them back on at some future point, any content in them will be lost.

Access uses a default template to create reports when using the AutoReport feature. However, you can use a customized form to serve as a template by using the Tools | Options menu selection. You can also import report objects from an outside source by using File | Get External Data | Import. Once imported, you can use Tools | Options to set it as the template.

You can easily adjust the size of each section by dragging the divider bars. In addition, you can create customized headers and footers based on groupings. Select View | Sorting and Grouping to open the Sorting and Grouping dialog box. Here it is shown as if you were going to group the records on the txtState field:

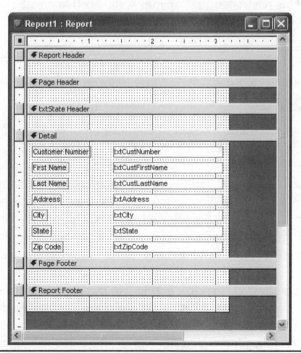

Notice that the Group Header is turned on. In addition, not only will the report group on the txtState field, but it will sort by that column in ascending order.

If you close this box now, the Design View of the report will reflect the new grouping section, as shown in Figure 13-2. You could then drag the txtState column, and related label, up to that grouping section. If you wanted to, you might have

Figure 13-2   *Report with new header grouping added*

another grouping within the txtState grouping that reflected, perhaps, the txtZipCode column. The possibilities are many.

As an alternative to the AutoReport tool, there is a Report Wizard that takes you through the report-building process step-by-step. In most cases, the wizard gives you a nice report with, if you choose it, groupings.

You may need to make some adjustments after using it. For instance, the name you give the report is the name that appears in the title. If you follow naming standards, you might use a name like rptCustomer. Do you want that to appear as the title of the report? Probably not!

What I do is name the report as I want the title to appear at the top of the report. Then, once the report is created, I rename it in the Database window. The report title retains the original name. As an alternative, you can go into Design View and manually change the title.

There are also specialized report capabilities for things like mailing labels and organizer pages. We'll look at examples of charts and mailing labels later in the chapter.

Because of all this report-writing capability, the need to create reports with VBA is actually minimized. Let's take a look at several scenarios using the wizard, and then using VBA.

Report Wizard

Let's assume we want to build a report of our customer list grouped by state and then by zip code within the state. First, open the Report Wizard by selecting the Create Report By Using Wizard option in the Reports Objects window. Then select tblCustomer as the data source, and use all the columns, as shown in Figure 13-3.

The next step, after clicking Next, allows you to decide the grouping. In this case, as shown in Figure 13-4, txtState is selected, with txtZipCode as the subgrouping. Within the groupings, you can do a sort on last name by selecting Next and then the txtCustLastName column and leaving the sort order as Ascending, as shown in Figure 13-5.

The next screen allows you to select a style. For this report, Stepped works nicely. The step after that allows you to select the format style. This example uses Corporate.

The final screen is where you select a name for the report. As mentioned earlier, this is also the title of the report. You can convert the name to proper format later on.

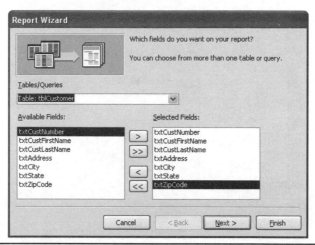

Figure 13-3   *Step one of the Report Wizard*

For the time being, let's use the name Customer List. After selecting Finish in the title screen, the report should look like Figure 13-6.

You can see how easy it is to build a nice report with groupings. However, there are some problems. Some of the labels are too wide, and the customer number falls

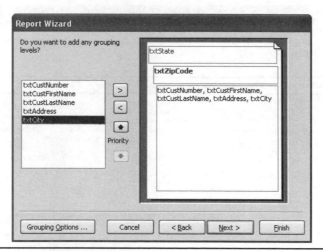

Figure 13-4   *Step two: grouping the data*

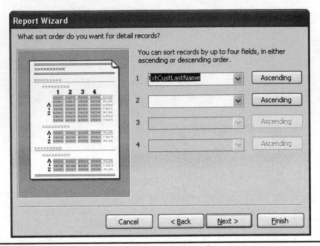

Figure 13-5 *Using the wizard to build a sort within the groupings*

between the last and first name. From here on, you can easily go into Design View and make some adjustments, as shown in Figure 13-7. The finished result is shown in Figure 13-8.

Customer List

Customer List

txtState	txtZipCode	Last Na	Customer N	First Na	Address	City
NJ						
	07622					
		Harris	103	Jack	1123 Oradell Aven	Oradell
	07642					
		Jones	101	John	123 Main Street	Hackens
	07689					
		Miller	104	Susan	890 5th Street	River Ed
	07698					
		Janson	105	Robert	222 Washington	Bergenfi
NY						
	10469					
		Smith	102	Jane	1519 Morris Aven	Bronx

Page: 1

Figure 13-6 *Finished report created in Report Wizard*

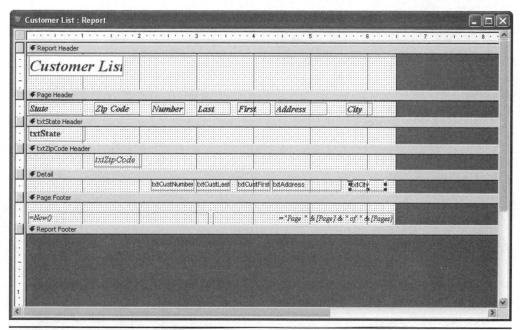

Figure 13-7   *Adjustments in Design View*

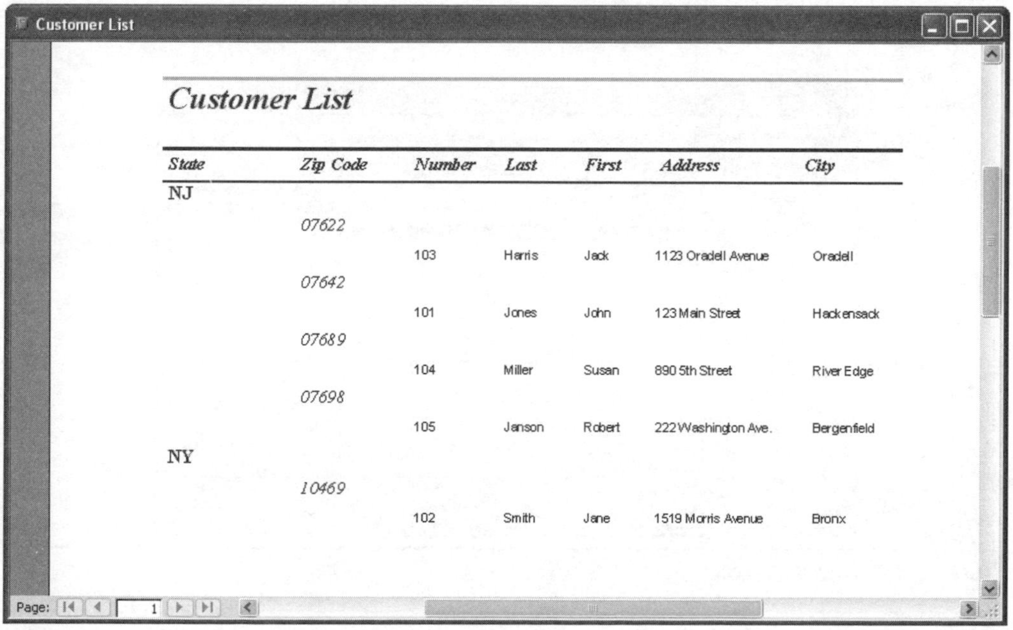

Figure 13-8   *Adjusted report*

As you can see, you need knowledge of both AutoReport and the wizard. Go to the Database window now, and change the name of the report to rptCustomer. At this stage, the title on the report, Customer List, will not be changed.

Specialized Reports

As mentioned earlier, there are some specialized report tools. In the first example, we are going to look at adding a chart to the report, and in the second, we are going to look at mailing labels.

Charts

You can easily add a chart to a report. Admittedly, our little bookstore has only a few customers, and their purchases are located in the tblPurchases table. Let's assume we want to create a report of their purchases and then append a chart at the end of the report in the report footer.

Let's begin by using AutoReport for tblPurchases, and then open the report in Design View. Once there, select Insert | Chart. If you bring your mouse pointer down to the Report Footer area, you should see the chart icon attached to the mouse pointer. Just click in the footer area. This should open a new wizard, as shown in Figure 13-9.

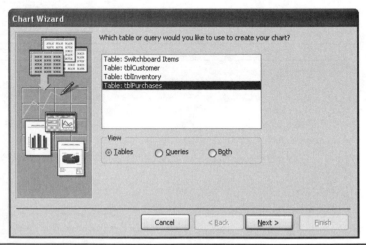

Figure 13-9 *Chart Wizard*

As you can see in the first screen of the wizard, tblPurchases is selected. You also could have based the chart on a query. After selecting Next, you decide what fields you want to use. In this case, we want txtNumber and curPurchasePrice, as shown in Figure 13-10. After selecting Next, you need to select the type of chart. The wizard gives you a choice of many different kinds of charts, but will automatically select one that seems appropriate. In this case, a 3-D column chart is selected, and this works well.

Select Next again, and the Chart Wizard brings you to the chart layout screen. As seen in Figure 13-11, Access made some default decisions. It decided to place the txtNumber field in the category, or x, axis and a calculated field, sumOfcurPurchases, in the value, or y, axis. For purposes of this example, we'll leave it at that.

The next screen will only be applicable when the chart needs to be regenerated for each new record. As an example, you may want to have a chart showing the total for each customer. In this case, however, we are using it just to summarize the data at the end of the report. For that reason, turn off the two field selections by selecting the <no field> option. The screen should look like Figure 13-12.

Since the total is a separate object inserted into the report, you have to give it a name. After selecting Next, you are taken to a screen to name the object, as shown in Figure 13-13. Once again, the name you enter here—Total of Purchases in the example—is the name that goes on the chart. Note also that the chart's legend is turned on. Now when you select Finish, you will see the Design View with the chart, as in Figure 13-14.

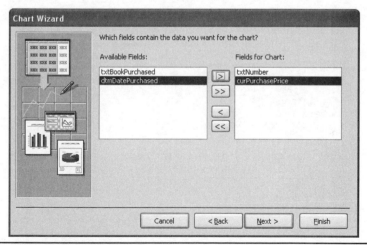

Figure 13-10   *Fields selected for chart*

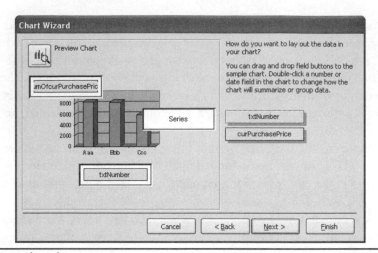

Figure 13-11 *Chart layout screen*

As mentioned in Chapter 10 with regard to naming the controls located in a form, it is also a good idea to rename the controls in the report. This is good programming practice and prevents possible errors when VBA needs to call those controls.

Don't worry if you see generic data in Design View. This is not the actual data yet. If you switch to Report View, it should look something like Figure 13-15. Of course, you can go back to Design View and fine-tune the position of the chart.

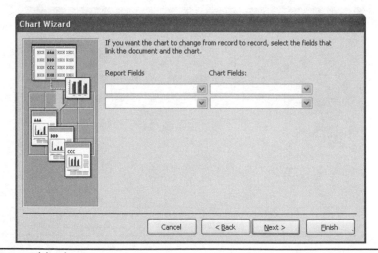

Figure 13-12 *Field selection screen*

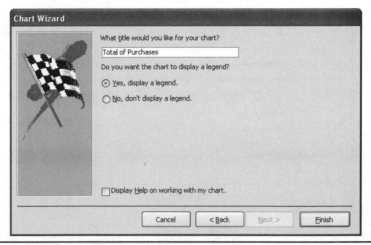

Figure 13-13   *Object name screen*

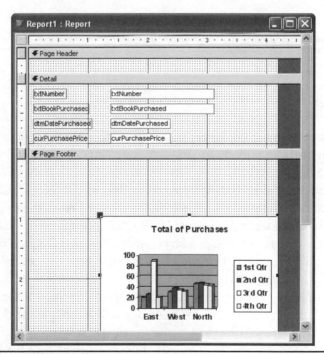

Figure 13-14   *Report design with chart*

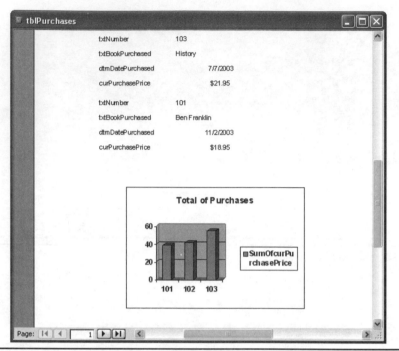

Figure 13-15 *Finished report*

Mailing Labels

Another specialized feature of Access is the ability to write reports formatted for the various Avery label numbers. Again, like charts, Access walks you through the process with the help of a wizard.

You can access the Label Wizard through the Reports Objects window. Once there, you begin by selecting New. You are taken to the first step, as shown in Figure 13-16. Here, the wizard is selected, with tblCustomer as the data source. After selecting OK, you are taken to a screen that allows you to pick the label type you want to use. You will be able to choose from the common Avery labels that come on sheets with three across.

After selecting Next, you are taken to a screen allowing you to select the text and font properties. For purposes of this example, we will leave it at the default settings (you may find a font size of 12 a little easier to read) and select Next.

The next screen is a little tricky if you have never worked with the Label Wizard before. Let's use Figure 13-17 as a guide. You not only transfer the columns you

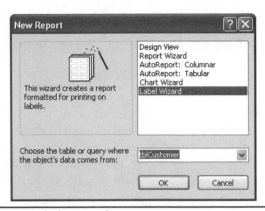

Figure 13-16   *First step in Label Wizard*

want to use on your labels, but you also need to position them exactly as you want them in the label. For example, you want a space between txtCustFirstname and txtCustLastName. The column txtAddress is on the next line. Finally, txtCity is followed by a comma and a space. Finish off the label with txtState, space, and txtZipCode.

The next screen asks you to decide the sort order. In this example, I am going to do the post office a favor and sort by txtZipCode. The final screen asks you to name your report. I selected rptLabelsCustomers.

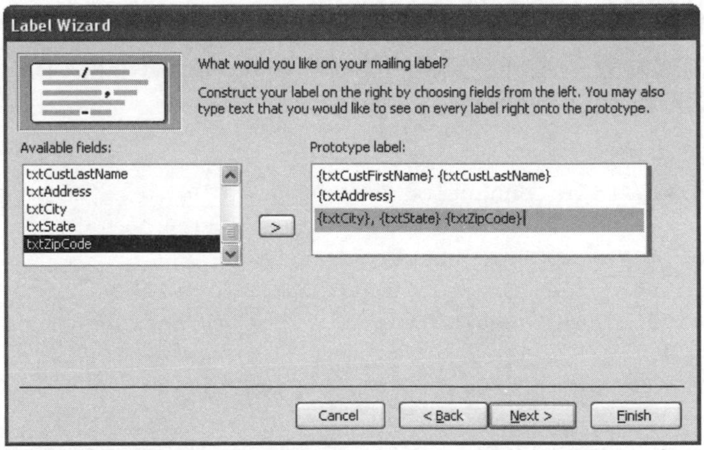

Figure 13-17   *Label construction screen*

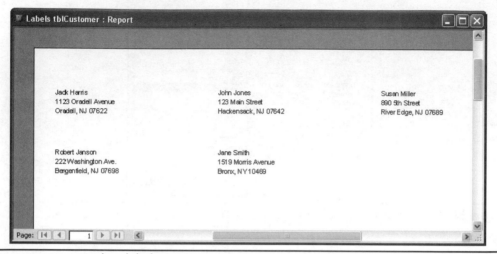

Figure 13-18   *Mailing label report*

Now open the report in preview mode, which, depending on how much data you have, will look something like Figure 13-18. As you can see, the entries are perfectly formatted to print on the Avery 5160 label sheet.

Calling the Report from VBA

As with forms, you can use the DoCmd to call your report within VBA. Let's take a look at the code that follows.

```
Sub runReport()
    Dim con As ADODB.Connection

     Set con = New ADODB.Connection
    con.Open "Provider=Microsoft.Jet.OLEDB.4.0;" & _
       "Data Source=C:\BegVBA\thecornerbookstore.mdb;"

    DoCmd.OpenReport "rptCustomer", acViewPreview

End Sub
```

We have one variation from the form here. If you enter the line with just

```
DoCmd.OpenReport "rptCustomer"
```

Access will assume you want to send the report directly to the printer. In order to prevent that from happening, for the time being, you need to add a second parameter of acViewPreview.

Of course, as in previous chapters, you could include the DoCmd within a decision structure to decide which report to run. In addition, you can include it as part of the Switchboard form created in Chapter 12.

Creating a Report Programmatically

Now that I have shown you all the reasons for not programmatically creating reports, let me show you how to do it on the off chance that you may need to do it for a project.

We are going to look at this in stages.

Creating an Empty Report

Access has a method of the Application object for creating an empty report: CreateReport. As the name implies, it creates an empty report with a page header, Detail section, and page footer. It is not attached to any database table and contains no controls. However, it is the first stage for programmatically building a report. It will also assign the report the default name of Report1, Report2, Report3, and so on.

In the following code, we set a variable as type Report, call the CreateReport method, and then save the results:

```
Sub NewReport()
    Dim rpt As Report
    Set rpt = createReport
    DoCmd.Close , , acSaveYes
End Sub
```

If you were to run this method, it would create the report. Then the DoCmd.Close call would save the report. As stated a moment ago, a default name is assigned. Figure 13-19 shows the results. If you opened Report1 in Design View, you would see something like Figure 13-20.

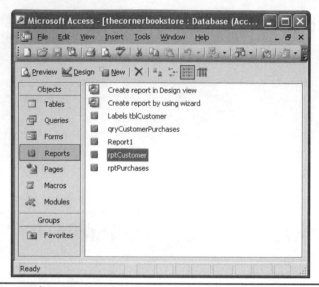

Figure 13-19   *Report object Report1*

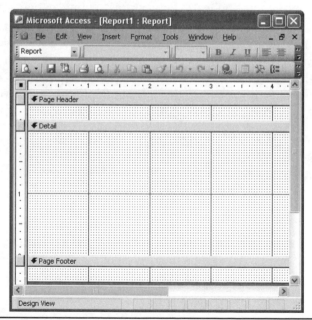

Figure 13-20   *Report1 in Design View*

You can modify the previous code to allow the user to create his or her own name, as follows:

```
Sub NewReport()
    Dim rpt As Report
    Dim strReportName As String

    strReportName = InputBox("Enter the report name", "Report Name")
    Set rpt = CreateReport
    DoCmd.Save , strReportName
    DoCmd.Close , , acSaveYes
End Sub
```

If you were to go ahead and run this method, you would get the input box shown here:

In this example I used MyReport as the name. Figure 13-21 shows that it was added as a report object to the database.

Adding Controls to the Report

To add controls to the report, you use another method of the Application object called CreateControlReport. In this example, we are going to create a simple report in order to show how to add controls using this method.

We will do this in stages so that you understand each step of the process. Let's start by adding variables to handle the report's labels and textboxes, and a variable for handling width:

```
Sub NewReport()
    Dim rpt As Report
    Dim strReportName As String
    Dim txtReportColumns As Access.TextBox
    Dim lblReportLabel As Access.Label
    Dim intWidth As Integer
```

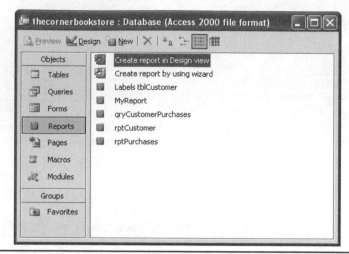

Figure 13-21 *Report objects with MyReport added*

The next thing to do is to set up the SQL for the record source:

```
strReportName = InputBox("Enter the report name", "Report Name")
Set rpt = CreateReport
rpt.RecordSource = "SELECT * FROM tblCustomer"
```

You could use any of the SQL concepts discussed in previous chapters.

We now need to add the controls to the report. We will add the column headings to the page header and the bound controls to the Detail section. While using ADO, the Detail section is the default section.

It is strongly suggested that you set the size of your Detail section. If you don't, the spacing between records could be abnormally large. VBA uses a measurement unit called a *TWIP*. One inch equals 1440 TWIPS.

To set the Detail section to be about a quarter of an inch, add the following code:

```
rpt.Section("Detail").Height = 350
```

Now we want to add the txtCustNumber column to the Detail section of the report with the following code:

```
Set txtReportColumns = CreateReportControl(rpt.Name, acTextBox, _
 , , "txtCustNumber")
```

Again, it is not necessary to indicate that you want this in the Detail section, because that is where the default placement is.

Let's now add a header for the customer number. We will put it in the page header, make it bold, and set the width and height:

```
Set lblReportLabel = CreateReportControl(rpt.Name, acLabel, _
acPageHeader)
    lblReportLabel.Name = "lblCustNumber"
    lblReportLabel.Caption = "Customer Number"
    lblReportLabel.Width = 2000
    lblReportLabel.Height = 300
    lblReportLabel.FontBold = True
```

Notice that you need to set the width and height because the default setting is 0.

We are now going to repeat the process for the Last Name column. The only difference is that we are going to adjust the position by an additional 3000 TWIPs:

```
Set txtReportColumns = CreateReportControl(rpt.Name, acTextBox, _
  , , "txtCustLastName", 3000)
```

Likewise, you can use the same techniques to add a column heading with the following code:

```
Set lblReportLabel = CreateReportControl(rpt.Name, acLabel, _
  acPageHeader, , ,3000)
    lblReportLabel.Name = "lblLastName"
    lblReportLabel.Caption = "Last Name"
    lblReportLabel.Width = 2000
    lblReportLabel.Height = 300
    lblReportLabel.FontBold = True
```

You can repeat the process for the First Name as follows:

```
Set txtReportColumns = CreateReportControl(rpt.Name, acTextBox, _
        , , "txtCustFirstName", 6000)

    Set lblReportLabel = CreateReportControl(rpt.Name, acLabel, _
      acPageHeader, , , 6000)
    lblReportLabel.Name = "lblFirstName"
    lblReportLabel.Caption = "First Name"
    lblReportLabel.Width = 2000
```

```
    lblReportLabel.Height = 300
    lblReportLabel.FontBold = True

 DoCmd.Save , strReportName
    DoCmd.Close , , acSaveYes
    DoCmd.OpenReport strReportName, acViewPreview
End Sub
```

If you were to run the report, either programmatically or within Access, you would see a result that looks something like this:

Summary

In this chapter, you learned how to build useful and attractive reports using the wizards that come with Access. You also saw an example of building a report programmatically, but in most situations, you are more likely to use the former, rather than the latter, technique.

As you saw in forms, and it works the same way here, you can use programming to assign a record source to the report. By doing that, you can build a limited number of generic reports and just assign the data source as needed.

With this chapter on reports, you've now concluded your overview of Access objects (tables, queries, forms, and reports). In the next chapter, you'll learn how to construct menus and menu items that can be used to programmatically run the code that uses Access objects.

Menus and Toolbars

In the previous two chapters, you saw how to interact with VBA through the use of forms and reports. However, you can interact through the use of command bars also. In this chapter, you will learn what command bars are and how to create and use one. We will also look at Access's built-in command bars and work with menus and submenus.

Understanding Command Bars

The term *command bar* is a catch-all term that encompasses toolbars and menus. As a matter of fact, the collection of all the toolbars, menus, and shortcut menus is referred to as the CommandBars collection. This includes the built-in command bars, as well as any customized ones you may create. The CommandBars collection is contained within the larger Application object.

To give you an idea how large Access 2003 is, it contains 178 command bars. This includes one menu bar, 126 shortcut menus, and 51 toolbars. Not all of the toolbars can be customized, as you will soon see.

Let's write a little bit of code to show which command bars are available to you. Before you begin, though, make sure that a reference to the Office object model has been added to your project by selecting the References item from the Tools menu of the VBA Editor window. When the References dialog box opens, check the box for the Microsoft Office x.0 Object Library if it is not already checked. (Checked items appear at the beginning of the Available References list box and are followed by unchecked items.) Then add the following code:

```
Sub listCommandBars()
   Dim comBar As CommandBar
   Dim comBarType As String

   For Each comBar In CommandBars
      Select Case comBar.Type

      Case msoBarTypeNormal
        comBarType = "Toolbar"
      Case msoBarTypeMenuBar
        comBarType = "Menu Bar"
      Case msoBarTypePopup
        comBarType = "Shortcut"
      End Select

      Debug.Print comBar.Index, comBar.Name, comBarType, comBar.Visible
   Next
End Sub
```

This will yield results in the Immediate window resembling those shown in Figure 14-1.

As you may have guessed, the CommandBar object is part of the Office library. We have printed out the properties:

▶ **Index** The position of the command bar within the entire CommandBars collection

▶ **Name** The name of the command bar

▶ **Visible** Whether the command bar is visible or not

The Type property will return what type of msoBar it is ("mso" stands for Microsoft Office). If you look in the Object Browser and search for the msoBarType, you will get the results shown here:

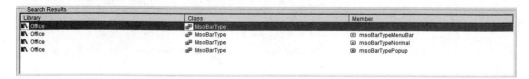

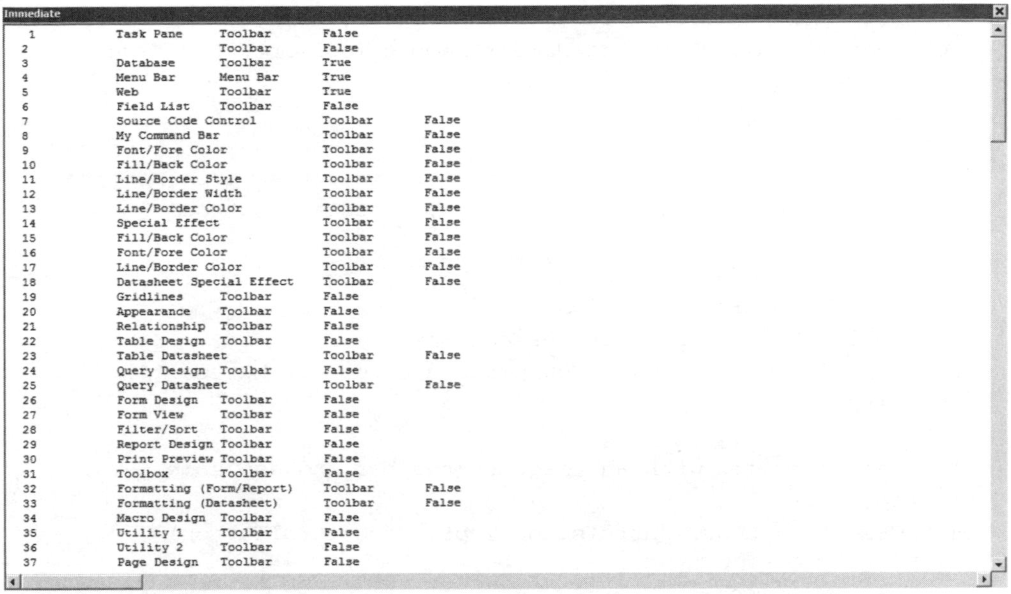

1	Task Pane	Toolbar	False		
2		Toolbar	False		
3	Database	Toolbar	True		
4	Menu Bar	Menu Bar	True		
5	Web	Toolbar	True		
6	Field List	Toolbar	False		
7	Source Code Control		Toolbar	False	
8	My Command Bar		Toolbar	False	
9	Font/Fore Color		Toolbar	False	
10	Fill/Back Color		Toolbar	False	
11	Line/Border Style		Toolbar	False	
12	Line/Border Width		Toolbar	False	
13	Line/Border Color		Toolbar	False	
14	Special Effect		Toolbar	False	
15	Fill/Back Color		Toolbar	False	
16	Font/Fore Color		Toolbar	False	
17	Line/Border Color		Toolbar	False	
18	Datasheet Special Effect		Toolbar	False	
19	Gridlines	Toolbar	False		
20	Appearance	Toolbar	False		
21	Relationship	Toolbar	False		
22	Table Design	Toolbar	False		
23	Table Datasheet		Toolbar	False	
24	Query Design	Toolbar	False		
25	Query Datasheet		Toolbar	False	
26	Form Design	Toolbar	False		
27	Form View	Toolbar	False		
28	Filter/Sort	Toolbar	False		
29	Report Design	Toolbar	False		
30	Print Preview	Toolbar	False		
31	Toolbox	Toolbar	False		
32	Formatting (Form/Report)		Toolbar	False	
33	Formatting (Datasheet)		Toolbar	False	
34	Macro Design	Toolbar	False		
35	Utility 1	Toolbar	False		
36	Utility 2	Toolbar	False		
37	Page Design	Toolbar	False		

Figure 14-1 *The command bar listing in the Immediate window*

Each type is itself a separate object. Understanding this is an important part of working with command bars in VBA.

Each of these command bar types can be called up using either their name or a numeric reference.

▶ **msoBarTypeNormal** This is a toolbar and has a numeric equivalent of 0.

▶ **msoBarTypeMenuBar** This is a menu bar and has a numeric equivalent of 1.

▶ **msoBarTypePopup** This is a shortcut menu and has a numeric equivalent of 2.

Creating a Toolbar

One of my favorite demonstrations for creating a toolbar, and one I use often in class, was shown to me by a couple of Microsoft programmers. Here it is:

```
Sub AddNewCB()
    Dim CBar As CommandBar, CBarCtl As CommandBarControl
    On Error GoTo AddNewCB_Err
```

```
' Create a new floating toolbar and make it visible.
Set CBar = CommandBars.Add(Name:="Sample Toolbar", Position:= _
    msoBarFloating)
CBar.Visible = True

' Create a button with text on the bar and set some properties.
Set CBarCtl = CBar.Controls.Add(Type:=msoControlButton)
With CBarCtl
    .Caption = "Button"
    .Style = msoButtonCaption
    .TooltipText = "Display Message Box"
    .OnAction = "=MsgBox(""You pressed a toolbar button!"")"
End With

' Create a button with an image on the bar and set some
' properties.
Set CBarCtl = CBar.Controls.Add(Type:=msoControlButton)
With CBarCtl
    .FaceId = 1000
    .Caption = "Toggle Button"
    .TooltipText = "Toggle First Button"
    .OnAction = "=ToggleButton()"
End With

' Create a combo box control on the bar and set some properties.
Set CBarCtl = CBar.Controls.Add(msoControlComboBox)
With CBarCtl
    .Caption = "Drop Down"
    .Width = 100
    .AddItem "Create Button", 1
    .AddItem "Remove Button", 2
    .DropDownWidth = 100
    .OnAction = "=AddRemoveButton()"

End With
Exit Sub
AddNewCB_Err:
MsgBox "Error " & Err.Number & vbCr & Err.Description
Exit Sub
End Sub
```

```
'****************************************************************
' This procedure is called from a button on the toolbar.
' It toggles the Visible property of another button on the bar.
'****************************************************************
Function ToggleButton()
    Dim CBButton As CommandBarControl
    On Error GoTo ToggleButton_Err
    Set CBButton = CommandBars("Sample Toolbar").Controls(1)
    CBButton.Visible = Not CBButton.Visible
    Exit Function
    ToggleButton_Err:
    MsgBox "Error " & Err.Number & vbCr & Err.Description
    Exit Function
End Function


'****************************************************************
'This procedure is called from a combo box on the toolbar.
'It adds a button to the bar or removes it
'****************************************************************
Function AddRemoveButton()
    Dim CBar As CommandBar, CBCombo As CommandBarComboBox
    Dim CBNewButton As CommandBarButton
    On Error GoTo AddRemoveButton_Err
    Set CBar = CommandBars("Sample Toolbar")
    Set CBCombo = CBar.Controls(3)
    Select Case CBCombo.ListIndex
        ' If Create Button is selected, create a button on the bar
        Case 1
            Set CBNewButton = CBar.Controls.Add(Type:=msoControlButton)
            With CBNewButton
                .Caption = "New Button"
                .Style = msoButtonCaption
                .BeginGroup = True
                .Tag = "New Button"
                .OnAction = "=MsgBox(""This is a new button!"")"
            End With
        ' Find and remove the new button if it exists.
        Case 2
            Set CBNewButton = CBar.FindControl(Tag:="New Button")
            CBNewButton.Delete
```

```
    End Select
    Exit Function
    AddRemoveButton_Err:
    ' If the button does not exist.
    If Err.Number = 91 Then
      MsgBox "Cannot remove button that does not exist!"
      Exit Function
    Else
      MsgBox "Error " & Err.Number & vbCr & Err.Description
      Exit Function
    End If
End Function
```

I know this seems like a lot of code, but it ties many concepts together that we will discuss. However, before you analyze it, let's try running it. Make sure you are in the original sub procedure adNewCB. Once you run it, a floating toolbar like the one shown here should appear:

If you click on each of the buttons, you will see various responses. Spend a few minutes and play with it.

Let's take a look at some of the code that was used. Near the beginning of the AddNewCB procedure, we have the following code:

```
Set CBar = CommandBars.Add(Name:="Sample Toolbar", Position:= _
     msoBarFloating)
  CBar.Visible = True
```

Notice that the code sets the object reference variable CBar (which represents the CommandBar object) to reference the value returned by the Add method of the CommandBars collection. Remember, the CommandBars collection is within the Application object and includes all the toolbars, menu bars, and shortcut menus. The Add method creates a new command bar, adds it to the collection, and returns a reference to it. In the call to the Add method, you give the command bar a name and declare that you want its position to be floating. It is also necessary to set its visibility to true. If not, you would need to turn it on manually.

You can tell that the new toolbar has been added to the collection by going into the Database window and selecting Tools | Customize. If you select the Toolbars tab and scroll to the end, you will see the customized toolbar added to the collection, as Figure 14-2 shows.

The next section of code adds a button to the toolbar:

```
Set CBarCtl = CBar.Controls.Add(Type:=msoControlButton)
   With CBarCtl
      .Caption = "Button"
      .Style = msoButtonCaption
      .TooltipText = "Display Message Box"
      .OnAction = "=MsgBox(""You pressed a toolbar button!"")"
   End With
```

CBarCtl is a command bar control object. You are adding it to the controls on the command bar (CBar) and making it a control of type msoControlButton, or a command button.

The caption is the text within the button, and the normal style of the caption is the property msoButtonCaption.

TooltipText is the tag that is shown when you roll the mouse over the button.

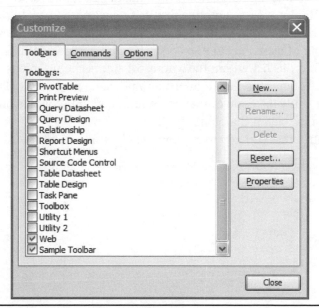

Figure 14-2   *The customized toolbar in the collection*

Finally, the onAction method defines what happens when the button is pressed. It returns a message box like this one:

The following block of code then adds a second control to the toolbar:

```
Set CBarCtl = CBar.Controls.Add(Type:=msoControlButton)
   With CBarCtl
      .FaceId = 1000
      .Caption = "Toggle Button"
      .TooltipText = "Toggle First Button"
      .OnAction = "=ToggleButton()"
   End With
```

Like before, you add the button to the command bar. However, there is one thing that is a little different. You will notice that you now use the FaceId property.

The FaceId property dictates the look, not the function, of a command bar button. A complete listing of these FaceId numbers is beyond the scope of this book. However, you can easily find this list within the Microsoft Access help screens.

This time, onAction calls the ToggleButton procedure, which is also defined in our code. If you study the code of that procedure, it simply toggles on and off the visibility of the first button that you added.

The next control that you add to the command bar is a combo box:

```
Set CBarCtl = CBar.Controls.Add(msoControlComboBox)
   With CBarCtl
      .Caption = "Drop Down"
      .Width = 100
      .AddItem "Create Button", 1
      .AddItem "Remove Button", 2
      .DropDownWidth = 100
      .OnAction = "=AddRemoveButton()"
   End With
```

Each of the items populating this combo box must be added with the AddItem method. You also give each item an Index reference in addition to the text. You will notice that the onAction method calls the AddRemoveButton procedure, which has also been supplied in the code.

Let's take a look at a section of this AddRemoveButton procedure:

```
Set CBCombo = CBar.Controls(3)
   Select Case CBCombo.ListIndex
      ' If Create Button is selected, create a button on the bar
      Case 1
         Set CBNewButton = CBar.Controls.Add(Type:=msoControlButton)
         With CBNewButton
            .Caption = "New Button"
            .Style = msoButtonCaption
            .BeginGroup = True
            .Tag = "New Button"
            .OnAction = "=MsgBox(""This is a new button!"")"
         End With
      ' Find and remove the new button if it exists.
      Case 2
         Set CBNewButton = CBar.FindControl(Tag:="New Button")
         CBNewButton.Delete
   End Select
```

Since this is the third control on the command bar, you set up a reference to it with CBar.Controls(3). Once that CBCombo object reference is set up, you use the ListIndex property to determine the index value of the item selected in the combo box.

You then send that to a Select Case structure that handles each of the possible combo box options. Notice that the FindControl method is used to find the next instance of the "New Button" tag and delete it.

Admittedly, this was only a light examination of the code. However, I think you should have enough information here to build sophisticated toolbars that will cover a variety of situations.

Note, if you try to run this code a second time, you will end up with the following error message:

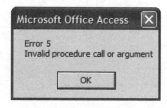

You would need to delete the toolbar using the Tools | Customize box in the Database window, or by using the following simple procedure.

```
Sub cmdBarDelete()
    CommandBars("sample toolbar").Delete
End Sub
```

Menus

Again, with a few variations, the little demonstration in this section is complements of some friends of mine at Microsoft. Like before, it shows some very interesting features. Here is the code:

```
Sub AddNewMB()
    Dim MBar As CommandBar, MBarCtl As CommandBarControl
    Dim MBarSubCtl As CommandBarControl
    On Error GoTo AddNewMB_Err

    ' Create a new menu bar and dock it on the left.
    Set MBar = CommandBars.Add(Name:="Sample Menu Bar", Position:= _
        msoBarTop, MenuBar:=True, Temporary:=False)
    ' Make the menu bar visible.
    MBar.Visible = True
    ' Prevent users from undocking the menu bar.
    MBar.Protection = msoBarNoMove

    ' Create a popup control on the bar and set its caption.
    Set MBarCtl = MBar.Controls.Add(Type:=msoControlPopup)
    MBarCtl.Caption = "Displa&y"

    ' Create 2 controls on the Display popup and set some properties.
    Set MBarSubCtl = MBarCtl.Controls.Add(Type:=msoControlButton)
    With MBarSubCtl
        .Style = msoButtonIconAndCaption
        .Caption = "E&nable ClickMe"
        .FaceId = 59
        .OnAction = "=ToggleClickMe()"
        .Parameter = 1
        .BeginGroup = True
    End With
    Set MBarSubCtl = MBarCtl.Controls.Add(Type:=msoControlButton)
```

```
    With MBarSubCtl
        .Style = msoButtonIconAndCaption
        .Caption = "Di&sable ClickMe"
        .FaceId = 276
        .OnAction = "=ToggleClickMe()"
        .Parameter = 2
        .BeginGroup = True
    End With


    ' Add another control to the menu bar.
    Set MBarCtl = MBar.Controls.Add(Type:=msoControlButton)
    With MBarCtl
        .BeginGroup = True
        .Caption = "&ClickMe"
        .Style = msoButtonCaption
        .OnAction = "=MsgBox(""You clicked ClickMe"")"
    End With


    ' Add a control to make this menu bar invisible and bring back
    ' the system menu bar.
    Set MBarCtl = MBar.Controls.Add(Type:=msoControlButton)
    With MBarCtl
        .BeginGroup = True
        .Caption = "&Set Visibility Off"
        .Style = msoButtonCaption
        .OnAction = "=SampleMenuDisable()"
    End With
    Exit Sub
AddNewMB_Err:
    MsgBox "Error " & Err.Number & vbCr & Err.Description
    Exit Sub
End Sub




'****************************************************************
' This procedure uses the Parameter property of a command bar
' control to execute a different action depending on which item
' you click on a popup menu.
'****************************************************************
Function ToggleClickMe()
    Dim MyMenu As CommandBar
    Dim MBarClickMe As CommandBarControl
    On Error GoTo ToggleClickMe_Err
```

```
    Set MyMenu = CommandBars("Sample Menu Bar")
    Set MBarClickMe = MyMenu.Controls(2)
    ' The ActionControl property of command bars returns the control
    ' whose OnAction property is running this procedure.
    With CommandBars.ActionControl
        Select Case .Parameter
            Case 1
                MBarClickMe.Enabled = True
            Case 2
                MBarClickMe.Enabled = False
        End Select
    End With
    Exit Function
ToggleClickMe_Err:
    MsgBox "Error " & Err.Number & vbCr & Err.Description
    Exit Function
End Function


'***************************************************************
' This function restores the original menu bar. Because there can
' only be one system menu bar, you must hide the sample menu bar
' when you want to bring back the previous system menu bar.
'***************************************************************
Function SampleMenuDisable()
    Application.CommandBars("Sample Menu Bar").Visible = False
    Application.CommandBars("Menu Bar").Visible = True
End Function
```

If you run the original procedure, you end up with the menu bar, shown here.

In the code, you create the menu bar as follows:

```
Set MBar = CommandBars.Add(Name:="Sample Menu Bar", Position:= _
        msoBarTop, MenuBar:=True, Temporary:=False)
    ' Make the menu bar visible.
    MBar.Visible = True
    ' Prevent users from undocking the menu bar.
    MBar.Protection = msoBarNoMove
```

You add the menu bar to the CommandBars collection as you did with the toolbar before. You even set its position at msoBarTop. You have to set its visibility, as before, to true. In this case, however, you prevent the user from undocking the menu by setting the Protection property to msoBarNoMove.

Again, like before, you add controls to the menu bar. The first of these is defined as follows:

```
' Create a popup control on the bar and set its caption.
Set MBarCtl = MBar.Controls.Add(Type:=msoControlPopup)
MBarCtl.Caption = "Displa&y"
```

This code adds a menu item (called a CommandBarControl object) to the "Sample Menu Bar" menu bar. The menu item's caption is "Display."

The following code then adds another menu item (or CommandBarControl object) to the menu item whose caption is Display:

```
Set MBarSubCtl = MBarCtl.Controls.Add(Type:=msoControlButton)
   With MBarSubCtl
      .Style = msoButtonIconAndCaption
      .Caption = "E&nable ClickMe"
      .FaceId = 59
      .OnAction = "=ToggleClickMe()"
      .Parameter = 1
      .BeginGroup = True
   End With
```

This means that when the user selects the Display menu item, a drop-down menu that includes the item "Enable ClickMe" appears. (Subsequent code also adds another menu item captioned "Disable ClickMe.") The string assigned to the OnAction property can be used to define a command or procedure that is to be executed when this menu item is selected.

Both the Enable ClickMe and Disable ClickMe items refer to the ToggleClickMe procedure. This procedure either enables or disables the ClickMe button. It retrieves a reference to the second control on the command bar (the one captioned "ClickMe"). It then looks at the value of the Parameter property, which is passed to the procedure defined by the OnAction property. Based on the value of this parameter, it decides whether to enable or disable the ClickMe button.

Even though this seems like a lot of code, based upon what you have learned already, it is pretty straightforward and easy to follow.

Submenus

In the preceding example, you have set the menu items as pop-ups. However, what happens if you just want to have additional items on submenus? Let's take a look at the following code:

```
Public Sub newSubMenu()
    Dim menuBar As CommandBar
    Dim newMenu As CommandBarControl
    Dim menuItem As CommandBarControl
    Dim subMenuItem As CommandBarControl

    Set menuBar = CommandBars.Add(menuBar:=True, Position:=msoBarTop, _
        Name:="Sub Menu Bar", Temporary:=True)
    menuBar.Visible = True

    Set newMenu = menuBar.Controls.Add(Type:=msoControlPopup)
    newMenu.Caption = "&First Menu"

    Set newMenu = menuBar.Controls.Add(Type:=msoControlPopup)
    newMenu.Caption = "&Second Menu"

    Set newMenu = menuBar.Controls.Add(Type:=msoControlPopup)
    newMenu.Caption = "&Third Menu"

    Set menuItem = newMenu.Controls.Add(Type:=msoControlButton )

    With menuItem
        .Caption = "F&irst Sub"
        .FaceId = "356"
        .OnAction = "myTest"
    End With

    Set menuItem = newMenu.Controls.Add(Type:=msoControlButton)

    With menuItem
        .Caption = "S&econd Sub"

        .FaceId = "333"
        .OnAction = "otherTest"
    End With

    Set menuItem = newMenu.Controls.Add(Type:=msoControlPopup)
```

```
menuItem.Caption = "Sub Menus"

Set subMenuItem = menuItem.Controls.Add(Type:=msoControlButton)

With subMenuItem
    .Caption = "Item 1"
    .FaceId = 321
    .OnAction = "firstMacro"
End With

Set subMenuItem = menuItem.Controls.Add(Type:=msoControlButton)

With subMenuItem
    .Caption = "Item 2"
    .FaceId = 432
    .OnAction = "secondMacro"
End With

End Sub
```

As you can see, we did a bit of modular construction here. You add menu items to the menu bar. Then you add submenu items to each of the menu items located on the menu bar.

As you can see in the code, it is a very repetitive pattern that can easily be extended to add even more levels of submenus. As a matter of fact, as a little experiment, why don't you try to add another level under the subMenuItems.

Summary

We have looked at three uses of command bars: toolbars, pop-up menus, and submenus. Even though it seems like a tremendous amount of coding, the patterns within each code are quite repetitive. You just need to repeat the pattern, with the appropriate adjustments, for each new menu or toolbar item needed.

We are now going to turn our attention to making adjustments to elements of the work environment, such as startup options.

Changing the
Access Environment

In the previous chapter, you learned how to manipulate command bars (menus and toolbars) using VBA. That changed how you could interact with Access. In this chapter, you will see how to change other environmental settings by using VBA. We are going to look at some simple startup procedures as well as changing and restoring default information. The second half of the chapter contains tables that you can use as a handy reference.

The Startup Properties

On several occasions you have already encountered the database startup properties. You can access them from the Database window by selecting Tools | Startup. You will see the dialog box shown in Figure 15-1.

Interestingly, each item in this box has a VBA equivalent. Table 15-1 lists the startup properties that correspond to the Startup dialog box interface items and the type of values they are.

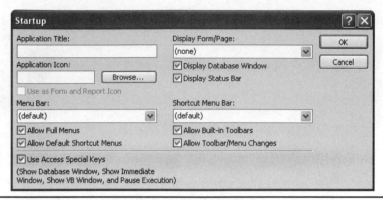

Figure 15-1 *The database startup properties dialog box*

Property	VBA Equivalent	Data Type
Application Title	AppTitle	String
Application Icon	AppIcon	String (Image name)
Display Form	StartupForm	String (Form name)
Display Database Window	StartupShowDBWindow	Boolean
Display Status Bar	StartupShowStatusBar	Boolean
Menu Bar	StartupMenuBar	Menu bar name
Shortcut Menu Bar	StartupShortcutMenuBar	Shortcut menu bar name
Allow Full Menus	AllowFullMenus	Boolean
Allow Default Shortcut Menus	AllowShortcutMenus	Boolean
Allow Built-in Toolbars	AllowBuiltinToolBars	Boolean
Allow Toolbar/Menu Changes	AllowToolBarChanges	Boolean
Allow viewing of code after an error (Note: While not specifically listed in the dialog box, this shuts off controls to access the code.)	AllowBreakIntoCode	Boolean
Use Access Special Keys	AllowSpecialKeys	Boolean

Table 15-1 *VBA Equivalents of Startup Properties*

The following code shows an example of changing some startup properties using the current database as the object.

```
Public Sub startupProperties()
   Dim myDatabase As Object
   Set myDatabase = CurrentDb
   myDatabase.Properties("AllowFullMenus") = True
   myDatabase.Properties("Allowtoolbarchanges") = True

End Sub
```

If you try to run this code and you get an error message, open the Startup dialog box and click OK. This lets Access populate the properties of the Application and Database objects as needed.

When you run the code, nothing seems to happen. However, try changing the two Boolean values to False as follows:

```
Public Sub startupProperties()
   Dim myDatabase As Object
   Set myDatabase = CurrentDb
   myDatabase.Properties("AllowFullMenus") = False
   myDatabase.Properties("Allowtoolbarchanges") = False

End Sub
```

If you now open the dialog box, notice that those fields are toggled off, as shown in Figure 15-2.

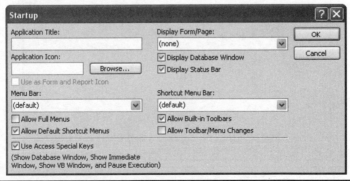

Figure 15-2   *The Startup dialog box with fields clicked off*

You can reset any values you set with the following code:

```
Public Sub startupProperties()
   Dim myDatabase As Object
   Set myDatabase = CurrentDb
   With myDatabase
      .Properties.Delete "AllowFullMenus"
      .Properties.Delete "AllowToolBarChanges"
    End With
    Application.RefreshTitleBar
End Sub
```

Changing Options

You can set the configuration options that are available in the Options dialog box, shown in Figure 15-3. (To see the Options dialog box, select Tools | Options.)

Let's say we want to shut off the Status Bar and the Startup Task Pane programmatically. To do this, we can call the Application object's SetOption method

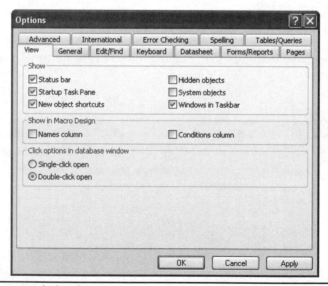

Figure 15-3   *Options dialog box*

and pass it two arguments: a predefined string indicating the option that we want to modify, and the new value of the option. The following code can accomplish that task:

```
Public Sub setOptions()
   With Application
      .SetOption "show status bar", False
      .SetOption "show startup dialog box", False
   End With
End Sub
```

Again, as with the Startup dialog box, you can look at the Options dialog box and see the corresponding options shut off.

The following sections give you the strings corresponding to the settings in each tab of the Options dialog box. Note that all of the options are found in Access 2003, although they are not all found in earlier versions.

Unfortunately, there is no Delete method to reset the defaults, as there is for the Properties collection that controls the startup procedures. Instead, you should save the original values to variables and then call on those variables to reset the property. You can find the original value of the property by calling the GetOption method before you call the SetOption method to change that option's value. It takes as its single argument the string shown in the String Argument column in the tables presented in the following sections.

To set the value of an option, you have to provide the SetOption method with not only the name of the option, but also with the value you'd like it to have. The rules for doing this are:

▶ If the option is represented by a checkbox in the interface, you can assign an Integer value of −1 or a Boolean value of True for On, and an Integer value of 0 or a Boolean value of False for Off.

▶ If the option is represented by a set of option buttons in the interface, you can assign a value of 0 if you'd like to programmatically select the first button, 1 if you'd like to programmatically select the second button, etc.

▶ If the item is represented by a list box or a drop-down list box in the interface, a value of 0 represents the first item, 1 represents the second, and so on.

▶ If the option is represented by a text box, it can be either a String, an Integer, or a Long (a long integer). As long as the string is in the appropriate format or numeric range, Access will automatically handle the conversion from a string to a nonstring data type, if necessary. To get some sense of the range and format of valid values, check the documentation and use the GetOption method to retrieve the existing setting.

View Tab

The options on the View tab and their string equivalents are as follows:

Option Text	String Argument	Data Type
Show, Status bar	Show Status Bar	Integer or Boolean
Show, Startup Task Pane	Show Startup Dialog Box	Integer or Boolean
Show, New object shortcuts	Show New Object Shortcuts	Integer or Boolean
Show, Hidden objects	Show Hidden Objects	Integer or Boolean
Show, System objects	Show System Objects	Integer or Boolean
Show, Windows in Taskbar	ShowWindowsInTaskbar	Integer or Boolean
Show in Macro Design, Names column	Show Macro Names Column	Integer or Boolean
Show in Macro Design, Conditions column	Show Conditions Column	Integer or Boolean
Click options in database window	Database Explorer Click Behavior	Integer

General Tab

The options on the General tab and their string equivalents are as follows:

Option Text	String Argument	Data Type
Print margins, Left margin	Left Margin	String
Print margins, Right margin	Right Margin	String
Print margins, Top margin	Top Margin	String
Print margins, Bottom margin	Bottom Margin	String
Use four-year digit year formatting, This database	Four-Digit Year Formatting	Integer/Boolean
Use four-year digit year formatting, All databases	Four-Digit Year Formatting All Databases	Integer/Boolean
Name AutoCorrect, Track name AutoCorrect info	Track Name AutoCorrect Info	Integer/Boolean

Option Text	String Argument	Data Type
Name AutoCorrect, Perform name AutoCorrect	Perform Name AutoCorrect	Integer/Boolean
Name AutoCorrect, Log name AutoCorrect changes	Log Name AutoCorrect Changes	Integer/Boolean
Recently used file list	Enable MRU File List	Integer/Boolean
Recently used file list, (number of files)	Size of MRU File List	Integer
Provide feedback with sound	Provide Feedback with Sound	Integer/Boolean
Compact on Close	Auto Compact	Integer/Boolean
New database sort order	New Database Sort Order	Long
Remove personal information from file properties on save	Remove Personal Information	Integer/Boolean
Default database folder	Default Database Directory	String

Edit/Find Tab

The options on the Edit/Find tab and their string equivalents are as follows:

Option Text	String Argument	Data Type
Default find/replace behavior	Default Find/Replace Behavior	Integer
Confirm, Record changes	Confirm Record Changes	Integer/Boolean
Confirm, Document deletions	Confirm Document Deletions	Integer/Boolean
Confirm, Action queries	Confirm Action Queries	Integer/Boolean
Show list of values in, Local indexed fields	Show Values in Indexed	Integer/Boolean
Show list of values in, Local nonindexed fields	Show Values in Non-Indexed	Integer/Boolean
Show list of values in, ODBC fields	Show Values in Remote	Integer/Boolean
Show list of values in, Records in local snapshot	Show Values in Snapshot	Integer/Boolean
Show list of values in, Records at server	Show Values in Server	Integer/Boolean
Don't display lists where more than this number of records read	Show Values Limit	Integer

Keyboard Tab

The options on the Keyboard tab and their string equivalents are as follows:

Option Text	String Argument	Data Type
Move after enter	Move After Enter	Integer
Behavior entering field	Behavior Entering Field	Integer
Arrow key behavior	Arrow Key Behavior	Integer
Cursor stops at first/last field	Cursor Stops at First/Last Field	Integer/Boolean
Auto commit	Ime Autocommit	Integer/Boolean
Datasheet IME control	Datasheet Ime Control	Integer/Boolean

Datasheet Tab

The options on the Datasheet tab and their string equivalents are as follows:

Option Text	String Argument	Data Type
Default colors, Font	Default Font Color	Integer
Default colors, Background	Default Background Color	Integer
Default colors, Gridlines	Default Gridlines Color	Integer
Default gridlines showing, Horizontal	Default Gridlines Horizontal	Integer/Boolean
Default gridlines showing, Vertical	Default Gridlines Vertical	Integer/Boolean
Default column width	Default Column Width	String
Default font, Font	Default Font Name	String
Default font, Weight	Default Font Weight	Integer
Default font, Size	Default Font Size	Long
Default font, Underline	Default Font Underline	Integer/Boolean
Default font, Italic	Default Font Italic	Integer/Boolean
Default cell effect	Default Cell Effect	Integer
Show animations	Show Animations	Integer/Boolean
Show Smart Tags on Datasheets	Show Smart Tags on Datasheets	Integer/Boolean

Forms/Reports Tab

The options on the Forms/Reports tab and their string equivalents are as follows:

Option Text	String Argument	Data Type
Selection behavior	Selection Behavior	Integer
Form template	Form Template	String
Report template	Report Template	String
Always use event procedures	Always Use Event Procedures	Integer/Boolean
Show Smart Tags on Forms	Show Smart Tags on Forms	Integer/Boolean
Show Windows Themed Controls on Forms	Themed Form Controls	Integer/Boolean

Pages Tab

The options on the Pages tab and their string equivalents are as follows:

Option Text	String Argument	Data Type
Default Designer Properties, Section Indent	Section Indent	String
Default Designer Properties, Alternate Row Color	Alternate Row Color	String
Default Designer Properties, Caption Section Style	Caption Section Style	String
Default Designer Properties, Footer Section Style	Footer Section Style	String
Default Database/Project Properties, Use Default Page Folder	Use Default Page Folder	Integer/Boolean
Default Database/Project Properties, Default Page Folder	Default Page Folder	String
Default Database/Project Properties, Use Default Connection File	Use Default Connection File	Integer/Boolean
Default Database/Project Properties, Default Connection File	Default Connection File	String

Advanced Tab

The options on the Advanced tab and their string equivalents are as follows:

Option Text	String Argument	Data Type
DDE operations, Ignore DDE requests	Ignore DDE Requests	Integer/Boolean
DDE operations, Enable DDE refresh	Enable DDE Refresh	Integer/Boolean
Default File Format	Default File Format	Integer
Default open mode	Default Open Mode for Databases	Integer
Command-line arguments	Command-Line Arguments	String
OLE/DDE timeout (sec)	OLE/DDE Timeout (sec)	Integer
Default record locking	Default Record Locking	Integer
Refresh interval (sec)	Refresh Interval (sec)	Integer
Number of update retries	Number of Update Retries	Integer
ODBC refresh interval (sec)	ODBC Refresh Interval (sec)	Integer
Update retry interval (msec)	Update Retry Interval (msec)	Integer
Open databases using record-level locking	Use Row Level Locking	Integer/Boolean

International Tab

The options on the International tab and their string equivalents are as follows:

Option Text	String Argument	Data Type
Right-to-Left, Default direction	Default direction	Integer
Right-to-Left, General alignment	General alignment	Integer
Right-to-Left, Cursor movement	Cursor movement	Integer
Use Hijri Calendar	Use Hijri Calendar	Integer/Boolean

Error Checking Tab

The options on the Error Checking tab and their string equivalents are as follows:

Option Text	String Argument	Data Type
Settings, Enable error checking	Enable Error Checking	Integer/Boolean
Settings, Error indicator color	Error Checking Indicator Color	Integer

Option Text	String Argument	Data Type
Form/Report Design Rules, Unassociated label and control	Unassociated Label and Control Error Checking	Integer/Boolean
Form/Report Design Rules, New unassociated labels	New Unassociated Labels Error Checking	Integer/Boolean
Form/Report Design Rules, Keyboard shortcut errors	Keyboard Shortcut Errors Error Checking	Integer/Boolean
Form/Report Design Rules, Invalid control properties	Invalid Control Properties Error Checking	Integer/Boolean
Form/Report Design Rules, Common report errors	Common Report Errors Error Checking	Integer/Boolean

Spelling Tab

The options on the Spelling tab and their string equivalents are as follows:

Option Text	String Argument	Data Type
Dictionary Language	Spelling dictionary language	Long
Add words to	Spelling add words to	String
Suggest from main dictionary only	Spelling suggest from main dictionary only	Integer/Boolean
Ignore words in UPPERCASE	Spelling ignore words in UPPERCASE	Integer/Boolean
Ignore words with numbers	Spelling ignore words with number	Integer/Boolean
Ignore Internet and file addresses	Spelling ignore Internet and file addresses	Integer/Boolean
Language-specific, German: Use post-reform rules	Spelling use German post-reform rules	Integer/Boolean
Language-specific, Korean: Combine aux verb/adj.	Spelling combine aux verb/adj	Integer/Boolean
Language-specific, Korean: Search misused word list	Spelling use auto-change list	Integer/Boolean
Language-specific, Korean: Process compound nouns	Spelling process compound nouns	Integer/Boolean
Language-specific, Hebrew modes	Spelling Hebrew modes	Integer
Language-specific, Arabic modes	Spelling Arabic modes	Integer

Tables/Queries Tab

The options on the Tables/Queries tab and their string equivalents are as follows:

Option Text	String Argument	Data Type
Table design, Default field sizes - Text	Default Text Field Size	Integer
Table design, Default field sizes - Number	Default Number Field Size	Integer
Table design, Default field type	Default Field Type	Integer
Table design, AutoIndex on Import/Create	AutoIndex on Import/Create	String
Query design, Show table names	Show Table Names	Integer/Boolean
Query design, Output all fields	Output All Fields	
Query design, Enable AutoJoin	Enable AutoJoin	Integer/Boolean
Query design, Run permissions	Run Permissions	Integer
Query design, SQL Server Compatible Syntax (ANSI 92) - This database	ANSI Query Mode	Integer/Boolean
Query design, SQL Server Compatible Syntax (ANSI 92) – Default for new databases	ANSI Query Mode Default	Integer/Boolean
Query design, Query design font, Font	Query Design Font Name	String
Query design, Query design font, Size	Query Design Font Size	Long
Show Property Update Options buttons	Show Property Update Options buttons	Integer/Boolean

Summary

In this brief chapter, we looked at some simple programmatic techniques to change the Access environment. You saw how to change the startup properties, as well as some optional properties. The chapter also provides some handy tables for reference.

We will now turn our attention to one of the most important topics you will need to deal with: security.

Advanced Access
Programming Techniques

Database Security

Y ou can start by asking two questions:

- ▶ Is the person accessing the database allowed to be there?
- ▶ If the person is allowed to be there, what is he or she allowed, or not allowed, to do?

These two questions lie at the heart of database security. In this age of malicious viruses and computer crimes, we have to be careful that our data, files, and programming code are not illegally accessed or retrieved.

In this chapter we explore security within Access and VBA. You will learn about user authentication, granting and revoking permissions, the Jet Sandbox, and ADOX programming techniques for security.

Access and Security

Since Access's growth from a home and boutique database package to a powerful tool that, in many cases, can be used as the backbone database of a website, the whole issue of security has been studied carefully. Let's first take a look at some of the simpler security techniques that can be used.

The User Interface

One of the simplest security techniques is to turn the Access user interface off. This can be done from within Access by going to Tools | Startup, as shown in Figure 16-1. This allows you to shut off the Database window and status bar, set a custom menu bar as the default, set a customized opening splash screen, and so on.

For smaller and less secure applications, this could be a very easy and nonprogrammatic way of securing them. It could restrict users' movements enough that they could not create a problem.

Setting a Password

Also for smaller and less secure database applications, you can set a password that would be required before obtaining unrestricted use of the database. This can be used for a two-level security system: those who have full access to the database, and those who have access only to the application.

Those who have the password can access virtually anything in the database; and those who do not can only access the application with its programmed restrictions.

If you have TheCornerBookstore database open, try setting a database password by selecting Tools | Security | Set Database Password. If you do that, you may end up with a message like this:

Figure 16-1   *The Startup dialog box*

In order to set the password, you need to open the database in an Exclusive mode. You can do this by first closing the database and then selecting File | Open. In the opening dialog box, click once on thecornerbookstore.mdb. In the lower-right corner, click on the down arrow of the Open button and select Open Exclusive:

Once that is completed, you can then select Tools | Security | Set Database Password, and you will be presented with the following dialog box:

You can now set the password you want to use. Access will store it in an encrypted format. Once it is set, you then have the option, by using Tools | Security | Unset Database Password, to shut that password off. You need the existing password for permission to unset it.

Creating a Password Programmatically

Up to this point in the book, the SQL code we have been using has been pretty generic in that it will run in any database environment. However, each database package has a small number of proprietary SQL statements that you can use.

Since Access is built on the Jet database engine, this is called Jet SQL in Access. One of the statements you can use is ALTER DATABASE PASSWORD. Because of this, you can write a fairly simple VBA program to set or change the password. The keyword NULL can be used to represent the old password. As an example:

```
Sub changePassword()
    Dim con1 As ADODB.Connection
    Dim strPassword As String

    strPassword = "ALTER DATABASE PASSWORD [smith] NULL;"

    Set con1 = New ADODB.Connection
    With con1
```

```
             = adModeShareExclusive
             .Open "Provider=Microsoft.Jet.OLEDB.4.0; " & _
             "Data Source=C:\BegVBA\thecornerbookstore.mdb;"
             .Execute (strPassword)
         End With
End Sub
```

This code assumes that you are accessing a remote database.

In this code, we made the new password the word "smith." As mentioned previously, NULL is used as the second argument because there is no password to replace.

As before, we had to set the mode of the connection to Exclusive (adModeShareExclusive).

Let's say we wanted to change the password of the database from smith to jones. Our code would need to reflect two things. First of all, the SQL string would look as follows:

```
strPassword = "ALTER DATABASE PASSWORD [jones] [smith];"
```

Again, notice that the first argument represents the new password, and the second argument represents the old password. However, you cannot change the password unless you open the database with the existing password. In order to do that, you need to add another line to the connection.

```
    With con1
        .Mode = adModeShareExclusive
        .Open "Provider=Microsoft.Jet.OLEDB.4.0; " & _
        "Data Source=C:\Books\Access\chap15\thecornerbookstore.mdb; " & _
        "Jet OLEDB:Database Password=smith;"
        .Execute (strPassword)
    End With
```

Finally, if you want to remove the password entirely, change the SQL string as follows:

```
strPassword = "ALTER DATABASE PASSWORD NULL [smith];"
```

As you can see, it is relatively easy to write VBA code to handle passwords.

Protecting the VBA Code

Beginning with Access 2000, you can now password protect your code modules. We can take a quick look at how to do that by going to the Visual Basic Editor and right-clicking on the project name in the Project window. Select TheCornerBookstore (or whatever your project name is) Properties. After you click on the Protection tab, you should see a dialog box like Figure 16-2.

Notice the Lock Project for Viewing option. This is a source of confusion for a lot of developers. If you leave that option turned off, the password you enter in the Password text box controls access only to the Project Properties dialog box; anyone can view and edit the VBA code. If you check the Lock Project for Viewing box, users will also need the password to get into the code.

This box will not take effect until you completely close the project and reopen it. If you want to remove the password, just open the dialog box and clear the password fields.

Compiling to an .mde File

If you really do not want anyone to get into the code, convert the file to an .mde file. This compiles all the modules into machine code (0's and 1's) and completely eliminates the editable code.

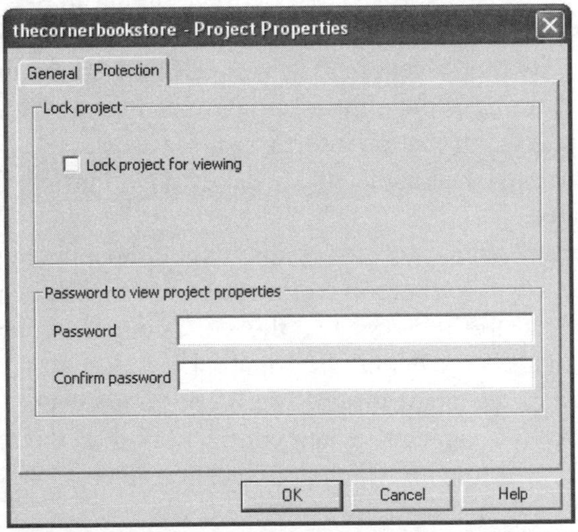

Figure 16-2   *The Project Properties Protection dialog box*

If you distribute the project, this technique offers some additional advantages over the usual compiled code. Your project size is much smaller, and because the code is compiled, it will run much faster. The downside is that you cannot edit the code in the .mde format. If you make any changes, you must go back to the original files, change them, and then recompile to the .mde format. Depending on how much code you have, this can be a time-consuming process.

As with many of the other security features, the original file must be opened in Exclusive mode. If your database is saved in the Access 2000 format, and you have either Access 2002 or 2003, you must first convert the 2000 database to the 2002/2003 format before you can compile it.

Once the database is converted and opened in an Exclusive mode, you can compile the database in Access by selecting Tools | Database Utilities | Make MDE File. Give the file a new name, and it will take some time to make the conversion.

As an interesting exercise, compare the size and speed of the .mde and .mdb files.

User-Level Security

To imagine user-level security, pretend you are a playwright. Your play has a number of characters, each having his or her own function in the play. You then hire actors and assign them to the characters in the play.

As you will be seeing, user-level security is very similar in that you set up roles that need to be performed in the database, and then you assign people to those roles.

When you work with user-level security, you will be working with two files: the standard .mdb file that tracks the objects and permissions of the database, and an .mdw file that contains identification information for users.

Using the play analogy, the characters are called a workgroup. Each workgroup needs an administrator.

You begin by starting a new Access session without opening any databases and selecting Tools | Security | Workgroup Administrator. You will be presented with the window shown in Figure 16-3. Notice that the workgroup information is being held under System.mdw. This is the default information.

Click on Create to create a new group. The Workgroup Owner Information dialog box, shown in Figure 16-4, appears. When you first bring up the screen, it should have the default information with which you installed Access. Before you make any changes, note the default information.

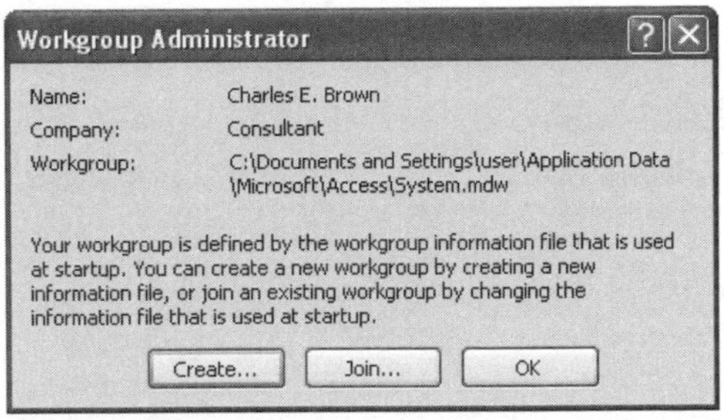

Figure 16-3   *Workgroup Administrator*

In order to form the new workgroup, you need to give the group a name, organization, and ID. The ID must be between 4 and 20 characters and is case sensitive. Again, the users will need this information to join the workgroup, so please keep good notes with this information.

After selecting OK, you will be prompted to enter the folder and name of the .mdw file that will contain the information. Again, record the default information before changing it. Do not add the .mdw; it will be added automatically.

Once you select OK, you will get one final chance to review the information, as shown in Figure 16-5. Select OK to accept the changes.

You now need to create an administrator. This is a user who will be assigned to this role. So you need to create a user by selecting Tools | Security | User and Group Accounts. In Figure 16-6, a new user called John Smith has been created. By default, each workgroup only has two initial groups: Admins and Users.

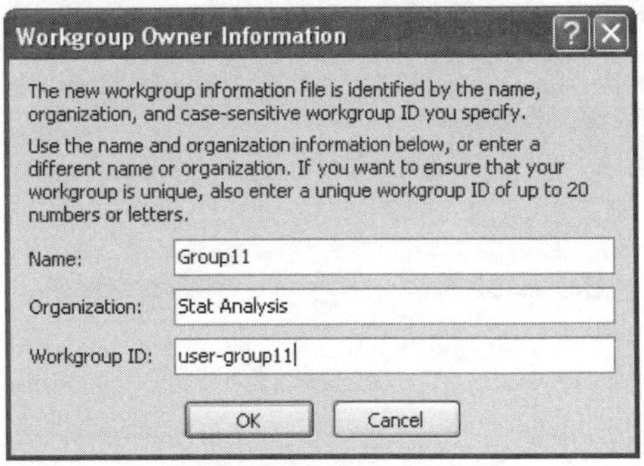

Figure 16-4   *Workgroup Owner Information*

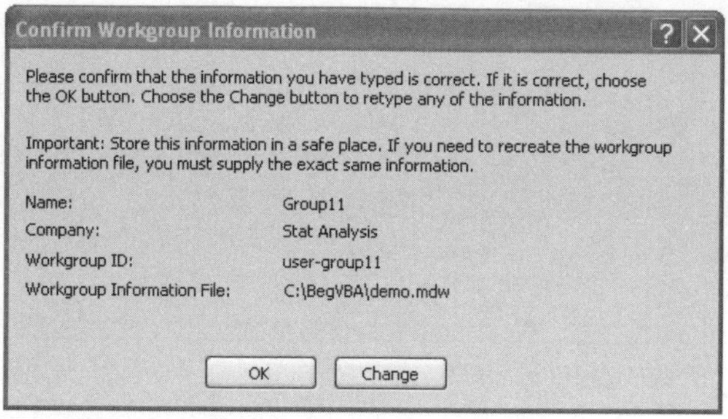

Figure 16-5   *Confirm Workgroup dialog box*

If you want to assign John Smith as an administrator, you select Admins and then click the Add button. John will now be a member of Admins and Users.

Initially, the Admin has no password. You can assign one here by clicking on the Change Logon Password tab.

Let's review something here for clarity. Initially, you created a new workgroup called Group11. Then, within Group11, you have two groups: Users and Admins. You create new users and, if necessary, assign them to the Admins group (or any group necessary within Group11).

The password assigned by the Change Logon Password tab is for the admin and not for the Group11 password, which we assume was assigned earlier.

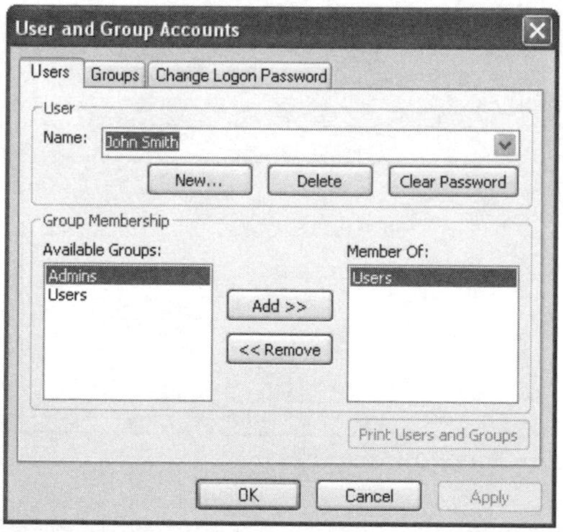

Figure 16-6   *User and Group Accounts*

Once all of this has been completed, you now need to assign the permissions. You need to have the database open and then select Tools | Security | User and Group Permissions. This dialog box is shown in Figure 16-7.

Here you can set the permissions for John Smith. As an example, you may want to give John all permissions for the tblCustomer object but only a Read Data permission for the tblInventory object. Or if John is assigned to a group created earlier, you may want to assign the permissions to the entire group. John would then have those permissions because he is a member of that group. In summary, you can assign permissions to either an individual or a group.

Changing Users Programmatically

Up to this point, we created the groups and granted the permissions manually. (We are assuming that the database you are connecting to is remote from where the code is located.) You can accomplish the same thing programmatically using VBA. In order to accomplish this, you need to use ADOX with ADOB.

A note is in order here. As I have stated several times throughout this book, ADO is a collection of prebuilt objects that facilitate the connection to, and manipulation of, databases. It is divided into libraries. The ADOB library is the core library for making connections and accessing the data inside the database. The ADOX library handles security issues in addition to its ability to build and change structures within the database.

Figure 16-7   *User and Group Permissions*

Please note that the code exhibits shown here are models. If you do test them, please do so in a noncritical environment because they could change system files.

Let's assume that you set up a secure database manually, and now you want to open it programmatically. When you create the connection code, you must reference the .mdw file and provide for the password as follows:

```
con1.Provider = "Microsoft.Jet.OLEDB.4.0"
con1.Properties("Jet OLEDB:System database") = "C:\BegVBA\demo.mdw"
con1.Open "Data Source=C:\BegVBA\thecornerbookstore.mdb; " & _
    "User ID = JohnSmith;Password =;"
```

Here you can see the reference to the .mdw file that contains the information for John Smith. Since John is the administrator, due to our earlier assignment, you want to make him the focus of the code to add and delete users and permissions.

When you want to add or delete users, you would employ the following code using the ADOX.Catalog object:

```
Sub addUser()

    Dim con1 As ADOX.Catalog
    Dim newUser As ADOX.User
    Dim userName As String
    Dim newPassword As String
    Set con1 = New ADOX.Catalog

    con1.ActiveConnection = _
        "Provider = Microsoft.Jet.OLEDB.4.0;" & _
        "Data Source=C:\BegVBA\thecornerbookstore.mdb;" & _
        "Jet OLEDB:System database=C:\begvba\demo.mdw;" & _
        "User id=johnsmith;Password=;"

    Set newUser = New ADOX.User
    newUser.Name = userName
    con1.Users.Append newUser
    con1.Users(newUser.Name).changePassword "", newPassword
End Sub
```

We made the connection to the data source as discussed earlier. We then used the Name attribute of the ADOX object called newUser to Append that name to the .mdx file of the active database. Finally, we set a password that is associated with that name.

This is a pretty straightforward code example. However, in my opinion, there is even an easier way to add and delete users, by using Jet SQL. As a beginner to VBA programming, you may find the following example, which does the same thing, a bit easier to follow because it does not employ the ADOX library:

```
Sub addUser()

    Dim con1 As ADODB.Connection
    Dim newUser As ADOX.User
    Dim strSQL As String

    Set con1 = New ADODB.Connection

    With con1
        .Provider = "Microsoft.Jet.OLEDB.4.0"
        .Properties("Jet OLEDB:System database") = _
          "C:\BegVBA\demo.mdw"
        .Open "Data Source=c:|BegVBA\thecornerbookstore.mdb;" & _
          "User ID=JohnSmith;Password=;"
        strSQL = "CREATE USER janedoe [mycat] NULL"
        .Execute (strSQL)
    End With
End Sub
```

Here we used Jet SQL to create a new user named janedoe and gave her a password of mycat. Since she is new, the old password was NULL.

If you were going to drop janedoe as a user, you could have simply made the SQL string as follows:

```
strSQL = "DROP USER janedoe"
```

I think you will agree that this is a little more straightforward and easier to follow than the previous code block. Jet SQL can also be used to grant the permissions to SELECT, INSERT, DELETE, and UPDATE.

As an example, I could have declared a second string variable, strGrants, and entered the following code for janedoe:

```
strGrants = "GRANT SELECT, UPDATE, INSERT, DELETE" & _
"ON TABLE tblCustomer TO janedoe"
.Execute (strGrants)
```

If you wanted to revoke her delete permission, you could use the following SQL string:

```
"REVOKE UPDATE ON TABLE tblCustomer FROM janedoe"
```

As I stated before, this could be an easier coding approach than using the ADOX library. However, this will only work with the Jet 4.0 engine. This engine ships with Access 2003 or if you are using an earlier version, can be updated at the Microsoft website. You will also find a complete list of permissions and syntax on the same site.

Security and Access 2003

With the release of Access 2003, there are two new security features previously unavailable: the Jet Sandbox, and Macro Security.

Jet Sandbox

There are three potential ways you can run a query in Access. The first way, which we saw in the chapter on Forms, is to build the query right into the form or report. The second way is to run the query through the command line shell (better known to most as the DOS prompt). This means you can actually run the Jet query through the DOS shell without even being in Access. This is rarely done and beyond the scope of this book. The third way is to build it into a module, as we have been doing through most of this book.

The first two techniques are loaded with dangers. As you saw, it is not that difficult for someone to gain access to the query code and make harmful changes to it that could allow improper access to, or destruction of, data.

Placing your code in a module, or even a macro, can offer extra levels of security. In a few moments, we are going to look at the Macro Security feature.

Unless you specifically shut it off, the Jet Sandbox, by default, will prevent potentially harmful code (code that could unexpectedly change or damage data) from form and report controls. You cannot shut it off in Access but must, instead, go into the registry to change the settings.

You need to look for the registry key:

```
HKEY_LOCAL-MACHINE\SOFTWARE\Microsoft\Jet\4.0\Engines\SandBoxMode
```

A full discussion, with a specific list of what the Jet Sandbox blocks, can be found in the help files that accompany Access 2003. Please note, before you make any changes to the registry, make sure you know what you are doing. You could inadvertently cause damage to the operating system and other programs on your computer.

Macro Security

In Chapter 1 we looked at macros. Essentially, VBA is the macro language of the Microsoft Office environment. Because of its popularity, there are a lot of places where developers can download macros to do various jobs. However, this has led to the propagation of viruses and security problems in macros.

Access 2003 addresses these issues with the introduction of Macro Security. You can access it by going to Tools | Macros | Security. You will see the dialog box shown in Figure 16-8.

There are three potential settings here:

▶ High will run only signed macros (which we will discuss shortly).

▶ Medium gives you the option of running an unsigned macro or not.

▶ Low will run anything and gives you virtually no protection.

It is interesting to note that this feature has been available for version 2000 of Word and Excel. However, Access implements it beginning in version 2003.

It is worth taking a few moments and discussing this whole concept of a digital signature. Basically, a digital signature is a certification that the code is virus free and safe to run.

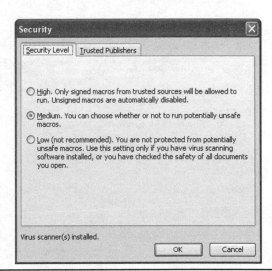

Figure 16-8   *Macro Security dialog box*

For testing purposes only, you can self-certify the code with a program that ships with Office 2003 called selfcert.exe. For true certifications, however, there are third-party certifiers who will test and verify the code. The most popular of these is a company called Verisign (www.verisign.com). These firms will provide you with a third-party validation and a digital certificate that is encrypted. The certificate must also be renewed on a regular basis.

When a digital certificate is obtained, there are two keys on it. A private key is encrypted into the file, and a public key is used for identification. If the file is changed in any way, the public key will not verify the private key.

As a demonstration, click on Start | All Programs | Microsoft Office | Microsoft Office Tools | Digital Certificate for VBA Projects. You should see the dialog box shown in Figure 16-9. This opening screen explains the process and warns about self-signed digital certificates. You can also obtain a list of third-party authorities here.

Once you give your certificate a name, click OK. You will be notified that the certificate was successfully created:

This is the first step. Let's assume that you now want to attach this certificate to a module you created in VBA. You would start by opening the module and selecting Tools | Digital Signature. The resulting dialog is shown in Figure 16-10.

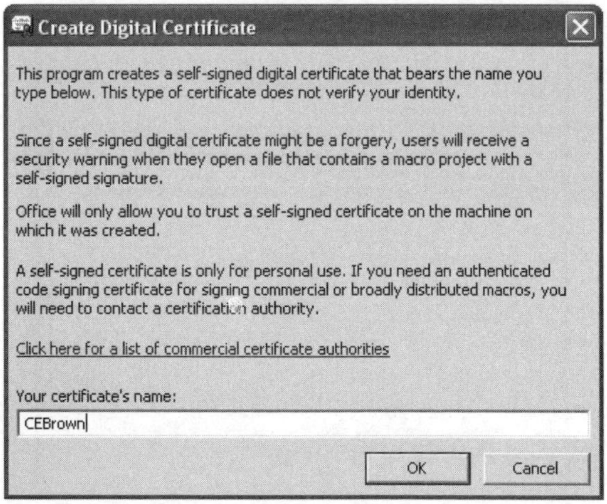

Figure 16-9   *Opening screen to create a digital certificate*

Figure 16-10   *Digital Signature attachment box*

Initially, the dialog box shows no signature at all. However, if you click Choose, it will bring up a list of certificates available on your computer, as Figure 16-11 shows.

The only one available, at this point, is the one you just created. By selecting it, you can either just attach it or view it first. If you choose View Certificate, you will see something like Figure 16-12. It is not verified by a third party, so there are warnings attached to it. You can also view various details about the certificate.

Select OK twice to return to the screen shown in Figure 16-10, and then select OK to attach the certificate. If you now save and close this session of TheCornerBookstore and start a new session, the dialog box shown in Figure 16-13 should appear.

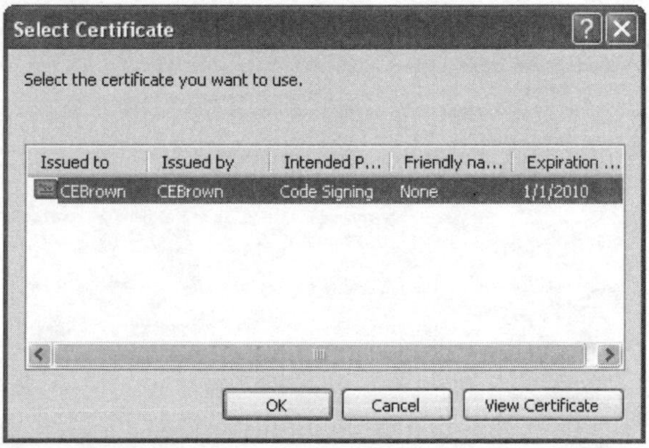

Figure 16-11   *List of available certificates*

Figure 16-12 *The digital certificate*

It is warning you because the certification has not been authenticated by a third party. You can select the option of always trusting this particular certifier by checking the box. If you feel safe with it, you can just go ahead and open it.

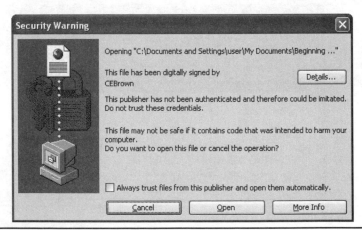

Figure 16-13 *Security Warning box*

Summary

The goal of this chapter was to give you a basic understanding of the various security tools you have available to you. We explored dialog boxes, passwords, users, and groups. We also looked at how to set permissions manually and with VBA code.

We then finished our discussion with an overview of the tools that are new to Access 2003. Specifically, we looked at the Jet 4.0 Sandbox and Macro Security. We also took a brief look at digital certificates.

We are now going to turn our attention to using Access with the other applications in Microsoft Office.

Access and the Microsoft Office Environment

I am sure it will come as no surprise that there are programming common denominators shared by all the Microsoft Office programs. This makes the interconnection of these programs fairly easy. In addition to interconnecting the programs, you can also perform internal functions such as creating custom menus and toolbars.

Many of the programming features we will be looking at in this chapter can apply to the other Office programs: Word, Excel, PowerPoint, and FrontPage. We are going to explore the objects common to Microsoft Office products, as well as ways of connecting these Office programs through VBA.

We start by looking at the objects necessary to search for a file. Then, we are going to start building a customized toolbar within Access. Finally we are going to look at some simple connections between Microsoft Access and Word, Outlook, and Excel.

Shared Objects

The Microsoft Office programs share approximately 14 programming objects. Some of them, such as DocumentProperty, Script, HTMLProject, and WebPageFont, are available in Word, Excel, and PowerPoint, but not available in Access. Another, AnswerWizard, is available in the Microsoft Office XP Developer Edition only.

One of the objects, Assistant, lets you control the Office Assistant. Unfortunately, many of the techniques needed are beyond the scope of this book.

In this section, we will focus on the most commonly used shared objects, beginning with the FileSearch object.

FileSearch Object

Many times you may want to check to see if a file exists before you attempt to open it (and cause a potential error). The FileSearch object, which is part of the Microsoft Office 11.0 Object Library and a shared object, works as if you searched for a file yourself.

As you have seen before, an object has properties and methods built into it that will do most of the programming work for you. All you need to do is call them when they are needed.

Let's begin by setting up a simple example as follows:

```
Sub findFile()
    With Application.fileSearch
        .NewSearch
        .LookIn = "c:\BegVBA"
        .FileName = "thecornerbookstore.mdb"
        .SearchSubFolders = True
            If .Execute() > 0 Then
                MsgBox "The file " & .FoundFiles(1) & " was found"
            Else
                MsgBox "The file is not found"
            End If
    End With
End Sub
```

If all works well, you should get the result shown here:

Let's discuss what just occurred. The NewSearch method resets all of the FileSearch properties This, of course, clears any previous search properties. Otherwise, the FileSearch object may "remember" some of its settings from one search to the next.

The LookIn property specifies the folder the search should take place in, while the FileName property specifies the name of the file you are searching for. Of course, you could easily modify these properties for other searches. As a matter of fact, you could easily use an input box to specify the search.

You can also set the SearchSubFolders property with the Boolean value of either True or False. This will specify whether or not you want subfolders searched.

The actual search begins with the Execute method. In this case, an If structure is used to decide whether the file was found. The Execute method returns a 0 if no files are found and a positive number if some are found; that is why you do a numeric test within the If statement. The method uses the FoundFiles collection used to hold the results of the search. Each member of the collection is a string that holds the path and name of a file that results from the search. In this case, we are just searching for one file. Notice that the collection is one-based: we retrieve the first item from position1 in the collection, not from position 0, as we do by default for an array.

If the Execute method returns multiple filenames and you're interested in all of them, you would need a loop to iterate the collection. In that case, you could use

```
FoundFiles.Count
```

as the upper boundary of a For loop with

```
FoundFiles(i)
```

to display the elements.

The following code is an example of this:

```
Sub findFile()
Dim i As Integer
   With Application.fileSearch
       .NewSearch
       .LookIn = "c:\BegVBA"
       .FileName = "*.mdb"
       .SearchSubFolders = True
           If .Execute() > 0 Then
               For i = 1 To .FoundFiles.Count
                  Debug.Print .FoundFiles(i)
               Next i
           End If
   End With
End Sub
```

The final result should look something like this:

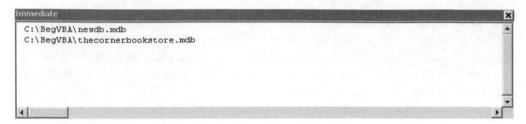

Your results will vary depending on the number of files you have.

CommandBar Object

The CommandBar object (which represents toolbars, pop-up menus, and menu bars) has many of the same properties and events as the FileSearch object. You may not realize it, but Access 2003 has 178 command bars built into it. Access 2002 has 173, and Access 2000 has 140. Don't believe me? Let's give this code a try:

```
Sub CommandBarCount()
   MsgBox "There are " & CommandBars.Count & " command bars"
End Sub
```

Depending on your version of Access (this is for Access 2003), you should see something like the following:

In case you are wondering where they all are, this count includes 1 menu bar, 50 toolbars, and 127 pop-up menus. Within the Microsoft Office Object Library, these are referred to by the names of their constants, as msoBarTypeMenuBar, msoBarTypeNormal, and msoBarTypePopup. However, before you can access them, you need to create a reference to them. You do this the same way you referenced ADO.

Select Tools | References and select Microsoft Office Object Library, as shown in Figure 17-1. As of this writing, version 11 of the library is the most recent.

NOTE

For a fuller treatment of creating and using Office menus and toolbars, see Chapter 14.

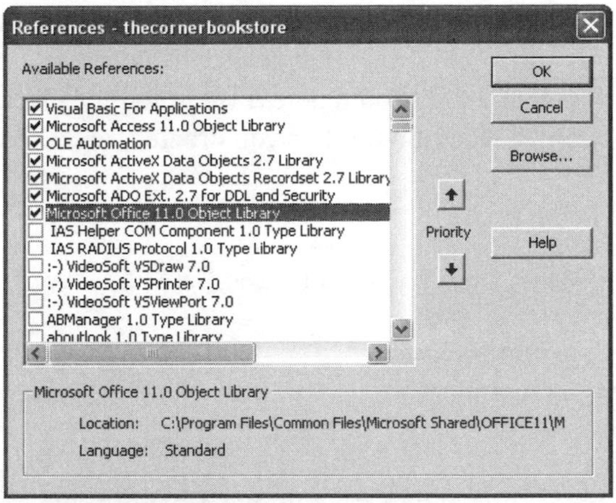

Figure 17-1   *The Microsoft Office Object Library reference*

Let's try building a command bar using VBA. You first need to create some object references. Notice the objects we are referring to.

```
Sub myCommandBar()
    Dim cmdBar As CommandBar
    Dim cmdButton As CommandBarButton
```

Notice that we created references for the CommandBar and CommandBarButton objects. A command bar button is a button that can be added to the toolbar to which you can assign customized programming.

We now need to build the bar as follows:

```
Set cmdBar = CommandBars.Add("My Command Bar")
    cmdBar.Visible = True
```

When setting, or creating, the command bar object, we call the method CommandBars, which in turn calls the method Add(). The Add() method assigns the command bar a name and then adds it to the project. We create the command bar and set the visibility to True. If you don't, you will need to manually turn the command bar on with View | Toolbars.

If you run this code now, you will see a blank command bar at the top with no controls on it yet. You could also verify the command bar with View | Toolbars:

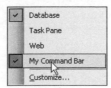

Well, let's add a button to our new command bar now. However, please note that before you can run this sub again, you *must* delete the command bar you just created. If you don't, you will get an error. You delete it by going into Access and selecting View | Toolbars | Custom. Select the toolbar you created, and then click the Delete button in the dialog box.

Let's add the following code:

```
Set cmdButton = cmdBar.Controls.Add(msoControlButton)
   With cmdButton
      .Caption = "My Button"
      .Style = msoButtonCaption
   End With
```

When we set the object, we called the command bar that we created, which then calls the Controls method where we use the Add method to add the control to the command bar.

Finally, with the With structure, we set the caption and style of the button. If you do not use the msoButtonCaption style attribute, the button may only appear when you roll the mouse over it.

NOTE

Instantiate *is the correct term for creating an object. However, VBA uses the keyword Set. I use "set" and "instantiate" interchangeably.*

If you run the code, you will end up with an, albeit, skimpy-looking command bar but, nonetheless, one fully functioning and able to do the job. Here is a sample:

From here on, you can build a macro or command code for the button, as you have seen throughout the book.

It is easy to add a second button. Just create a second instance of the cmdButton and add it to the command bar:

```
Set cmdButton = cmdBar.Controls.Add(msoControlButton)
   With cmdButton
      .Caption = "My Second Button"
      .Style = msoButtonCaption
   End With
```

Now your command bar will look something like this:

Connecting with Other Microsoft Office Products

In order to connect with Word, Excel, and Outlook, you need to create a reference to them. Open Tools | References, as shown in Figure 17-2.

Notice that there are references for

▶ Microsoft Office 11.0 Object Library

▶ Microsoft Excel 11.0 Object Library

▶ Microsoft Word 11.0 Object Library

▶ Microsoft Outlook 11.0 Object Library

All of these need to be activated, and then select OK.

For data access between Acess and the other Office applications, Office relies on a set of ISAM drivers. Up to this point, the only drivers we have been using are those connected with an ODBC database. However, these drivers are made available in order to connect with non-ODBC sources such as Word or Excel. There are even

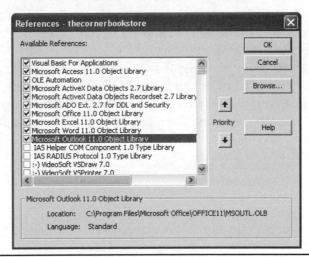

Figure 17-2   *The References dialog box*

third-party ISAM drivers to connect with other non-Microsoft programs. As an example, Borland has ISAM drivers that allow you to connect Paradox with Word or Excel.

The syntax for various ISAM drivers may vary a bit depending on the driver. Even within the Microsoft Office environment you will see some variations. For that reason, you will see some variations in syntax between connections with Outlook, Word, and Excel. As you work through the various examples, the differences will be obvious. In most cases, you can use the syntax verbatim in your projects.

There is one common factor, however: in the background, you are not actually working within Word, Excel, and Outlook. You are actually going to create new instances, or objects, of the application. You will see variations on two function calls: CreateObject and GetObject. Why do you need to do this? If you did not have this capability, you would need to have the application open in order to work with it. However, by creating an object, the application can be open or closed. As you look at the following code examples, you will see this.

Connecting with Excel

In my experience, the connection between Access and Excel is the most common. It is not unusual to use data from both sources within a project.

Many times, you may want to create your recordset from an Excel spreadsheet rather than from an Access table. The implications of this are enormous. Now you can handle data within Access from another source and treat it, in essence, the same way. As you will see, it is not that much different from opening an internal Access table.

Included with the download for this chapter's files is a worksheet called myCustomers.xls. I will assume you put it in a directory called BegVBA. Each of the column headers will serve as a field name.

One thing, while not essential, is highly recommended: you should give the dataset on the Excel sheet a range name. In our sheet, I called it "customers."

Here is a simple example that will open the Excel worksheet, myCustomers.xls, create a recordset with the data in the sheet, and then print it in the Immediate window.

```
Sub openWorksheet()
    Dim con1 As New ADODB.Connection
    Dim rec1 As ADODB.Recordset

    con1.Open "Provider=Microsoft.Jet.OLEDB.4.0;" & _
        "Data Source=C:\BegVBA\myCustomers.xls;" & _
        "Extended Properties=Excel 8.0;"

    Set rec1 = New ADODB.Recordset
```

```
      rec1.Open "customers", con1, , , adCmdTable

      Do Until rec1.EOF
         Debug.Print rec1("txtNumber"), rec1("txtBookPurchased")
         rec1.MoveNext
      Loop
End Sub
```

As I stated at the beginning of this section, there are variations in syntax of the ISAM drivers with Word, Excel, and Outlook. In this one, there are three arguments separated by a semicolon. The first argument is the provider, which, in this case, is Microsoft.Jet.OLEDB.4.0. The second is the data source. The final argument extends the Excel 8.0 engine to include the ISAM driver. Excel versions 97 through 2003 use the 8.0 engine.

As stated at the outset, it is easier to use the worksheet if you use a range name in the worksheet. While you could indicate the range manually, any changes to the sheet could easily cause the data to fall out of that range.

Beyond that, everything is quite the same as if you had opened it in Access, with the result in the Immediate window, as shown here:

```
Immediate
   101          How to Write Books
   102          Murder at Midnight
   102          Beginning VBA
   103          History
   101          Ben Franklin
   103          Cooking 101
```

As we have in the past, we could also set a variable and perform calculations. However, the results of the calculation cannot be written back to the worksheet. The recordset is, by default, read only.

You can also use the GetObject method discussed earlier. This will allow you to actually run a macro in an Excel worksheet. While open, you can treat it as if you had opened the actual application. Let's look at an example. (Note: This code is for example purposes; you will need to create the Excel macro first.)

```
Sub runWorkbook()
   Dim myWorkBook As Excel.Workbook

   Set myWorkBook = GetObject("c:\BegVba\myCustomers.xls")
   myWorkBook.Application.Run "myMacro"
End Sub.
```

If, for some reason, Access cannot find the Excel macro, you will get the following error message:

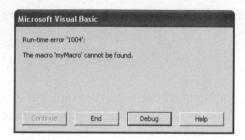

After the macro has done its job, you can save and close the workbook with the following code:

```
myWorkBook.Application.Activeworkbook.Save
myWorkBook.Application.Quit
```

Connecting with Outlook

As you may know, Outlook has a number of folders in which it stores various categories of information. It has folders for calendars, deleted items, emails, contacts, and so on. In addition, you can create custom folders to suit any need. You can use VBA to access information contained within these folders.

NOTE

The code in this section assumes that you are working with the standard Outlook folders. If there is any sort of customization (such as creating your own work folders and putting them in your own directories), you will need to make the appropriate adjustments to the code. In addition, I strongly suggest that you back up your Outlook folders before attempting to test this code. It could change your live data.

When working with the folders, you would first need to create a library to hold the folder information. This library is referred to as a *namespace*. All the information is then sent to that namespace where the individual items can be referenced.

Let's look at the following code example for clarity.

```
Sub myAddressBook()
    Dim myOutlook As Outlook.Application
    Dim myInformation As Namespace
    Dim mycontacts As Items
```

```
    Dim myItems As ContactItem

    Set myOutlook = CreateObject("Outlook.Application")
    Set myInformation = myOutlook.GetNamespace("MAPI")
    Set mycontacts = myInformation.GetDefaultFolder(olFolderContacts).Items

    For Each myItems In mycontacts
       Debug.Print myItems.FirstName, myItems.LastName, myItems.EmailAddress
     Next
End Sub
```

You first reference a new instance of an Outlook object, which is called myOutlook. Then set up the namespace, or library, to hold the information. This is called myInformation. However, like any library, the information is not just tossed in there randomly. It needs a record. In this case, the record is an Item called myContacts. And then, within the Item, you put the details of the contact with the ContactItem. This is where you list the individual fields of the contact.

VBA uses a namespace protocol called MAPI. VBA then uses the GetDefaultFolder method to locate the contacts folder (called olFolderContacts) and then retrieve the Items within that folder. If you use customized folders, you need to define them here and not use the GetDefaultFolder method.

The final part just prints out the information in the Immediate window.

The thing to remember is that we created an instance of Outlook, as we did with Excel earlier, and used it to retrieve information.

With just a slight modification, you could add a contact through VBA. We will use the method CreateItem():

```
Sub AddAContact()
    Dim myOutlook As Outlook.Application
    Dim myItems As ContactItem

    Set myOutlook = CreateObject("Outlook.Application")
    Set myItems = myOutlook.CreateItem(olContactItem)

    With myItems
       .FirstName = "John"
       .LastName = "Smith"
       .EmailAddress = "johnsmith@smith.com"
       .Save
     End With
End Sub
```

If you were to look at your contacts now, you should see the record for John Smith. Of course, you could have gotten elaborate and created input forms in order to type the information in.

Deleting a record is a little more involved. You have to enter criteria for deleting and then loop through all the records to see if they meet that criteria. However, as you will see in the following code, it is still just a variation on what we have been doing:

```
Sub DeleteaContact()
    Dim myOutlook As Outlook.Application
    Dim myInformation As Namespace
    Dim myContacts As Items
    Dim myItems As ContactItem

    Set myOutlook = CreateObject("Outlook.Application")
    Set myInformation = myOutlook.GetNamespace("MAPI")
    Set myContacts = myInformation.GetDefaultFolder(olFolderContacts).Items

    For Each myItems In myContacts
        If myItems.Email1Address = "johnsmith@smith.com" Then
            myItems.Delete
        End If
    Next
End Sub
```

As you can see, this is just a slight variation of the code using the .Delete method for the ContactItem.

Again, once VBA has accessed the data, it can easily be manipulated and used as necessary.

Connecting with Word

Because of Microsoft Word's ability to open and merge with Access data, the need to use VBA is limited. In many cases, using a macro within Word and then calling it up, as shown in the Excel section, will do the trick quite nicely. However, let's take a look at a few techniques should the occasion arise to use them.

Let's take a look at printing a form letter using the data from an Access table. To clear up a misconception, you would not use VBA to create the form letter, but just to create the link to the data. The form letter itself would need to be created in Word using standard mail-merge techniques before running VBA.

```
Sub MailmergeLetter()
    Dim myLetter As Document
    Documents.Open FileName:="C:\BegVBA\myFormLetter.doc"
    Set myLetter = Documents("myFormLetter.doc")

    myLetter.MailMerge.OpenDataSource _
        Name:="C:\BegVBA\thecornerbookstore.mdb", _
        Connection:="TABLE tblCustomer"
End Sub
```

The process is pretty straightforward. With the ISAM driver, you open the document and, within the document, open the data source. Within the data source, you specify the table to be connected to.

If you wanted to, you could specify that you want the document merged to a new document and use only records 1 to 3, as follows:

```
Sub MailmergeLetter()
    Dim myLetter As Document
    Documents.Open FileName:="C:\BegVBA\myFormLetter.doc"
    Set myLetter = Documents("myFormLetter.doc")

    myLetter.MailMerge.OpenDataSource _
        Name:="C:\BegVBA\thecornerbookstore.mdb", _
        Connection:="TABLE tblCustomer"

        With myLetter.MailMerge
            .Destination = wdSendToNewDocument

            With .DataSource
              .FirstRecord = 1
              .LastRecord = 3
            End With
            .Execute
        End With
End Sub
```

Notice in this that we had to issue the .Execute command. If you did not issue that, you would end up with the dataset from the previous merge. The .Execute triggers the new merge with the new parameters.

Summary

Once you see the syntax for the ISAM drivers, as demonstrated in this chapter, the connection process is fairly straightforward. They use techniques learned in earlier chapters to create and manipulate a recordset.

We looked at connections with Microsoft Word, Excel, and Outlook. In addition, we created a custom toolbar and searched for a file.

With all of this interaction, security can be a problem. In the next chapter, we are going to turn our attention to maintaining database security.

CHAPTER 8

Access and the Web

For many businesses, the future is the Web. Because of that, we see the Microsoft Office environment becoming more web friendly with each release. To help coordinate this even further, Microsoft has substantially beefed up the capabilities of FrontPage 2003.

In this chapter, we explore the techniques needed to put Access on the Web. This topic could be a book in itself, but we will only be doing an overview some of the technology involved.

Among the technologies we will explore are dynamic technologies, Data Access Pages, and XML (Extensible Markup Language). You will also use concepts you have learned so far, such as events and SQL, in a web environment.

The Mechanics of the Web

I would imagine that most of you regularly surf the Web. As a matter of fact, you may have obtained this book online from a site like Amazon.com. In order to do that, you need to use a web browser, such as Internet Explorer, Netscape, or Opera.

Browsers use a basic language called HTML, which stands for Hypertext Markup Language. This is not really a computer language (it does not have loop or decision-making capabilities) but is a way of identifying components of the web page you are looking at.

It is beyond the scope of this book to discuss the mechanics of HTML. If you want to learn more, I strongly recommend the book *HTML: A Beginner's Guide* (Second Edition), by Wendy Willard (McGraw-Hill/Osborne, 2002).

What does any of this have to do with Microsoft Access? Let's look at a potential scenario. When you call up a website, the "www" address you type in is called the URL (Uniform Resource Locator). Your request goes out, through your web connection, over a series of routers that ensure it gets to the right location. Once it arrives at the destination, your request is read by a piece of software called the web server. This server then searches its files for the HTML page you requested, addresses it with your return address, and sends it back to your computer. Your browser receives this HTML packet, unwraps it, reads the code, and displays it on your computer. All of this happens in seconds.

While this seems pretty straightforward, there is one little problem. Let's change the scenario slightly. Let's say you go to Amazon.com and get its home page. There is usually a box where you can type in the book, or types of books, you are looking for. This is called a *web form*. Once you click on the search button, your request is sent back to Amazon.com and the results are returned to you.

Does Amazon.com have HTML pages prebuilt for every possible scenario? That would involve the storage of millions, or tens of millions, of web pages. There is a better solution! Let's add one step to our original scenario.

Let's say you used the web form to request books about VBA. When Amazon's web server receives the request, it passes it to a database server. The database then finds the list of VBA books and returns that list to the web server. The web server then sends the list to a *dynamic technology* (such as CGI, ASP, ASP.NET, or JSP), which we will discuss shortly, that will write the HTML page (using a template) and pass it back to the web server. The web server then sends the HTML page back to your browser as discussed before.

So, as you can see, the HTML pages are written on-the-fly. Out of several dynamic technologies that perform the function of writing the HTML page, the most common is Active Server Pages (ASP). This comes built into professional versions of Microsoft Windows. Of the other names you may hear, ColdFusion, Java Server Pages (JSP), and PHP, the newest is Microsoft's ASP.NET. Each of these technologies has pros and cons, but they all do more or less the same thing.

Behind this dynamic technology is a database program to save and retrieve the requested data. Most of the larger sites use database servers such as Oracle or Microsoft SQL Server. However, Microsoft Access is now nicely positioned to serve as the database "backbone" of small- to medium-sized sites (there are no magic numbers as to when it is appropriate).

Data Access Pages

It is beyond the scope of this book to examine all the ins and outs of web design. Instead, we are going to focus on the tools available in Access—specifically, we are going to look at Data Access Pages.

A Data Access Page looks and feels like an Access form or report. Like forms and reports, it is tied into tables or queries. However, it uses HTML code so that data can be accessed through a web browser and viewed on the Web. The data can even be edited in the web browser.

As an example of how to use this, let's say you design an Access database for ABC Corporation. Let's say there is a data entry form that needs to be used by the New York and Los Angeles offices. Further, let's assume there are reports that need to be seen by the Paris office.

Using Data Access Pages in conjunction with Internet technologies will allow you to handle this scenario easily. Each of the offices can access the forms and reports as easily as they would if the database was located right there.

Here is a word of warning, however: Data Access Pages were introduced in Access 2000. The format used changed in Access 2002 and again in Access 2003. Thus, if you design the Data Access Page in Access 2003, and the workstations in Los Angeles, Paris, and New York are using Access 2000, the Data Access Page may not work properly. Also, if you design the page in one version of Access, you cannot open it in Design View in another version of Access.

This problem can be remedied by installing Office Web Components for Office 2003 on the workstations that will be accessing the Data Access Pages.

The examples shown here were created using Access 2003. If you are using a different version, you may see some variations in functionality.

Up to this point, forms and reports have been part of an Access database. However, Data Access Pages are stand-alone files. Access will show them as Pages objects, but they are external files. The reason for this is that you can point the browser to a Data Access Page like you would any other URL. A good knowledge of web technologies, coupled with a program like FrontPage 2003, is essential to successfully deploying these pages.

Generating a Data Access Page

To create a Data Access Page, you begin by going to Pages in the Objects list, as shown in Figure 18-1. As you can see, like forms and reports, Data Access Pages can be generated in either Design View or by using the wizard. Let's create our first page by using the wizard and connecting it to tblCustomer.

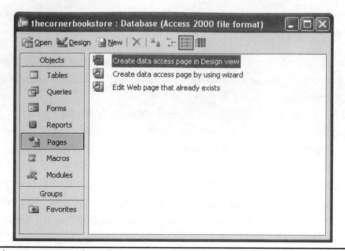

Figure 18-1 *The Pages window*

The first screen should be familiar to anyone who has built a form or report using the wizard. As shown in Figure 18-2, it allows you to select the table or query that the page will be attached to, and the fields you want to use.

As you can see, our web page is based on all the fields in tblCustomer. Once that is done, select Next. You should see a screen similar to Figure 18-3.

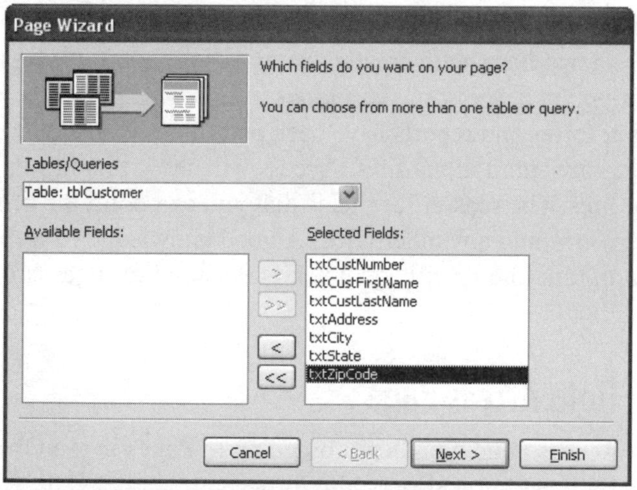

Figure 18-2 *First step in the Page Wizard*

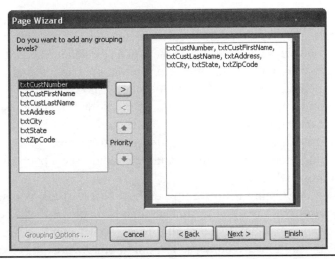

Figure 18-3   *Step 2 of the Page Wizard*

This allows you to decide if you want to group the data together in any particular way. That concept is discussed in Chapter 13 about reports. For this example, we are not going to use a grouping. Instead, just click on Next, which produces the screen shown in Figure 18-4.

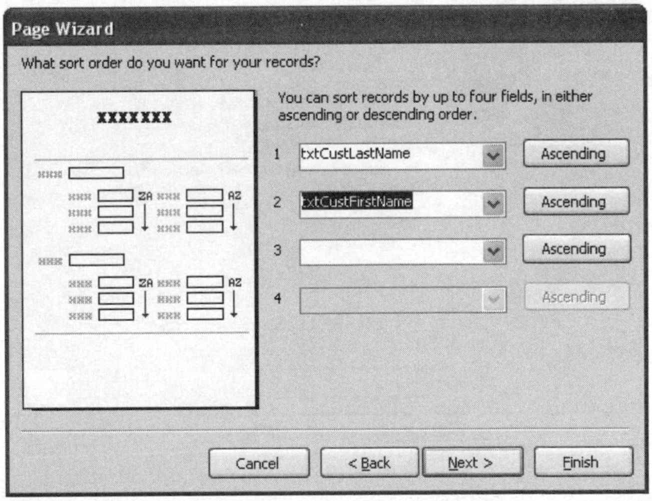

Figure 18-4   *Step 3 of the Page Wizard*

In this screen you decide how you want the data sorted. If the page is already associated with a query, that may be decided already. However, since our example is based on a table, we are going to sort it on the txtCustFirstName and txtCustLastName fields. The proper SQL code string will be written in the background.

After clicking Next, you are brought to the screen shown in Figure 18-5. This last screen allows you to name the Data Access Page. We will be discussing naming more in a bit. However, for the time being, you should use the identifying prefix of dap. In this example, the Open the Page option is also selected.

Once all is completed, click on Finish and you should see a page similar to the one shown in Figure 18-6.

There are two interesting things going on here. First of all, you see the fields much like you would on any other form. But what is unique is that Access created a web-based navigation bar that, like a regular form, allows you to move through the records, change the sort, filter records, and so on. In other words, it is like any normal form you work with—the only difference being that it is web based.

Remember, this form is built using HTML. Let's take a brief look behind the scenes by selecting View | HTML Source. You will see something like Figure 18-7.

This is called the Microsoft Script Editor; it allows you to view and edit the underlying HTML and related code. The necessary coding to properly connect the

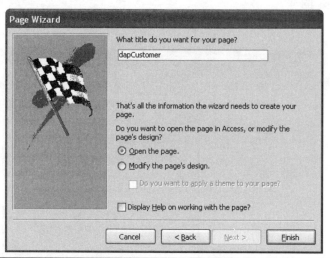

Figure 18-5   *Final step of the Page Wizard*

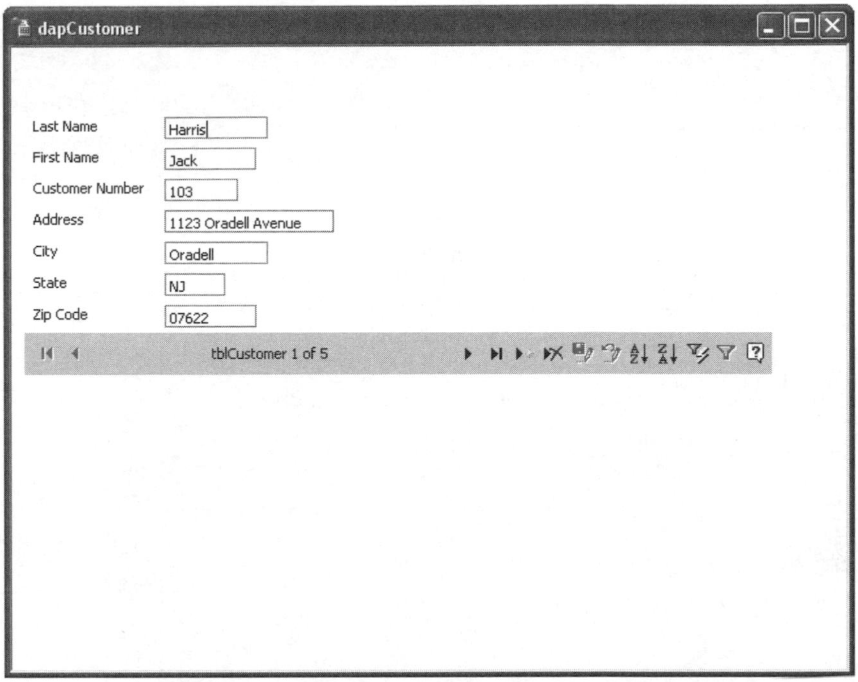

Figure 18-6   *A Data Access Page*

form to the table is also written, as well as JavaScript code to handle issues such as browser validation and navigation.

I strongly suggest that unless you are very familiar with HTML, JavaScript, and database connection strings, you do not change any code here.

Saving the Data Access Page

As I stated from the outset, a Data Access Page is an external file that needs to be named and saved outside of the database environment. The file has an extension of .htm, which indicates that it is an HTML file. *Where* you save it is another matter.

This is where a program such as FrontPage will come into play. Using it, in conjunction with a web server such as IIS (which comes as part of the Windows 2000 or XP Professional software), directory structures would be set up to hold the files of the website. The proper directory structure, and placement of the Data Access Page, would need to be determined in advance. As you are about to see, this can be critical.

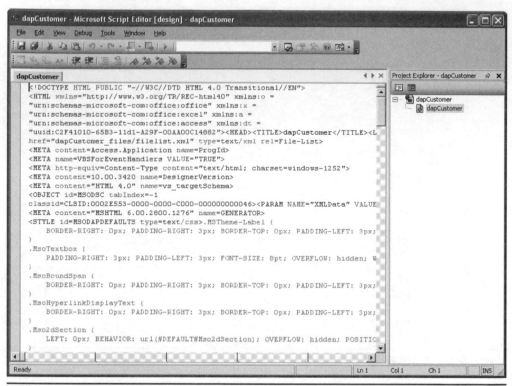

Figure 18-7 *The Microsoft Script Editor*

If you use IIS, in most cases, the file will need to be saved to a folder under c:\inetpub\wwwroot in order for it to be used in the web server environment.

The name we gave the example Data Access Page, dapCustomer, needs to be taken to another step. As soon as you go to close the page, you will see the prompt shown here:

After selecting Yes, you are taken to the standard Windows Save As screen using dapCustomer as the suggested name, as shown in Figure 18-8. This is where you need to decide where it is going to be placed. Again, this is a function of the website directory structure your particular project is employing.

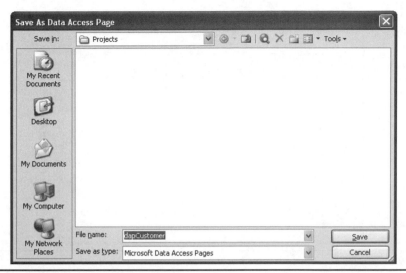

Figure 18-8   *Save As Data Access Page*

Once you select Save, you are brought to a rather cryptic message:

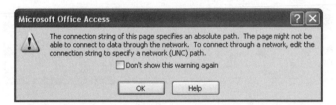

In order for a website to access a database, there must be code written that tells the website where to find the database structure (just like we have had to put that information into our VBA code). This is called a *connection string*. Unfortunately, due to the way networks and web servers work, the connection string that Access writes might not work and may need to be edited.

Once you select OK, Access will go ahead and do the best job it can to ensure that the web page functions properly (from my experience, most of the time it runs fine). Access recognizes the Data Access Page as an object, even though it is an external file. Now the Pages window should look like Figure 18-9.

As an interesting exercise, you can test your new page in the web browser by opening the browser, selecting File | Open, and maneuvering to the directory that contains your Data Access Page. Since it has the file extension of .htm, and is written in HTML, the browser should have no difficulties opening it with the connection string, written by Access, that provides the connection to the table tblCustomer.

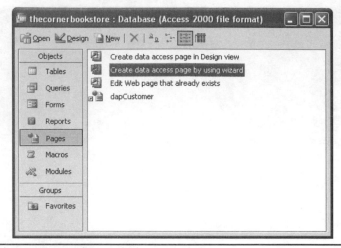

Figure 18-9   *The Pages window with the new object*

If you want to delete a Data Access Page, Access will prompt whether you want to delete the whole file or just the link to the database:

Creating a Data Access Page in Design View

Creating a Data Access Page has some similarities to creating a form. However, there are some differences. If you use the Pages window in Access, you can double-click on the Create Data Access Page in Design View option. You will receive the warning shown here, regarding the version conflicts discussed earlier:

Once you select OK, you are presented with the window shown in Figure 18-10. Notice that the design area is divided into sections. Along the top, you can click to

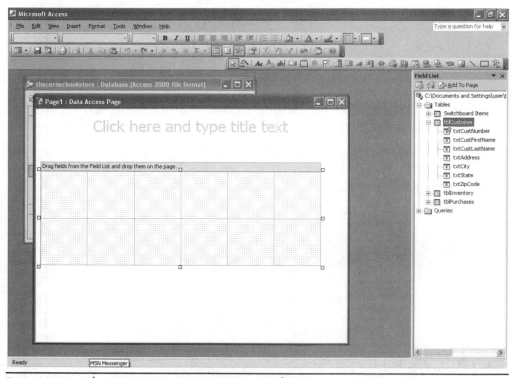

Figure 18-10   *The Data Access Page Design window*

enter a title for your page. There is a two-row grid in the middle of the page, which we will use shortly. On the right of the window, there is a list of tables and queries.

If you click on the plus (+) symbol just to the left of the table or query name, you will see the field list associated with it. As an example, suppose I open the tblCustomer field list. I can then take a field, txtCustNumber for example, and drag it where I want to place it on the grid. As soon as I do that, Access automatically creates the navigation controls you saw earlier. Your grid should look something like Figure 18-11.

You can add the fields you want and test the page by selecting View | Page View. Notice in the field list that you have all the tables and queries of your database listed. What would happen if you tried to drag a field from tblPurchases onto the design grid? Access will open up a Relationship Wizard window, as shown in Figure 18-12.

The options in this window are pretty easy to follow. Figure 18-12 has the information filled in. I related tblPurchases to tblCustomer by relating txtNumber to txtCustNumber. The bottom of the window shows that many relationships are on the tblPurchases side.

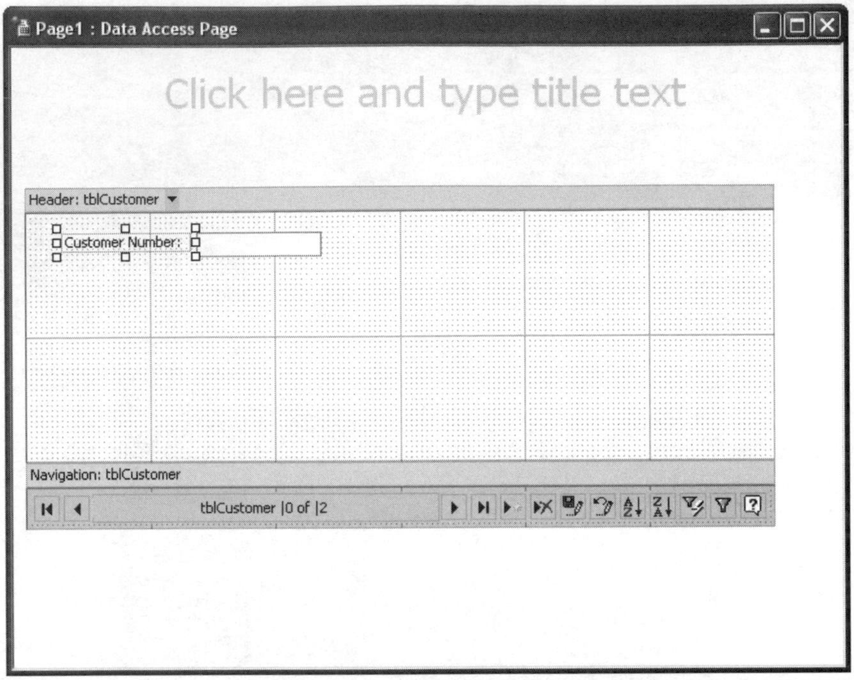

Figure 18-11   *The Data Access Page Design window with a field added*

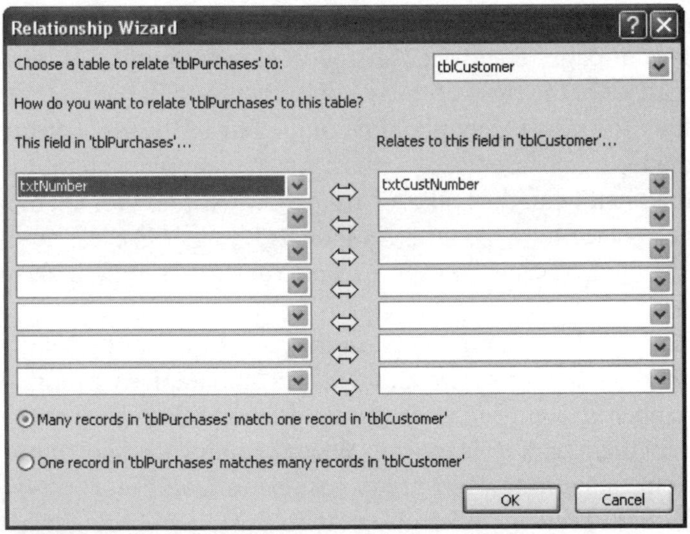

Figure 18-12   *Relationship Wizard window*

Once you have the Data Access Page set up the way you want it, you can select File | Save As to save it. (Remember, it will be saved as an external file.) You will see a dialog box like this:

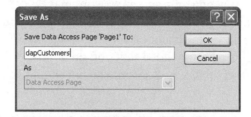

In this example, I used the name dapCustomers. Once you have given it a name, you will then see the standard Windows Save As dialog box, where you decide where the HTML file will be located. As before, once that decision is made, it will prompt you and write the proper connection string for you.

One final point needs to be made here. If you examine the properties of the controls inside a Data Access Page, you will notice that attributes such as color, size, and so forth, use HTML attributes instead of the settings you arc used to in Access. For instance, color uses a hexadecimal code, and size uses pixels. Figure 18-13 shows what a Property sheet looks like for the Pagc element.

Data Access Pages and VBA

You are going to find some serious compatibility issues between versions of Access if you try to work with Data Access Pages and VBA. Access 2000 offered a method called CreateDataAccessPage to create a new page. However, any attempts to run this page will result in an Error 13 in Access 2003.

Figure 18-13   *Properties for a Data Access Page*

The CreateDataAccessPage method accepts two parameters. The first is the path where the page is going to be stored. The second is a Boolean value of True or False. True means that you are going to create a new Data Access Page, and False means that you are just creating a connection to an existing page.

From there on, some rather advanced programming techniques are required to populate the page with the controls necessary.

In most situations, it is recommended that you do not use VBA to create the Data Access Page. There are very few situations in which it should be necessary to do that.

XML (Extended Markup Language)

As a beginner, you will probably not be designing XML documents, but if you use Data Access Pages, you may come across XML. It is one of the major topics in web design. For that reason we are going to take a brief look at the technology.

When you work with HTML, you work with a limited number of available tags (<head>, < body>, < h1>, etc.). These tags describe the structure of the document. You can also design Cascading Stylesheets (CSS) to format these tags. But is the structure of the document that simple?

If you want to connect a database to the web page, as you will probably be doing often with Access, you may need to use tags that reflect the structure of your database. For instance, within the body, you may need tags to reflect the last name, first name, address, and so on. Each one of these tags may need its own formatting rules.

XML permits you to design your own tags to reflect the structure of the database. Once the tags are defined, you can use them as you would any other HTML tag. This adds greatly to the ability to control the design and look of your web page.

Just as an example, here is an XML programming structure, with data from two records:

```
<?xml version="1.0" encoding="UTF-8"?>
<dataroot xmlns:od="urn:schemas-microsoft-com:officedata"
xmlns:xsi="http://www.w3.org/2001/XMLSchema-instance"
xsi:noNamespaceSchemaLocation="tblCustomer.xsd" generated="2003-12-14T15:17:12">
    <tblCustomer>
        <txtCustNumber>101</txtCustNumber>
        <txtCustFirstName>John</txtCustFirstName>
        <txtCustLastName>Jones</txtCustLastName>
        <txtAddress>123 Main Street</txtAddress>
        <txtCity>Hackensack</txtCity>
        <txtState>NJ</txtState>
        <txtZipCode>07642</txtZipCode>
```

```
    </tblCustomer>
    <tblCustomer>
        <txtCustNumber>102</txtCustNumber>
        <txtCustFirstName>Jane</txtCustFirstName>
        <txtCustLastName>Smith</txtCustLastName>
        <txtAddress>1519 Morris Avenue</txtAddress>
        <txtCity>Bronx</txtCity>
        <txtState>NY</txtState>
        <txtZipCode>10469</txtZipCode>
    </tblCustomer>
</dataroot>
```

Notice that there is a hierarchy of structure, with <dataroot> being the highest level, <tblCustomer> being the next, and finally, the fields being the lowest. Also, for every opening tag, there is a corresponding closing tag. What is not obvious is that all tags are case sensitive.

You can have Access set up XML pages for you by first clicking on the table you want to set them up for, and then using File | Export. Once you are in the Export dialog box, select XML as the file type. Once you decide where the file needs to be saved (depending on the directory structure of the web server), you click on Export. You will see the dialog box shown here:

You have a choice of three types of exports. The Data option creates a file with an .xml file extension and exports the structure and data. The code you just looked at is an example of that type of structure.

A Schema creates a file with an .xsd file extension. This will set up the structure without the data.

Finally, Presentation works like a Cascading Style Sheet and uses the file extension .xsl. It formats how the data will look on the web page. The following code excerpt reflects a typical XSL structure:

```
<?xml version="1.0" ?>
- <xsl:stylesheet version="1.0" xmlns:xsl="http://www.w3.org/1999/XSL/Transform"
xmlns:msxsl="urn:schemas-microsoft-com:xslt" xmlns:fx="#fx-functions" exclude-
result-prefixes="msxsl fx">
  <xsl:output method="html" version="4.0" indent="yes"
```

```
xmlns:xsl="http://www.w3.org/1999/XSL/Transform" />
- <xsl:template match="//dataroot"
xmlns:xsl="http://www.w3.org/1999/XSL/Transform">
- <html>
- <head>
  <META HTTP-EQUIV="Content-Type" CONTENT="text/html;charset=UTF-8" />
  <title>tblCustomer</title>
 <style type="text/css" />
  </head>
  <body link="#0000ff" vlink="#800080">
  <table border="1" bgcolor="#ffffff" cellspacing="0" cellpadding="0" id="CTRL1">
  <colgroup>
  <col style="WIDTH: 1.2187in" />
  <col style="WIDTH: 0.9375in" />
  <col style="WIDTH: 0.9375in" /
  <col style="WIDTH: 1.4062in" />
  <col style="WIDTH: 0.9375in" />
  <col style="WIDTH: 0.9375in" />
  <col style="WIDTH: 0.9375in" />
  </colgroup>

  <tr>
  <td>
  <div align="center">
  <strong>Customer Number</strong>
  </div>
  </td>
  <td>
  <div align="center">
  <strong>First Name</strong>
  </div>
 </td>
  <td>
  <div align="center">
  <strong>Last Name</strong>
  </div>
  </td>
```

You can also create VBA code in ADO 2.7, which will export XML (although, once again, it is rarely done):

```
Sub exportXML()
    Application.exportXML acExportTable, _
    "tblCustomer", _
    "c:\accessvba\Customer.xml", _
    "CustomerSchema.xml"
End Sub
```

As I said at the outset, entire books are devoted to the topic of XML. This section serves as a brief introduction.

Summary

In this chapter, we had a look at getting some of your data on the Internet. Although Access's Data Access Pages feature does not have some of the niceties of full dynamic languages (such as ASP or ASP.NET), it can get you up and running quickly. As you saw, we were able to set up the pages quickly and edit the data within a web browser. You were even able to quickly and easily write XML to facilitate the placement and formatting of data on the web page.

Once you have your database on the Web, you may find the demands on your database growing. As this demand grows, you may find Access running less efficiently. For that reason, we will now turn our attention to using the built-in upsizing tools to migrate your database from Microsoft Access to the more robust Microsoft SQL Server.

Upgrading

There is a chance that at some point or another, your application may grow beyond Microsoft Access. Imagine a scenario like this: You own a small store and decide to put your catalog on the Internet. You keep your catalog details on Access for easy updating. Your small site, initially, gets a few visitors a day and Access is working fine.

You then decide to start taking orders online. You suddenly have new security issues that Access may, or may not, fully address. A year or so down the road, your website is getting several hundred visitors an hour; and many are complaining that the site is running very slow. You may have reached the limitations of Access. If that is the case, the upgrade path of least resistance is Microsoft SQL Server.

NOTE

Do not confuse Microsoft SQL Server with the SQL query language.

In this chapter, we are going to examine the ways to upgrade your database to SQL Server while you continue using Access as a front end to access the SQL Server engine. This will require a brief discussion of user-defined functions, stored procedures, Transact SQL, and views.

Admittedly, this chapter will present only a brief overview. A full discussion of Microsoft SQL Server would fill a book by itself.

As of this writing, Microsoft has made a SQL Server available for approximately $50. This has most of the features of the Enterprise Edition but can only be used on a single machine for noncommercial applications. It is ideal for learning this product and for studying the examples shown in this chapter.

In addition, Microsoft has a 120-day trial available for free download at http://www.microsoft.com/sql/evaluation/trial/default.asp. Be warned, however: the download is approximately 350 megabytes, and you will need about 550 megabytes for it to expand. The $50 may be a more viable alternative.

Microsoft Access vs. SQL Server

When you access data with Access, you actually access the tables directly. First of all, this could create some serious security issues. Secondly, it also severely limits how many people can access the data simultaneously and how efficiently the requests can be handled.

On the other hand, SQL Server handles all requests through, as the name implies, a server. This means both better security and better efficiency. This will become obvious as we progress through this chapter.

Let's start by listing some of the advantages that SQL Server offers:

▶   Improved security because of the strong use of groups and roles.

▶   Better client handling (the ability to handle a greater number of visitors more quickly and securely) because of server access, as opposed to file access. SQL Server can handle hundreds of users at the same time.

▶   Larger database sizes. Access has a limitation of 2GB, while SQL Server can handle terabytes.

▶   Users have no access to the database file, while Access users access the data directly from the database file.

These improved features come at a price:

▶   Licensing costs are not inexpensive. Depending on circumstances, licensing could run to $10,000 +.

▶   Depending on how much traffic SQL Server will handle, you may need to purchase dedicated hardware to handle the resources.

▶   You will need to learn many additional skills, such as writing stored procedures, server management, and using T-SQL.

Access Data Projects

Very few developers would dispute the fact that Microsoft is evolving Access toward greater integration with SQL Server. Access 2002 introduced *Access Data Projects* to facilitate this. This is a new file type, with the file extension of .adp, which creates a common ground between SQL Server and traditional .mdb files. Prior to Access 2000, you had to create linked tables from Access to SQL Server.

Beginning with Access 2003, ADP files can create actual SQL Server objects while still working in the familiar Access GUI environment. In simpler terms, Access is serving as the GUI for SQL Server. In addition, features have been added to SQL Server to make it more Access-like. As an example, Figure 19-1 shows the Table Design window in SQL Server. While it is not identical, it is remarkably close to the Table Design window in Access.

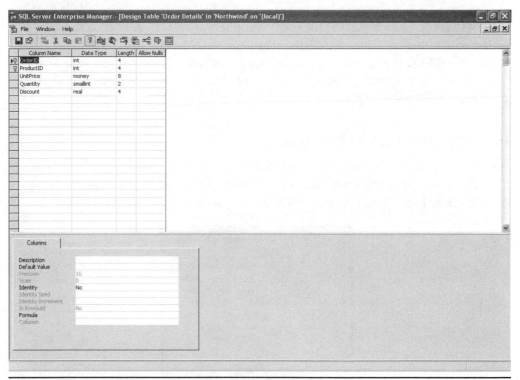

Figure 19-1 *Table Design window in SQL Server*

Because of this evolving integration, *upsizing* (the term used when migrating from Access to SQL Server) is not as daunting a task as you may think. As we move through this chapter, we will examine the upsizing mechanics. As you will see, it is not simply a matter of opening the file with a different program.

When a database is created in SQL Server, two files are created (as opposed to the single .mdb file of Access). The first has the file extension .mdf, and the second has the file extension .ldf.

The .mdf file contains the database that SQL Server will be using. The .ldf file contains a log of all the actions, or transactions, that have taken place in the database. In other words, it provides a history of what occurred within the database. A full discussion of how to use these files is well beyond the scope of this book. As a matter of fact, it would probably be a book in itself.

An Access Data Project, or ADP, allows you to use the easy-to-use features of Access to access the data in the SQL Server engine. The ADP file stores all of the objects created in Access (forms, reports, VBA code, etc.). The data itself is held on SQL Server. Note that ADP files will work only with SQL Server. If the data is stored on another database management system, such as Oracle, ADP cannot access it. However, SQL Server does have tools for accessing data in other systems.

Matters such as security, stored procedures (a stored procedure is precompiled SQL), functions, and views are handled by SQL Server.

Upsizing Your Access Database

Before you begin, you must make sure that SQL Server is up and running. If you installed it, you should see an icon in the Windows System Tray, which, if you double-click on it, should open the SQL Server Service Manager shown here.

You should also insure that each table in your Access database has a primary key. If a table does not, SQL Server will upsize the table in a read-only mode. Also, make sure that none of the object names (tables, forms, fields, etc.) have spaces in them. If they do, you would need to refer to them with the use of square brackets in SQL Server. For instance, if you were referring to a table called Address Book, you would need to use [Address Book] because of the space.

One invaluable tool that many developers use is SSW Upsizing Pro. This is a third-party tool that will analyze the existing Access database for potential problems before the upsizing process begins. You can get details and obtain a trial version at http://www.ssw.com.au/ssw/UpsizingPRO/. While the tool is not inexpensive, it could save you hours of troubleshooting.

Once the database is ready for conversion, you use Access itself to perform the conversion to a SQL Server database. Click Tools | Database Utilities | Upsizing Wizard from within Access. You should now see step 1 of the Upsizing Wizard.

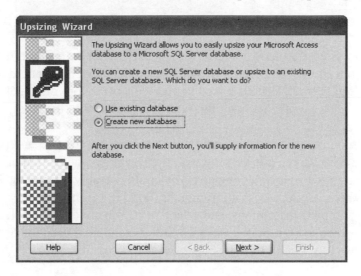

Here you can either create a new SQL Server database or use an existing one. In most cases, you are going to create a new SQL Server database to put your existing Access database into.

When you select Next, you should see step 2 of the wizard, shown here.

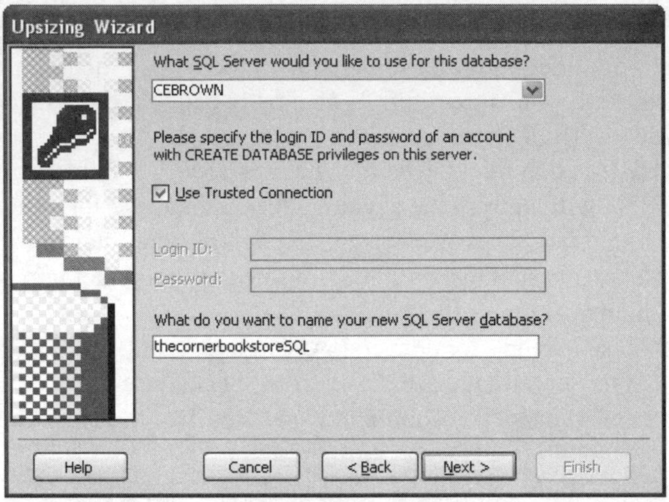

You need to select the name of the server where SQL Server resides. In most cases, there is only one name. However, in very large applications, there could be multiple instances of SQL Server. You also need to provide a name for your database. By default, the wizard uses the name of the Access database with the string "SQL" appended to it.

Depending on permissions, you may need to provide a user ID and password to access SQL Server. If you are working with the Development Edition of SQL Server and just running it on your own computer, you could probably just use the Use Trusted Connection check box to access it through the Windows administrator.

Once you complete the options, and select Next, you are asked to select the tables you want to upsize to SQL Server (step 3). In this example, I used the double right-pointing arrows to select all of the tables from the Access database.

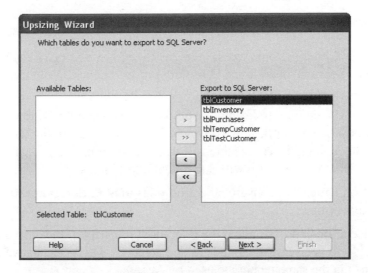

Once the tables are selected, click Next. You are brought to the screen shown here.

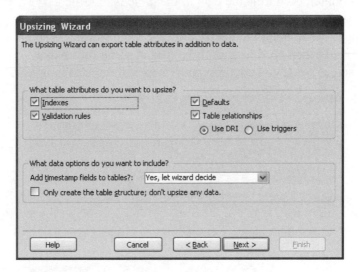

This allows you to select several additional options:

▶ Indexes will convert your Access indexes (remember, a primary key is an index) into SQL Server-type indexes. SQL Server uses indexes a little differently, and searches, by leaving this option on, will be a lot more efficient.

▶ Defaults will attempt to keep your field defaults when upsizing the tables. In most cases, it will work fine. However, if for some reason the wizard cannot upsize the default, the entire table will be skipped for upsizing. Again, a program such as SSW Upgrade Pro will flag potential problems.

▶ Validation Rules will convert validation rules to SQL Server constraints if you select this option.

▶ Table Relationships will retain the referential integrity of the database. This means it will keep cascading updates and deletions. DRI (Declarative Referential Integrity) is the same technique used by Access.

▶ Timestamps allows SQL Server to add a Timestamp field to each table, which will be updated each time the data in the table is modified.

Finally, you have an option to upsize only the table structures and to leave the data behind. You would then need to import the data at some future date.

After you select Next, you are brought to step 5 of the Upsizing Wizard.

Again, you are presented with a variety of options:

▶ Create a New Access Client/Server Application will move the tables into SQL Server and the user objects (forms, reports, and VBA code) into the ADP file. You can also browse to select the location for the new ADP file.

▶ Link SQL Server Tables to Existing Applications will create two copies of the tables: the SQL Server tables and the original .mdb tables with the prefix _local added. Unless you are very familiar with SQL Server processes, I strongly suggest that you do not select this option and leave it set for Create a New Client/Server Application. It could create difficulties.

▶ No Application Changes means that no changes will be made to the original .mdb file. All this will do is create the tables in SQL Server. There will be no connection between the original file and SQL Server. Again, I strongly suggest that you do not select this feature initially.

After selecting Next, you are brought to the final screen of the wizard.

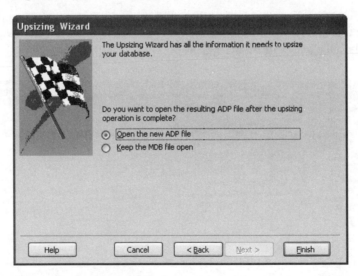

You can choose whether you want to open the new ADP file or stay in the existing MDB file. In this case, we are going to assume you want to open the ADP file.

After selecting Finish, the conversion begins. The process could take anywhere from several minutes to several hours, depending on the complexity of the database and the amount of data that needs to be upsized.

Upon completion, Access will produce a multipage report on the process. It is not a bad idea to print it out as a record. The report will also be kept as an Access Snapshot file in the same folder as the ADP file.

Working with an ADP File

The ADP file can be opened like any other Access file. However, notice the title bar on the top of the Database window, as shown in Figure 19-2. It reflects the fact that Access is now linked to a SQL Server database.

Access uses this ADP file to serve as the front-end GUI for SQL Server. At first, the differences may not seem like much, but there are many. As an example, if you click on the Queries category under Objects, you will notice several operations you have not seen in a standard MDB file. This is shown in Figure 19-3.

Stored Procedures

As an example, you can create stored procedures. A stored procedure is precompiled SQL code that is stored within the SQL Server database. Doing it this way makes the query considerably faster and more secure.

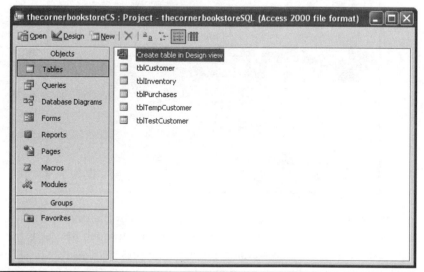

Figure 19-2   *The Database window in the ADP file*

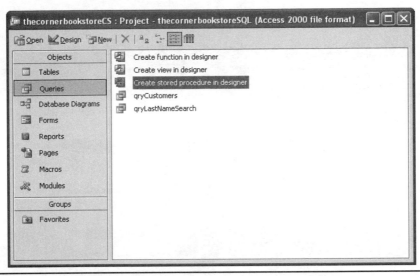

Figure 19-3   *The Queries category*

If you select the Create Stored Procedure in Designer option, you are presented with a screen similar to the query builder screen in an MDB file. This is shown in Figure 19-4. You select tables as you would in building a query. You even drag a field from one table to another in order to create a link. The only difference is that you can either check the boxes or drag them to a vertical column to select them. You can even set sort order and criteria as you would in a query.

Unlike queries, a stored procedure cannot be run unless it is saved first. To do this, just click on the Save icon and enter the name of the stored procedure in the Save As dialog box, as shown in Figure 19-5. Once you do that, you can run it as you would a query by simply clicking on the Exclamation icon.

Using buttons on the toolbar, you can turn the three sections of the designer window on and off. The three sections are

► The diagram that shows the tables

► The grid that shows the design grid

► The SQL window, which shows the SQL code

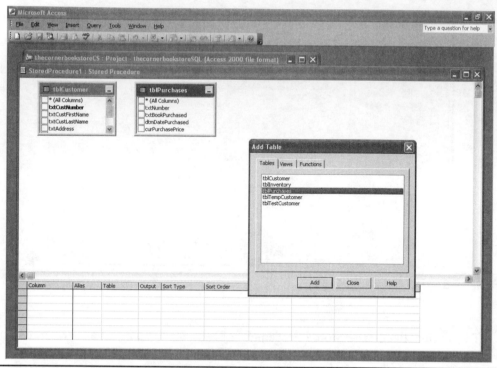

Figure 19-4   *The stored procedure designer*

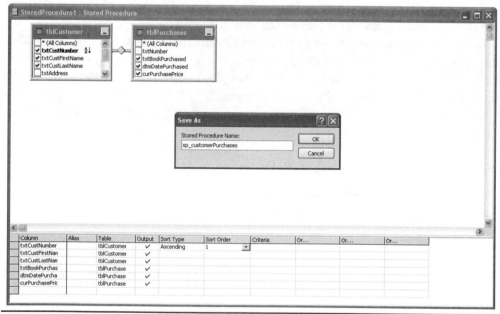

Figure 19-5   *Saving a stored procedure*

Views

A view is a way to access your data. It allows you to create a table containing a subset of your data on-the-fly. You would create a view from the queries window as you would a stored procedure. However, there is one additional step in order to make the data editable. You need to select View | Properties (see Figure 19-6).

So what does this mean to you? Let's look at actual SQL code from a recent project I did:

```
SELECT
store.storename, store.address, store.city, store.state, store.zipcode,
store.manager, store.storeNumber, sales.storesales, sales.Itemssold
FROM
store INNER JOIN sales ON store.storeNumber = sales.storeID
```

By saving this code as a view, the only front-end SQL that would be needed is

```
SELECT
vw_sales.*
FROM
Vw_Sales
```

Figure 19-6   *The View Properties dialog box*

In addition to being more efficient, it hides (programmers use the word "encapsulates") the actual SQL. This lends itself to greater efficiency.

You can set a permission to update the data by selecting the Update Using View Rules option.

Summary

In this chapter, we moved out of Access and briefly into the world of Microsoft SQL Server. I don't think it would come as any surprise that whole books are written on this subject.

We looked at how to take an existing Access MDB file and upsize it to SQL Server. We even took a brief look at some of the features that are different from Microsoft Access.

Application Development

Multiuser Applications

W hen Access was introduced, it was positioned primarily as a single-user, single-desktop database application. Since its introduction, however, networking has become virtually ubiquitous, and many web pages rely on Access as their data store. This means that an Access database is more and more likely to be accessed by multiple users (or to serve multiple simultaneous requests to a web server).

That multiple users can access an Access database simultaneously raises two issues. The first is performance: if an application is not designed and code is not written to be efficient, an application often runs more and more slowly as more data is added to it and as more users access it.

The second issue is resource contention: you must make sure that data accessed and changed by one user is not overwritten (and corrupted) by data from another user, or that one user is not locked out of the database for a protracted period while another user accesses it exclusively.

In this chapter, we'll examine some of the basic techniques you can use to make sure that multiuser applications perform efficiently, with minimal contention for resources.

Sharing the Database

The presence of a multiuser or networked environment, of course, implies that a database can (and almost certainly will) be opened by more than one user at a time. However, if Access is not configured for users to share a database and they attempt to open a database already opened by another user or process, they will see a warning like this one:

Once the dialog box is closed, Access will simply ignore the Open command, a frustrating experience for the end user of an application.

You can configure Access to automatically open a database in shared mode by selecting Tools | Options, which opens the Options dialog box, shown in Figure 20-1. Click on the Advanced tab if it is not already showing. The setting in the Default Open Mode group box determines whether Access opens a database for exclusive or shared use by default. You should make sure that Shared is checked before closing the dialog box.

Two additional points concerning the Default Open Mode setting are worth mentioning. First, by default, it is set to Shared, so unless it's been changed from its default at some point, you may not actually have to change the setting. Second, it is an Access sessionwide setting, rather than an individual database setting. That is, you don't have to individually configure each database to be opened in Shared mode, since the setting applies to all Access sessions as a whole.

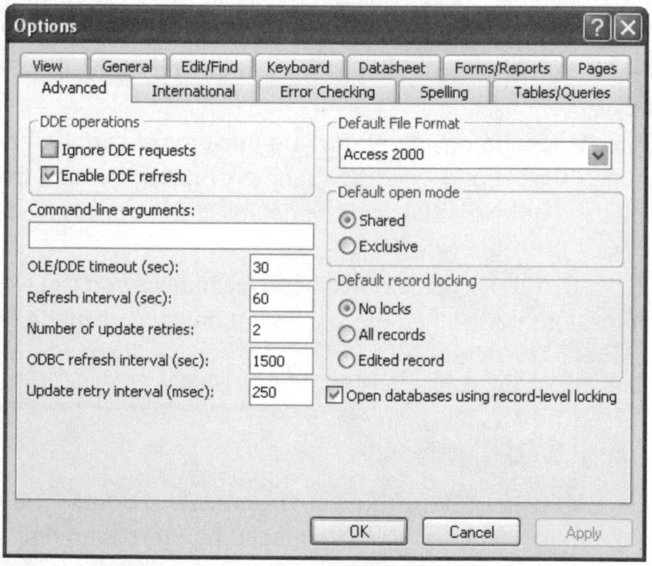

Figure 20-1   *Advanced tab of the Options dialog box*

Handling Resource Contention and Conflicts

Whenever multiple users have access to data, and especially when at least one of those users has the ability to modify or update that data, the possibility of contention arises. One possible scenario involves updates to data and goes something like this: User A accesses a recordset that includes record 1. User B then accesses a more or less identical recordset that includes record 1 as well. User B deletes the record. User A then updates the record that user B deleted. In order to handle conflicts such as this, a record locking scheme is typically used. In this section, we'll examine the facilities that Access provides to lock records in order to maintain the integrity of data in a multiuser environment.

Actually, we have to examine record locking in two different environments. If data is accessed purely through the Access interface, Access provides its own scheme of record locking, which can be configured through the Access user interface. If data is accessed programmatically using ADO and you make updates to data using the ADO Recordset object, your ADO code is responsible for handling resource contention and conflicts.

NOTE

Record locking is only in effect for databases on network shares. When a user accesses a database on a network share, Access creates a special record locking information (.idb) file that controls which records are locked. If a database is not on a network share, record locking settings are ignored.

Setting the Refresh Interval

The refresh interval determines how long it takes for data changed by one user to be displayed in the session of a second user. The refresh interval is set by the Refresh Interval (Sec) text box on the Advanced tab of the Options dialog box; it represents the number of seconds after which Access will refresh a user's data. The lower the value (and therefore the shorter the refresh interval), the more network traffic is generated just to update the display of records that a user is already displaying, but the more accurate the data will be. Conversely, the higher the value, the less network traffic, but the greater the probability that a user's form data will be inaccurate. The refresh interval, an Integer whose value can range from 1 to 32,766 seconds, is expressed as the number of seconds between refreshes.

The refresh interval is an Access-wide setting that applies to all databases opened by Access. Although there isn't a form property that allows you to override the default refresh interval on a form-by-form basis, you can call the Form object's Refresh method to update data displayed by the form.

Setting the Update Interval

Two additional settings control how often Access will attempt to update an edited record that is locked. The setting in the Number of Update Retries text box on the Advanced tab of the Options dialog box determines how many attempts Access will make to save an edited record that is locked. The default value is 2, although it can be an Integer ranging from 0 to 10.

The Update Retry Interval (Msec) text box determines how much time (in thousandths of a second) must elapse before each new attempt to save the edited record. The default value of this setting is 250 (an attempt is made to commit the edits to a locked record every 2.5 seconds), though its value is an Integer ranging from 0 to 1000.

In setting these values, you should recognize the trade-off involved here: setting them to higher values virtually insures that in the event of record contention, a record eventually will be saved. On the other hand, the time required to do this can degrade performance on the user's system to a ridiculous degree. For instance, if both properties are set to their maximum values, the user may have to wait up to 1 minute 40 seconds (10 seconds x 10 tries) to update a single record. On the other hand, setting them too low increases the likelihood that Access will abandon an update if a record is locked.

Record Locking in the Access Interface

A record locking scheme locks records when they are being edited by a particular user so that other users cannot edit them. Record locking reduces the likelihood that collisions will occur when multiple users are updating data simultaneously.

Access allows you to configure the record locking scheme used for forms bound to data in tables or in queries. Record locking for bound forms is controlled by the Default Record Locking group box on the Advanced tab of the Options dialog box (shown earlier in Figure 20-1). The dialog box offers three types of record locking:

▶ **No Locks**   This is actually a misnomer, since it represents an optimistic locking scheme. Access locks a record only when a user has saved changes to an edited record. (Actually, Access may lock a page of data, which is a buffer containing the current record and possibly the records that surround it that is 4KB in size in Access 2000 and later versions and 2KB in size in earlier versions.) That is, once a user clicks the Save button, selects the File | Save menu option, or navigates away from a modified record to save changes, Access locks a record. The record is not locked while the user is actually editing it. No Locks is the default setting, and it minimizes locking conflicts. Its goal is to insure that updates are atomic—that is, that a record isn't updated by two users at the same time, causing it to have inconsistent values from both users. This option is best used when the probability that more than one user will edit the same record is very small.

▶ **All Records**   Access locks the entire table whose records are being edited. Although this is the safest alternative, it is also the most restrictive, since it can easily result in multiple users being locked out of a database completely for long periods of time.

▶ **Edited Record**   This is a pessimistic locking scheme and is probably the most commonly used form of locking in a multiuser environment. Access locks the record (or the page containing the record, which is a 2KB or 4KB buffer that includes the record) edited by a user as soon as that user begins the editing process, and releases the lock once the edits have either been saved or abandoned.

To make the differences among locking types clear, let's imagine a scenario in which two users are editing the same record in the tblCustomer table. Table 20-1 shows the effect of the three locking schemes.

Although optimistic locking is clearly different from pessimistic locking and database locking, the latter two lock types are not clearly differentiated from one another in the first scenario. However, if we consider a second scenario, in which User A attempts to edit and save a record at the beginning of the database and User B attempts to edit and save a record at the end of the database (and more than one page away from the record being edited by User A if page-level locking is in effect), you will see the differences, as shown in Table 20-2.

Event	No Locks	Edited Record	All Records
User A navigates to record	No effect	No effect	No effect
User B navigates to record	No effect	No effect	No effect
User A begins edit	No effect	Lock placed	Lock placed
User B begins edit	No effect	User B locked out	User B locked out
User A begins to save record	Lock placed	--	--
User A's save completed	User A saves record; lock released	User A saves record; lock released	User A saves record; lock released
User B saves record	User B saves record	User B saves record	User B saves record

Table 20-1   *Effect of Locking Schemes when Two Users Edit the Same Record*

Event	No Locks	Edited Record	All Records
User A navigates to record	No effect	No effect	No effect
User B navigates to record	No effect	No effect	No effect
User A begins edit	No effect	Lock placed	Lock placed
User B begins edit	No effect	No effect	User B locked out
User A begins to save record	Lock placed	--	--
User A's save completed	User A saves record; lock released	User A saves record; lock released	User A saves record; lock released
User B saves record	User B saves record	User B saves record	User B saves record

Table 20-2 *Effect of Locking When Two Users Edit Different Records*

In this scenario, when User A is editing and saving a record, User B is also able to edit and save a record using pessimistic locking, but is locked out of the database if using the No Locks option.

If a user attempts to edit a locked record, Access displays the dialog box shown here:

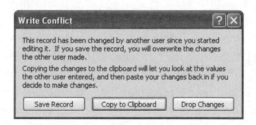

The user can save the changes despite the fact that another user has modified the record, abandon the changes and copy them to the Windows Clipboard (which allows them to be recalled and reviewed later), or simply discard the changes.

Like many of the other settings on the Advanced tab of the Options dialog box, the Default Record Locking setting applies to the Access application as a whole, and not to the individual database application that is opened.

You can override the default locking method for an individual form by assigning one of these three values—No Locks, All Locks, or Edited Record—to its RecordLocks property. You can also override the default locking method for the data in a report by assigning one of two values (No Locks or All Locks) to its RecordLocks property. The original value of the property is determined by the value assigned in the Default Record Locking group box.

Along with the type of locking, you can also determine whether one or possibly more records are locked. The Open Databases Using Record-Level Locking option on the Advanced tab of the Options dialog box, which appears in Access 2000 and later versions, allows you to lock only the record that a user is editing, or to lock a page that includes the record being edited by a user. The page size also varies depending on the Access version. For Access 98 and earlier versions, the page size is 2KB; for Access 2000 and later versions, it is 4KB. (The number of locked records, of course, depends on the size of an individual record.)

Setting Options Programmatically

Many of the options available through the Options dialog box in the Access user interface can also be set programmatically by calling the SetOption method of the Access Application object. The method's syntax is

```
SetOption(OptionName, Setting)
```

where *OptionName* is a predefined String argument containing the name of the option to be set, and *Setting* is the value to which the option should be set. Valid values of *Setting* and their data types depend on the option being set. The options discussed in this chapter have the values shown in Table 20-3.

Record Locking with ADO

The settings that we've examined so far have applied to bound forms based on tables and queries and are applied automatically by Access. However, if your forms use ADO recordsets to display editable data, you must implement record locking programmatically. In the section "Assigning Recordsets Dynamically" in Chapter 12,

User Interface Name	*OptionName* Parameter	Setting Values
Default Open Mode	Default Open Mode for Databases	An Integer: 0 for shared, 1 for exclusive
Refresh Interval (Sec)	Refresh Interval (sec)	An Integer from 1 to 32,766
Number of Update Retries	Number of Update Retries	An Integer from 0 to 10
Update Retry Interval (Msec)	Update Retry Interval (msec)	An Integer from 0 to 1000
Default Record Locking	Default Record Locking	An Integer: 0 for No Locks, 1 for All Records, 2 for Edited Record
Open Databases Using Record-Level Locking	Use Row Level Locking	Integer: −1 for True (record level), 0 for False (page level)

Table 20-3   *Parameters and Values for the SetOption Method*

you have already briefly seen how this is done by setting the LockType property of the ADO Recordset object to one of four possible values:

▶ adLockReadOnly to lock the entire recordset

▶ adLockPessimistic to lock a record while it is being edited

▶ adLockOptimistic to lock a record while it is being saved

▶ adLockBatchOptimistic to lock out users while records are updated in batch mode

The type of lock can be specified as a parameter to the Open method of the Recordset object, or it can be assigned to the Recordset object's LockType property before the recordset is opened. For example, the following code sets properties separately before calling the Open method:

```
Private Sub Form_Open(Cancel As Integer)

    Dim con As ADODB.Connection
    Dim recSet As ADODB.Recordset
    Dim strFrmNm As String

    Set recSet = New ADODB.Recordset
    recSet.CursorType = adOpenKeyset
    recSet.LockType = adLockOptimistic

    Set con = New ADODB.Connection
    con.Open "Provider=Microsoft.Jet.OLEDB.4.0;" & _
        "Data Source=C:\BegVBA\thecornerbookstore.mdb;"

    recSet.Open "SELECT * FROM tblCustomer", con
    Set Me.Recordset = recSet

    recSet.Close
    con.Close
    Set recSet = Nothing
    Set con = Nothing

End Sub
```

The following code is identical, except that it sets the locking type in the call to the Open method:

```
Private Sub Form_Open(Cancel As Integer)

    Dim con As ADODB.Connection
    Dim recSet As ADODB.Recordset
    Dim strFrmNm As String

    Set recSet = New ADODB.Recordset
    Set con = New ADODB.Connection

    con.Open "Provider=Microsoft.Jet.OLEDB.4.0;" & _
        "Data Source=C:\BegVBA\thecornerbookstore.mdb;"

    recSet.Open "SELECT * FROM tblCustomer", con, adOpenKeyset, adLockOptimistic
    Set Me.Recordset = recSet

    recSet.Close
    con.Close
    Set recSet = Nothing
    Set con = Nothing

End Sub
```

When ADO rather than Access is managing the recordset you're working with, it's also important to recognize that the type of recordset your application uses has a vast impact on performance. For a brief discussion of the types of ADO recordsets and their impact on performance, see Chapter 12.

Improving Application Performance

Users quickly grow tired of waiting for a slow application to respond. Performance is particularly a problem in a network environment, where multiple users can be running an application and requesting its data simultaneously, and your application data has to share network resources with all of an organization's other applications. In this section, we'll examine some steps that you can take to optimize the performance of your multiuser Access application.

Separating Data from Other Access Objects

Obviously, the major reason for making a centralized database available over the network for users to share is that the data it contains is dynamic to some degree. If data were static, once the data was assembled, it could simply be distributed to each user and run on his or her desktop. A network to share data would be unnecessary, and issues of performance and network traffic need never arise.

Generally, though, if you look at the components of your Access application, you'll find that most of them are in fact static. Except for periodic maintenance and upgrades, objects such as forms, reports, queries, and macros tend to change little if at all. The data stored in tables is the dynamic part of an Access application. Yet, if all database objects are stored in one centralized database, each time users access the application, they receive these same static objects along with dynamic data. Sending the same static data, like forms and code, over the network again and again is a real drag on performance. Instead, it is much more efficient to use the network only to send the dynamic data of a database application, and to load the static form, report, and query objects from the user's local system.

To address this issue, Access (from Access 97 on) offers a utility that allows you to split your database into a front end that resides on the user's desktop and a back end that resides on a single machine and is shared by all users of the application. Called the Database Splitter, this utility can be accessed by selecting Tools | Database Utilities | Database Splitter.

Before using the splitter and dividing your database application into components, it's best to make a backup copy of your original database. To do this, select File | Back Up Database. Access closes the open database file and opens the Save Backup As dialog box, a standard File Save dialog box. As you can see in Figure 20-2, Access suggests a filename that consists of your original database filename along with the date of the backup. Feel free to assign a filename and a directory of your choice. Then select the Save button to begin the backup. When the backup is completed, Access will reopen the original database.

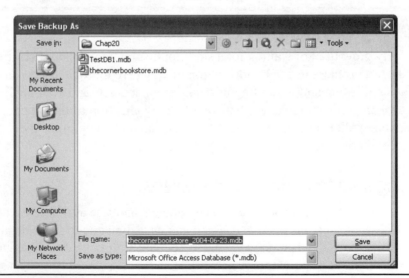

Figure 20-2   *Save Backup As dialog box*

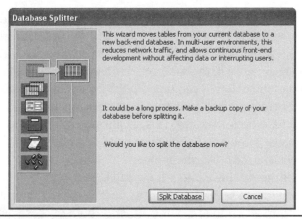

Figure 20-3   *First screen of the Database Splitter Wizard*

When you launch the Database Splitter Wizard, Access displays the dialog box shown in Figure 20-3, which allows you to cancel the operation if you've forgotten to back up your database or if you've launched the wizard in error. If you select the Split Database button, Access prompts you to select a name and location for the back-end part of the database, as Figure 20-4 shows. This consists of the Access objects that you will store on a single system (your database server) and that typically are fairly dynamic, such as your nonstatic database tables. In forming a recommended filename, Access simply adds the substring "_be" to your existing filename. You can change it or accept the default. Click the Split button when you're satisfied with the name and location of your back-end database component.

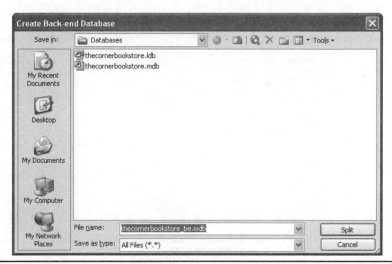

Figure 20-4   *The Database Splitter Wizard's Create Back-end Database dialog box*

Eventually, depending on the number of objects in your database and its size, Access should display a dialog box informing you that the database has been successfully split. This means that your Access database (.mdb) file has been separated into two distinct files: all tables have been saved in the back-end database file, while all queries, forms, reports, macros, and modules have been saved in the front-end file. This front-end file is a modified version of your original database file (in our case, thecornerbookstore.mdb), except that its tables have been removed. This is indicated by the icon beside each table in the front-end database's Tables window, shown in Figure 20-5, which shows that links to the tables have replaced the tables themselves.

Once you've split the database into a front and a back end, you can copy the front-end file to individual users' machines, as well as move the back-end database file to another location. Of course, moving either or both of these database files usually breaks the front-end database's links to the back-end tables. For your application to work, you must update these links to reflect the current location of the back-end database. Otherwise, the front end of your application will simply be unable to locate the back end, and you'll see an error dialog box like this one:

To correct this problem, Access provides the Linked Table Manager, which you can activate by selecting Tools | Linked Table Manager, or by right-clicking on one of the front-end linked tables and selecting Linked Table Manager from the pop-up menu.

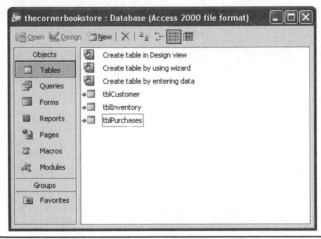

Figure 20-5   *The Tables window of a front-end database*

Access then opens the Linked Table Manager dialog box, shown in Figure 20-6. The dialog box lists the linked tables in the current database and shows the location of the physical tables to which they point. You can select the links that you'd like to update, then click the OK button. Access will then display a File Open dialog box that prompts you for the new location of the back-end database file. If Access finds all of the physical tables in the file you've selected, it will update the remaining links as well. Otherwise, it will prompt you for each remaining table whose link it can't resolve.

When it finishes, Access will display a dialog box informing you that the links have been successfully updated. Wherever possible, you should make sure that the links are correct before you distribute the client component of your database application to individual users.

In most cases, the default behavior of separating tables in a back-end database file from everything else in a front-end database file is acceptable. But if one or more of your tables contain static data (like a state or a zip code table), you might want to include it in the front-end database so that its data doesn't contribute to network traffic. You can do this by opening the front-end database file and performing the following steps:

1. Select the linked table in the Tables window, and then select Edit | Copy.

2. Select Edit | Paste. Access displays the Paste Table As dialog box shown in Figure 20-7.

3. In the dialog box, assign a unique name to the table (it can't be the same as the linked table), select the Structure and Data (Local Table) option, and then click OK.

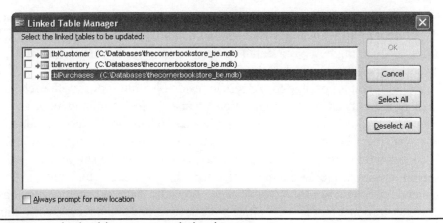

Figure 20-6   *Linked Table Manager dialog box*

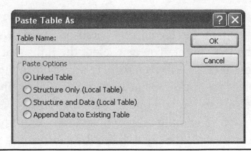

Figure 20-7   *The Paste Table As dialog box*

You can then delete the original linked table and rename the new table. In addition, you can open the back-end database file and delete the file that you've just added to your front-end database file.

Although splitting a database can significantly boost an application's performance, it also has one major drawback: each time you make changes to the static database objects, like forms, reports, and queries, you have to redistribute the front-end component to your users. Depending on how often your application changes and how many users there are, this can be a real nuisance. Because of this, it makes sense to split your database only when its supposedly static portions have become more or less stable. Alternatively, you may want to include more "dynamic" static objects in the back-end of your database application, so that they continue to be sent across the network, while more "static" objects continue to reside in the front-end component.

Centralization vs. Decentralization

Whether you should split your database is only part of a larger question of what the overall architecture of your application should be and how centralized it should be. In addition to deciding how your database application is to be distributed, if it is to be distributed at all, you should decide how Access is to be distributed.

At one extreme, it is possible for Access to reside on a file server, with each user downloading not only an Access application but also Access itself and all of its associated library files. This allows for complete centralization of Access, reduces the cost of Access licenses, minimizes hard disk storage requirements, and allows for the use of diskless workstations. But it also increases the load on the single file server and results in an enormous increase in network traffic. In many cases, this will be a load that the network cannot bear and that Access, especially since it was engineered as a single-desktop product first and a multiuser product second, cannot efficiently support.

At the other extreme is a decentralized solution, where Access (and possibly the front end of Access applications) resides on each desktop, and a single file server is responsible for providing the data for front-end requests. This, of course, places a copy in the hand of each user, which maximizes licensing fees, consumes more disk space, and has greater hardware costs. It also offers the best performance.

In between the two extremes are a number of possible solutions. It is possible to install Access on a single file server, for instance, but to install many of its libraries on individual users' machines. By splitting up the elements of your architecture and locating some on the client and some on the server, you may be able to optimize a number of goals (performance, administrative control, cost, and efficiency) at once.

Compiling Your Code

At runtime, VBA code executes in a compiled environment. This means that before it is run, the source code that you write is translated into executable code by a VBA language compiler. This differs from an interpreted environment, where source code is translated into executable code as the source code is encountered.

Access compiles its VBA code dynamically before running it. This means that if your code calls a function that has not been compiled, the module that contains it will be compiled automatically before it is executed. As a result, you don't have to make sure that all of your code is compiled; Access will handle the compilation process for you. The downside, though, is that compilation can be time consuming. The first time that the code in a module is run, the application's performance can be noticeably slower because of the compilation process. (Once the code is compiled, though, performance should improve.)

In addition to its effect on performance, uncompiled code has another undesirable side effect: it is not necessarily syntactically correct, and may not compile at all. For instance, if you've made a modification to a code module but have never subsequently tested the code, it may not have been compiled. And if your modification itself introduced an error, that error may be discovered at runtime by the user, when Access is unable to compile the module's code.

You can eliminate this performance bottleneck and insure that your code will compile by compiling the code yourself. Access in fact provides two methods to do this. The first and simplest method involves selecting the Debug | Compile <project_name> menu option, which causes Access to compile all of a project's VBA code. At a minimum, it's a good idea to compile all VBA code when you've finished coding and are ready to place your code in production.

The second option is to create and distribute a compiled .mde file, instead of the conventional Access .mdb file. This not only compiles your code, but also removes all source code, thus hiding it from prying eyes and making it impossible for the users of your application to see or to modify your source code. It also compacts the destination database, which makes it possible to compile the front end of a split database (discussed in the section "Separating Data from Other Access Objects" earlier in this chapter).

An .mde file also disables the following features that are commonly available to users from the Access interface:

▶ The ability to create or modify forms, reports, or modules. (Note that the user can continue to create new tables and queries and to modify existing tables and queries.)

▶ The ability to insert modules or class modules in the VBA Editor.

▶ The ability to add, delete, or change references to libraries in the VBA Editor.

▶ The ability to view existing modules or "code behind forms" in the VBA Editor.

To create an .mde file, select Tools | Database Utilities | Make MDE File. When the Save MDE As dialog box appears, enter the name of the .mde file (by default, it will be given the same name as the .mdb file from which it is created) and select the directory where you'd like the file to be saved. When you select the Save button, Access will close the open .mdb file, create the .mde file, and then reopen the .mdb file.

If the .mde file becomes the production version of your application, be sure to keep the .mdb file in a safe place. Since the .mde file no longer includes your source code in text form, you can make no further modifications to the application. Instead, you'll have to make modifications to the latest version of the .mdb file and recompile it into an .mde file.

Writing Optimized VBA Code

Because multiuser applications tend to perform more slowly than single-user ones, it is especially important in a multiuser application to write optimized code. Performance that is acceptable or barely acceptable in a single-user application easily becomes unacceptable in a networked environment. In this section, we'll examine three of the major techniques that you can use to improve your code's performance. Although all three techniques apply equally to both single-user and multiuser environments, they can have the greatest impact on performance in a multiuser or networked environment.

One of the greatest performance gains comes from taking advantage of early binding. *Binding* refers to the point at which the identity of an object becomes known. *Early binding* means that the identity of an object is established when the code is compiled and before it is actually run, so that all information about the object (such as its methods and method parameters) can be verified. *Late binding* means that the identity of an object becomes known only as code is run.

In VBA, you use late binding by using the generic Object data type. To get a sense of what this means, the following code, which originally appeared in Chapter 12, opens an Access form using early binding:

```
Sub runForm()
    Dim con As ADODB.Connection                    ' con is early bound

    Set con = New ADODB.Connection
    con.Open "Provider=Microsoft.Jet.OLEDB.4.0;" & _
        "Data Source=C:\BegVBA\thecornerbookstore.mdb;"

    DoCmd.OpenForm "frmCustomer"
End Sub
```

The following is a late-bound version of the same code:

```
Sub runLate()
    Dim con As Object ' con is late-bound

    Set con = New ADODB.Connection
    con.Open "Provider=Microsoft.Jet.OLEDB.4.0;" & _
        "Data Source=C:\BegVBA\thecornerbookstore.mdb;"

    DoCmd.OpenForm "frmCustomer"
End Sub
```

Here, the precise object type of the **con** variable can only be resolved when VBA encounters the Set keyword, rather than when **con** is declared by the Dim statement. The result is that, on my system, the second version of the code took twice as long to run as the first. The conclusion is clear: use early binding wherever possible.

The final two performance tips that we'll look at focus on code executed in loops. Since loops execute multiple times, they tend to consume a relatively large proportion of total execution time. If the code within a loop is poorly written, it can severely degrade overall performance.

One technique for minimizing the time that code within a loop executes is to exit the loop as soon as possible using the Exit Do (for Do loops) or Exit For (for For and For Each loops) statements. Although it may seem obvious, the fact that a loop can be exited "prematurely" is frequently forgotten when coding.

For instance, if you are working with a large recordset and looping through each of its records, you can save a significant amount of time by exiting the loop once you have finished, rather than iterating each of the records in which you are no longer interested. Similarly, if you are using a loop to examine a number of controls for a particular property value and you find that value, you can immediately exit the loop without examining any additional controls. The exact improvement in performance attributable to prematurely exiting a loop varies depending on the number of iterations of the loop that are eliminated.

Second, every operation within a loop necessarily occurs every time the loop is executed. Sometimes, though, those operations actually need to be performed only once and are not dependent on the loop. Variable declaration is a case in point. Take the following code fragment, for example:

```
Public Sub Loops()

    Dim con As ADODB.Connection
    Dim rs As New ADODB.Recordset
    Dim strList As String

    Set con = New ADODB.Connection

    con.Open "Provider=Microsoft.Jet.OLEDB.4.0;" & _
        "Data Source=C:\BegVBA\thecornerbookstore.mdb;"

    rs.CursorLocation = adUseServer
    rs.Open "SELECT * FROM tblCustomer", con, adOpenStatic, adLockOptimistic

    Do While Not rs.EOF
        ' Variable should be declared outside of loop
        Dim strName As String
        strName = rs!txtCustFirstName & " " & rs!txtCustLastName
        strList = strList & strName & vbCrLf
        rs.MoveNext
    Loop
    MsgBox rs.RecordCount & " records: " & vbCrLf & strList

    Set rs = Nothing
    Set con = Nothing
End Sub
```

The strName string variable is declared inside the loop, which means that it is declared anew each time the loop executes. If you move the variable declaration outside of the loop, this code executes approximately 25 percent faster than if the variable is declared inside the loop.

Summary

In this chapter, you've learned some of the basic factors that you need to consider when creating a networked or multiuser application. You've learned about resource contention and ways to handle and minimize it in the Access interface and using ADO. You've also learned about the merits of centralized versus distributed architectures, including some of the ways that you might split your database application to improve performance. Finally, you've learned some techniques for improving performance in both a single-user and a multiuser environment.

Beyond Microsoft Access

So far, this book has focused on using databases within the Access environment and on writing VBA code that runs within the Access environment. However, the tools you've used and the skills you've developed while reading this book are applicable to a wide variety of programming environments. Similarly, you can leverage the knowledge you've acquired in the course of reading this book to programmatically access the data stored in Access databases without actually having to be in the Access environment. This is because Access programming makes use of two relatively standard tools:

► Visual Basic for Applications (VBA), the programming language used by Access. The same programming language is used in the other Microsoft Office applications, as well as in Microsoft's retail Visual Basic product. In addition, Microsoft's scripting language, VBScript, is really a scaled-down version of VBA that is most commonly used as the programming language for Microsoft's Active Server Pages (ASP).

► ActiveX Data Objects (ADO), the data access technology used in Access programming. Although Access can use ADO for programmatic data access, ADO itself is a more or less language- and product-independent technology that exists as a stand-alone component apart from Access. This means that it can be used to manipulate Access data outside the Access environment.

This chapter examines some of the areas in which you can leverage the skills you've learned to develop programs that run in environments other than Access.

VBA and Microsoft Office

In Chapter 17, you learned that some of the components used by Access, such as its command bars, are actually shared by all Office applications. VBA is another one of those components. VBA is the programming language used by each of the applications included in Office (as is the VBA Editor, the tool for editing VBA code). So with the knowledge of Access programming that you've acquired so far in this book, you're in an excellent position to begin programming with any of the other Office applications.

 NOTE

Microsoft Outlook is a partial exception to this rule. Outlook is a relative latecomer to the VBA environment, and in its initial versions, it used VBScript as its programming language. Today, although it continues to use VBScript and a special Notepad-like editor for form-level programming, it uses VBA and the VBA Editor for application-level programming.

Rather than starting from scratch, in order to work effectively with a particular Office application, you simply have to familiarize yourself with the basics of that application's object model. (An *object model* is a set of classes that, along with their properties, methods, and events, exposes an application's functionality. A *class* is a sort of template from which an object is created.) ADO, for instance, is a generalized object model for data access (that is, it's product independent), while the Application object that you've used in the course of this book is part of the Access object model. And each of the other Office applications has its own object model.

The Office object models themselves vary in complexity. Of the major applications in Office XP, the largest object model belongs to Word, with 245 classes and 251 enumerations (an *enumeration* is a group of related constants), while the smallest is Outlook, with 67 classes and 54 enumerations. Since even the smallest object model is far too extensive to cover in a single chapter, we'll look at a relatively simple example of how you might retrieve data from your Access database from Excel.

Let's take a look at Excel and its programming environment by actually running the application. When you launch Excel and open its VBA Editor (Tools | Macros | Visual Basic Editor), you see the familiar interface shown in Figure 21-1. The Code window occupies the right side of the screen, while the Project Explorer is on the upper-left side and the Properties window is on the lower-left side. The Project Explorer contains different objects than the Project Explorer in Access, since Excel's basic working objects are worksheets and workbooks.

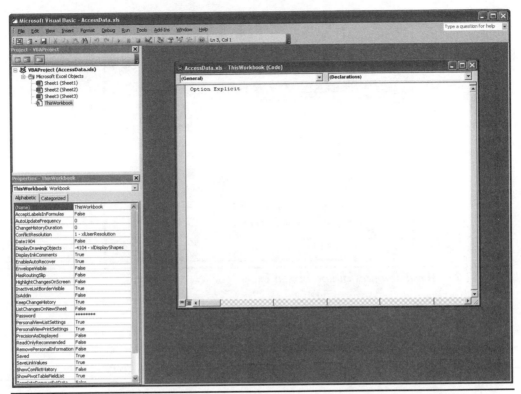

Figure 21-1 *The VBA Editor in Excel*

If you select Tools | References from the VBA Editor menu, you see the familiar References dialog box, shown in Figure 21-2. Some of the references themselves are also familiar. Excel, like Access, automatically adds references to Visual Basic for Applications, OLE Automation, and the Microsoft Office Object Library. As you might expect, though, Excel automatically adds some different references to its projects than Access does. Whereas Access automatically adds references to the Microsoft Access Object Library, the Microsoft ActiveX Data Objects Library, and the Microsoft DAO Object Library, Excel adds a reference to the Microsoft Excel Object Library. In order to retrieve data from our sample database, thecornerbookstore.mdb, you should add a reference to the Microsoft ActiveX Data Objects Library to your Excel project.

Since Excel has some limited database capabilities (one of the predominant uses of Excel, in fact, is as a flat-file database), you would expect that it should provide support for data access. And in fact it does. The Excel object model includes a QueryTables collection object that holds QueryTable objects, each of which represents a table built from data returned by an external data source. The QueryTables collection is a child object of the Worksheet object, and is returned by its QueryTables property.

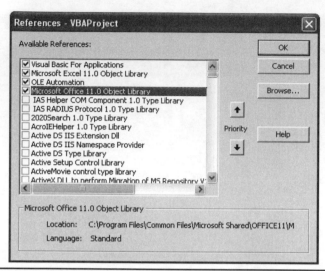

Figure 21-2 *The References dialog box in Excel*

To retrieve data and add a QueryTable object to the collection, you call its Add method, which can take data from a variety of data sources (in our case, an ADO recordset) and inserts it into a specified range in the worksheet. Here is the code to do this:

```
Public Sub ImportCustomerData()

    Dim con As ADODB.Connection
    Dim rs As New ADODB.Recordset
    Dim ws As Worksheet
    Dim qt As QueryTable
    Dim app As New Excel.Application

    ' Open recordset with customer data
    rs.CursorType = adOpenForwardOnly

    Set con = New ADODB.Connection
    con.Open "Provider=Microsoft.Jet.OLEDB.4.0;" & _
        "Data Source=C:\BegVBA\thecornerbookstore.mdb;"

    rs.Open "SELECT * FROM tblCustomer", con

    ' Add Customer table to active worksheet
    Set ws = Application.ActiveSheet

    Set qt = ws.QueryTables.Add(rs, Range("A2"))
```

```
    qt.RefreshStyle = xlOverwriteCells
    qt.Refresh True
End Sub
```

To enter this code, select Insert | Module from the VBA Editor menu. Then double-click on the module (which VBA automatically names Module1) in the Project Explorer. This opens a Code window containing the module's code. You can then proceed to enter the code, and when you are finished, you can run it by selecting the Run button on the VBA Editor toolbar. The result should resemble Figure 21-3.

Much of this code should be familiar—it's largely the same as the code used to bind a recordset to a form in Chapter 12. The difference is that since you are using Excel, you must bind your recordset to a worksheet and so must use the Excel object model. Most of the code here, however, is a combination of VBA code and ADO code that can run unmodified under both Access and Excel.

There's a second difference that's even more significant. Note that although this data can be edited in the Excel environment, changes cannot be saved back to the Access database. This becomes a local copy that is independent of the original Access table from which it was formed; the table in Access will not be updated to reflect any changes made to the data in the Excel spreadsheet.

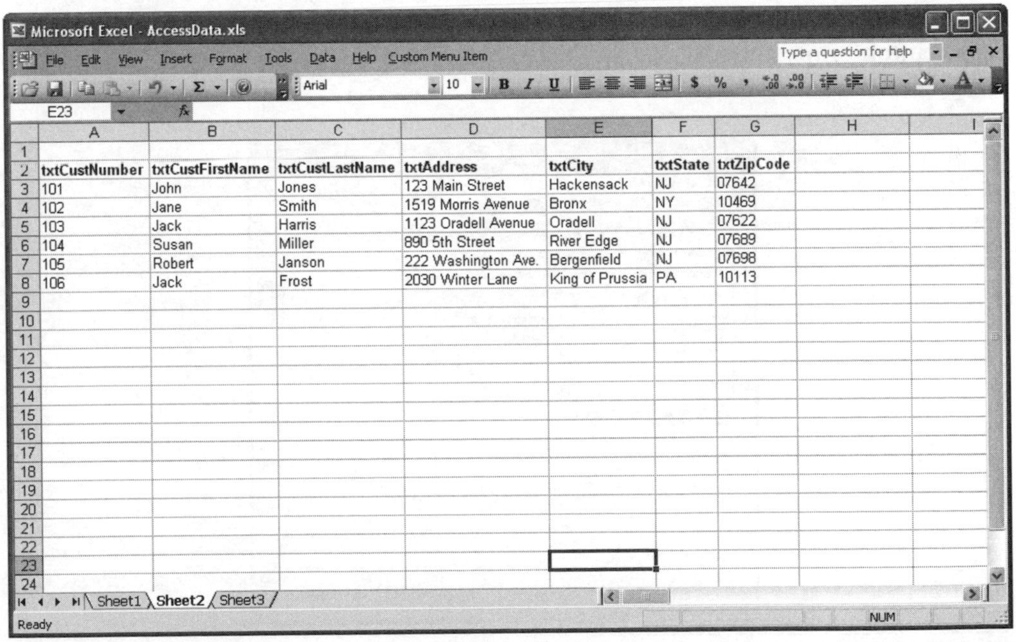

Figure 21-3   *The Customer table in Excel*

NOTE

Excel provides a number of methods for retrieving data in Access tables and queries and importing them into an Excel spreadsheet. This isn't meant to be a definitive treatment of how to import Access data. Instead, it's intended to illustrate that the knowledge of Access VBA programming you've gained from this book can be applied readily outside the Access programming environment.

To make it easier for others (as well as for yourself) to activate your data access routine, you can do one or more of the following:

▶ Attach it to a toolbar or menu item programmatically, as illustrated in Chapter 17.

▶ Attach it to a toolbar or menu item through the user interface. To do this, right-click on the menu and select Customize from the pop-up menu, or select Tools | Customize to open the Customize dialog box. On the Commands tab, select Macros from the Categories list box. The Customize dialog box should now resemble Figure 21-4. If you want to create a menu item, drag the Customize Button icon to the position on a menu where you'd like it to appear. If you want to create a toolbar button, drag the Custom Button icon to the toolbar on which you'd like it to appear. (The toolbar must already be visible.) Finally, right-click on the newly added toolbar or menu item to open a pop-up menu, select the Assign Macro option, and select the macro that you'd like to assign to the button or menu item.

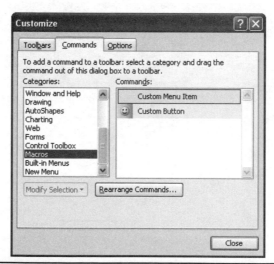

Figure 21-4 *Excel's Customize dialog box*

▶ Call it from an event procedure, such as the Open event that is fired when a worksheet opens. To do this, go to the Visual Basic Editor, double-click on ThisWorksheet in the Project Explorer to open the worksheet's Code window, select Workbook in the window's Objects drop-down list, and select Open in the window's Members drop-down list. Then call the procedure from the event handler, so that the code appears as follows:

```
Private Sub Workbook_Open()
    ImportCustomerData
End Sub
```

In this case, the procedure will run automatically whenever the workbook is opened.

Visual Basic

Microsoft's retail Visual Basic product consists of four components, as shown in the References dialog box in Figure 21-5. (You can open the References dialog box by selecting Project | References.) The first component is Visual Basic for Applications, the same programming language found in Access and the other Office applications. The second, described as "Visual Basic runtime objects and procedures," is a runtime module. The third, described as "Visual Basic objects and procedures," consists of Visual Basic forms and controls. The fourth is OLE Automation, which makes it possible to connect

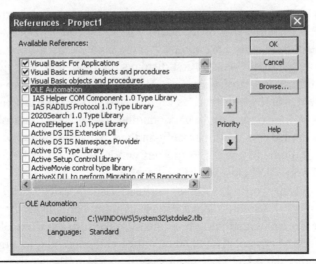

Figure 21-5 *The Visual Basic References dialog box*

to other components and access their object models. Two of these references—to VBA and to OLE Automation—are present in Access projects as well as in Excel projects.

Since access to data residing in databases is central to application programming, it is not surprising that Visual Basic provides a rich collection of tools for supporting data access while reducing the need for coding. These include

▶   The Data Control, a service component that retrieves a DAO recordset and provides individual records from it to other bound data controls. (A service component is a control whose primary purpose, rather than to provide an interface, is to provide some service—in this case to distribute data—to other controls.)

▶   The DBList and DBCombo controls, which bind to a Data Control and display an entire column of a recordset in a list box or combo box, respectively.

▶   The ADO Data Control, another service component that retrieves an ADO recordset and provides individual records to other bound data controls.

▶   The DataList and DataCombo controls, which bind to an ADO Data Control and display an entire column of a recordset in a list box or combo box, respectively.

▶   The DataGrid control, which displays an entire recordset using a spreadsheet-like interface.

In addition, most of the intrinsic Visual Basic controls include support for data binding through their properties, which can be set using the Properties dialog box as well as programmatically.

Data binding using Visual Basic is an extensive topic that has been the focus of entire books. This section will simply attempt to show you how easy it is to use the ADO Data Control to retrieve and update Access data.

When you launch Visual Basic, it first displays the modal New Project dialog box. When you select the Standard EXE option, Visual Basic opens a form in a design window in the center of the interface, as Figure 21-6 shows. The left side of the Visual Basic window is occupied by a toolbox containing Visual Basic controls, while the Project Explorer appears on the upper right and the Properties window on the lower right. This is a good time to use the Properties window to change the form's Caption property from "Form1" to "Customer Database."

Since the ADO Data Control is not an intrinsic Visual Basic control, you'll have to add it to your project. To do this, select Project | Components from the Visual Basic menu. When the Components dialog box opens, make sure the Controls tab is selected; then find and check Microsoft ADO Data Control in the list box, as Figure 21-7 shows. An icon representing the ADO Data Control will appear in the toolbox, which now

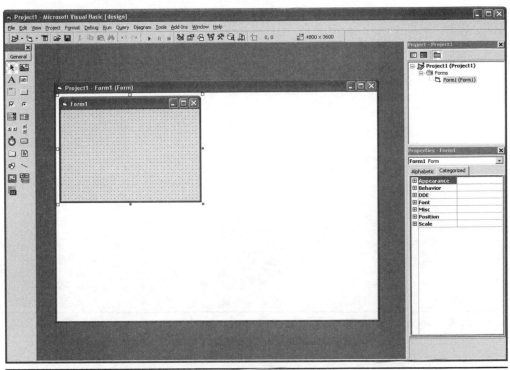

Figure 21-6   *A Standard EXE project in Visual Basic*

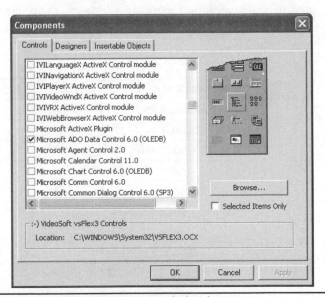

Figure 21-7   *Controls tab of the Components dialog box*

Figure 21-8 *Toolbox with the ADO Data Control added*

resembles Figure 21-8. Double-click on it, and Visual Basic will place the control on the form.

Visual Basic automatically assigns a name of Adodc1 to the control. You can leave the name unchanged, but you should set the properties of the ADO Data Control as shown in Table 21-1.

Property	Value
BackColor	Button Face
Caption	\<blank\>
CommandType	1 – adCmdText
CursorLocation	3 – adUseClient
CursorType	2 – adOpenDynamic
EOFAction	2 – adDoAddNew
LockType	2 – adLockPessimistic
Mode	adShareDenyNone
RecordSource	SELECT * FROM tblCustomer

Table 21-1 *Properties of the ADO Data Control*

The final property whose value needs to be set is the ConnectionString. Visual Basic makes this easy and also helps to make sure that your connection string is correct. When you select the ConnectionString property and click on the button with the ellipsis to the right of the property's text box, Visual Basic opens the Property Pages dialog box shown in Figure 21-9. Select the Use Connection String option button, and then click on the Build button. Visual Basic opens the Data Link Properties dialog box with the Provider tab selected, as Figure 21-10 shows. Select the Microsoft Jet x.x OLE DB Provider, and click on the Next button. Visual Basic takes you to the Connection tab.

In the Connection tab, shown in Figure 21-11, you can select the name of the database you'd like to connect to. If you're uncertain of its name and location, you can click on the ellipsis to the right of the text box. This opens the Select Access Database dialog box, a standard File Open dialog box that lets you navigate the file system and select your database file. You can provide a user name and password, if access to your database requires them. And finally, once you've finished, you can click the Test Connection button to see if the ADO Data Control can build a correct connection string based on the data you've provided.

The values assigned to the data control's properties merit some further explanation. First, as you can see from the finished form shown in Figure 21-12, the ADO Data Control's interface consists of four scroll buttons and a text area whose contents are defined by the control's Caption property. You could hide the control completely by setting its Visible property to False (True is the default), or you could use it to display some additional information about the record being displayed. But instead, we've chosen to simply delete its caption (which by default is set to Adodc1) and change the text area to be the same color as the scroll bars. Second, note that we're using the control to create a dynamic recordset that should reflect changes to the Access database made by other users. (If you don't remember what a dynamic recordset is, see the discussion of the CursorType property in Chapter 12.)

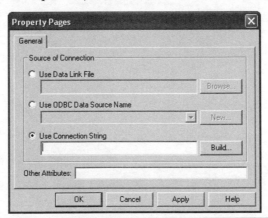

Figure 21-9   *The first step toward building a connection string*

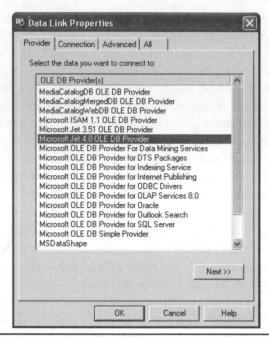

Figure 21-10   *Selecting a data provider*

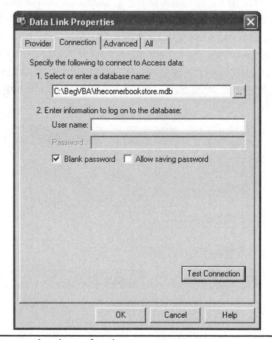

Figure 21-11   *Selecting a database for the connection*

Next, add four Label controls and seven TextBox controls to the form by clicking on each control in the toolbox and then "drawing" and sizing each control on the form. (The Label control appears as an icon with the letter *A* in the toolbox; the TextBox control is to the right of the Label control.) Again, you should place them on the form so that they resemble Figure 21-12.

Once all of the controls are positioned on the form, select all of the text boxes by clicking on the first, then clicking on each successive text box while you hold down the CTRL key. This allows you to change all common properties of these controls to a single value. In the properties window, change the DataSource property to Adodc1, the name of the ADO Data Control. Then select each of the controls individually and change their properties, as shown in Table 21-2.

Control	Property	Value
Label1	Name	lblCustNo
	Caption	Customer Number:
Text1	Name	txtCustNo
	Text	<blank>
	DataField	txtCustNumber
Label2	Name	lblName
	Caption	Name:
Text2	Name	txtFirstName
	Text	<blank>
	DataField	txtCustFirstName
Text3	Name	txtLastName
	Text	<blank>
	DataField	txtCustLastName
Label3	Name	lblAddress
	Caption	Address:
Text4	Name	txtAddress
	Text	<blank>
	DataField	txtAddress
Label4	Name	lblCityState
	Caption	City, State ZipCode:
Text5	Name	txtCity

Table 21-2   *Setting the Properties and Values for the Controls*

Control	Property	Value
	Text	\<blank\>
	DataField	txtCity
Text6	Name	txtState
	Text	\<blank\>
	DataField	txtState
Text7	Name	txtZipCode
	Text	\<blank\>
	DataField	txtZipCode

Table 21-2   *Setting the Properties and Values for the Controls* (continued)

When you're finished, your form should resemble the one shown in Figure 21-12.

Next, run the form by selecting Run | Start or clicking on the Start button on the toolbar. The result should resemble Figure 21-13.

This is a little more cumbersome than creating a bound Access form, but nevertheless it is quite easy. And although you defined some property values and used a series of property sheets to have the ADO Data Control create your ADO connection string, you haven't done any coding. Just as if you were working with an Access form, you could, if you wanted, use VBA to attach code to some of the controls' events, but you already have a fairly functional application.

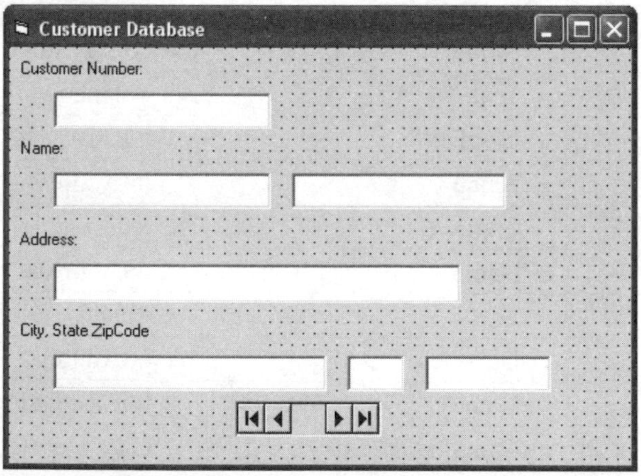

Figure 21-12   *The finished form in design mode*

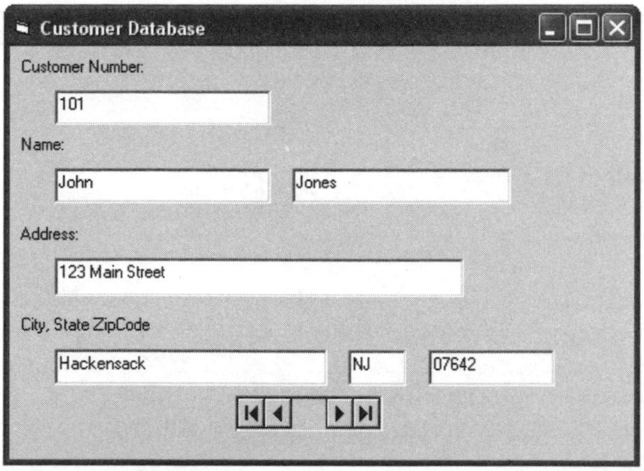

Figure 21-13   *The finished application*

VBScript

VBScript (or Visual Basic Scripting Edition) is a "lightweight" scripting language from which some of the features of VBA (like file access or access to the Win32 API) have been removed. (Many of these features are still available, though, through additional components, such as Microsoft Scripting Runtime, that are included with VBScript.) VBScript has four major applications:

▶ The programming language for Outlook forms

▶ A programming language for Windows Script Host, a collection of components for Windows system administrators and power users

▶ A client-side scripting language for Microsoft Internet Explorer

▶ A server-side scripting language for Active Server Pages, Microsoft's object model to extend Internet Information Server and create dynamic web pages

If your system has access to Internet Information Server, you can create web pages that display data from your Access databases by using VBScript and ADO. The following code, for instance, when saved as an .asp file in a virtual folder, displays the contents of the Customer table, as Figure 21-14 shows.

```
<% Option Explicit %>
<HTML>
<HEAD>
<TITLE>The Corner Bookstore Customer Table</TITLE>
<%
```

```
<!-- #INCLUDE VIRTUAL="C:\Program Files\Common Files\System\ado\adovbs.inc" -->
%>
<SCRIPT LANGUAGE="VBSCRIPT" RUNAT="SERVER">


Function GetRecordset()
    On Error Resume Next
    Dim con, rs

    Set con = CreateObject("ADODB.Connection")
    Set rs = CreateObject("ADODB.Recordset")

    con.Open "Provider=Microsoft.Jet.OLEDB.4.0;" & _
        "Data Source=C:\BegVBA\thecornerbookstore.mdb;"

    rs.CursorType = adOpenForwardOnly
    rs.CursorLocation = adUserClient
    rs.Open "SELECT * FROM tblCustomer", con
    Set GetRecordset = rs
End Function

</SCRIPT>
</HEAD>
<BODY>
<H1><CENTER>The Corner Bookstore</CENTER></H1>
<H2>Customer List</H2>
<TABLE>
<%
    Dim rs, fld

    Set rs = GetRecordset()

    ' Iterate fields for field names
    Dim strField
    Dim iPos


    Response.Write "<TR>"
    For Each fld in rs.Fields
        strField = fld.Name

        ' Remove "txt" from field name
        iPos = Instr(strField, "txt")
        If iPos = 1 Then strField = Mid(strField, 4)
        ' Spell out "customer" in field name
        iPos = Instr(strField, "Cust")
        If iPos = 1 Then strField = "Customer " & Mid(strField, 5)
        Response.Write "<TH>" & strField & "</TH>"
```

```
   Next
   Response.Write "</TR>"

   ' Position pointer to beginning of file
   rs.MoveFirst

   ' Display records
   Do While Not rs.EOF
      Response.Write "<TR>"
      For Each fld in rs.Fields
         Response.Write "<TD>" & fld.Value & "</TD>"
      Next
      Response.Write "</TR>"
      rs.MoveNext
   Loop
%>
</TABLE>
</BODY>
</HTML>
```

A good deal of the code consists of HTML statements, either directly or through code inserted into the output stream by the ASP Response.Write statement. The remainder of the page consists of VBScript and ADO code. Much of it is more or less identical to the code used to display the Customer table in Excel earlier in this chapter. The remaining code simply iterates the recordset's fields to display their

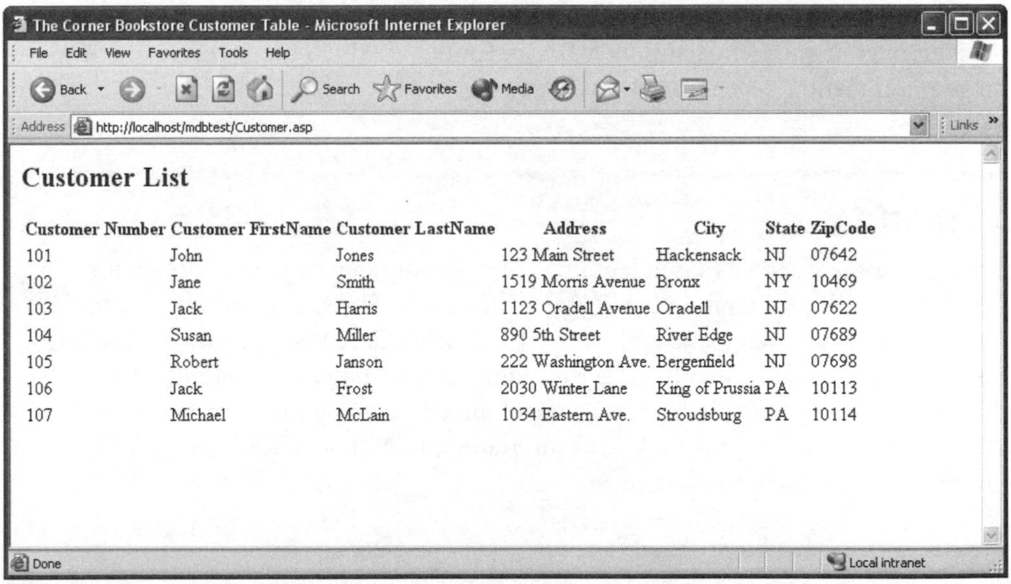

Figure 21-14   *Output from an Active Server Page built with VBScript*

names and then iterates the recordset itself to display the values of each field in each record. Once again, this is a more or less straightforward extension of VBA code with which you're already familiar.

Although you may be unfamiliar with many of the details needed to create ASP pages—you may not know how to configure IIS, what the ASP object model is like, or what syntax is required in ASP pages—nevertheless, given your knowledge of VBA and ADO, you have a firm basis to begin developing web applications with ASP if you choose to do so.

Transition to Microsoft .NET

Microsoft .NET represents Microsoft's next-generation application development framework. It is accompanied by .NET-enabled languages, particularly Visual Basic .NET and Visual C# .NET. Although Visual Basic .NET is a fully object-oriented language that differs in significant ways from Visual Basic, VBA code and Visual Basic .NET code are recognizably similar, and some code written for Visual Basic even compiles and runs successfully in a .NET environment.

Along with a new version of Visual Basic, the .NET platform includes a new data access technology, ADO.NET. Here too, although ADO.NET differs in significant ways from its predecessor, ADO, the code is recognizably similar to ADO.NET code.

The point of all this is that as you make the transition to the .NET platform and the next generation of Microsoft development tools and technologies, the skills you have already acquired by learning VBA and ADO will help you to more quickly master application development for .NET.

Summary

This chapter has shown that in learning Access programming, you're beginning to develop a set of programming skills that can be transferred to a number of other programming environments, including Microsoft Office, Visual Basic, and Active Server Pages developed with VBScript. Similarly, despite the differences between the current generation of Microsoft's development technologies and Microsoft's .NET platform, your skills in Access programming will help you more quickly learn how to develop .NET applications.

APPENDIX

The DoCmd Object

O ne of the more interesting objects in the Access object model is DoCmd. DoCmd originally appeared in Versions 1.0 and 2.0 of Access Basic, before a standardized version of Visual Basic for Applications became the programming language of Access. With the incorporation of VBA into Access, DoCmd then changed from a language component to a portion of the object model. In any case, it remains one of the more unique features of Access, notable for the diversity of its functionality. This appendix documents the methods supported by the DoCmd object.

The methods of the DoCmd object also correspond more or less directly to "macro actions" that are available in the Action column of the Macro dialog box. However, a few macro actions (MsgBox, RunApp, RunCode, SendKeys, SetValue, StopAllMacros, and StopMacro) were not implemented as members of the DoCmd object, since they are readily available as parts of VBA itself.

In Access, the DoCmd object is returned by the DoCmd property of the Application object. Since Application is a global object (that is, its members can be called from code without requiring that a reference to an Application object be instantiated), the methods of the DoCmd object can be called as follows:

```
DoCmd.<method_name>
```

In the syntax statements, parameter names are indicated in italics. For example, in the statement

```
DoCmd.SetWarnings WarningsOn
```

WarningsOn is the method's single parameter. This is the name that you use if you are using named arguments in calling a method. For example:

```
DoCmd.SetWarnings WarningsOn:=True
```

If you are using positional arguments, you replace the parameter placeholder with the value you want to pass to the method.. For example:

```
DoCmd.SetWarnings False
```

Many of the method calls have optional arguments, which are indicated by brackets in the syntax statements in this appendix. In general, these can be omitted, except that if you are using positional arguments, commas serving as placeholders must be present to indicate omitted optional values that precede an optional value that is provided. If you are using named arguments, all optional arguments can simply be omitted.

AddMenu

AddMenu, which was added as a method of the DoCmd object in Access 2000, is intended to add menu items taken from macro commands that have been assigned a group macro name to a form's menu bar or its pop-up menu. However, I was unable to get the method to work reliably.

ApplyFilter

Applies a filter to a table, form, or report.

Syntax

```
DoCmd.ApplyFilter [FilterName][, WhereCondition]
```

with the following parameters:

FilterName

The name of a filter saved as a query, or of a query to which a filter condition is to be attached.

WhereCondition

The WHERE clause of a SQL statement (the filter).

Example

```
Private Sub cmdFilter_Click()

Dim strState As String, strFilter As String

strState = InputBox("Enter state whose customers will be shown:")
' If null string, clear filter
If strState = "" Then
    DoCmd.ShowAllRecords
Else
    strFilter = "txtState = '" & strState & "'"
    DoCmd.ApplyFilter , strFilter
End If
Debug.Print Me.Filter

End Sub
```

Comments

► Calling the ApplyFilter method is equivalent to setting the Filter property of a form.

► The *WhereCondition* clause does not actually include the SQL WHERE keyword, as the example shows.

► To clear a filter, you can either assign a null string to a form's Filter property or call DoCmd.ShowAllRecords.

► Either the *FilterName* or the *WhereCondition* argument should be supplied. If both are supplied, *WhereCondition* is used.

Beep

Makes a sound using the computer's built-in speaker.

Syntax

```
DoCmd.Beep()
```

Example

The following code causes the computer to sound a beep whenever the user enters a non-numeric value in the zip code field:

```
Private Sub txtZipCode_Change()
   If Not IsNumeric(Me.txtZipCode) Then
      Beep
   End If
End Sub
```

Comments

▶ The Beep method corresponds to the intrinsic VBA Beep statement.

▶ The duration and frequency of the beep are hardware dependent.

▶ On systems with sound cards, the beep is defined by the sound assigned to the Default Beep program event in the Control Panel Sounds applet.

▶ Although calls to DoCmd.Beep or the Beep statement may be appropriate in some cases (such as particular kinds of data entry errors), they are rarely used in VBA programming.

CancelEvent

Cancels a cancelable event (an event that has a Cancel parameter).

Syntax

```
DoCmd.CancelEvent()
```

Example

The following example displays a dialog asking the user whether he or she wants to save changes to a record. If the user clicks the No button, then the CancelEvent method is called to cancel the update.

```
Private Sub Form_BeforeUpdate(Cancel As Integer)
   If MsgBox("Are you sure you want to save changes to this record?", _
            vbYesNo Or vbInformation, "Confirm Upate") = vbNo Then
      DoCmd.CancelEvent
   End If
End Sub
```

Comments

▶ The CancelEvent method can only be called inside an event procedure.

▶ Calling the CancelEvent method is equivalent to setting an event handler's Cancel parameter to True.

▶ If an event is not cancelable (has no Cancel parameter), calls to the CancelEvent method have no effect.

Close

Closes the window of an Access object.

Syntax

```
DoCmd.Close([ObjectType][, ObjectName][, Save])
```

with the following parameters:

ObjectType

An AcObjectType constant indicating the type of object to close. Possible values are acDataAccessPage, acDefault (the active window), acDiagram, acForm, acFunction, acMacro, acModule (a VBA module), acQuery, acReport, acServerView, acStoredProcedure, and acTable.

ObjectName

A String indicating the name of an object of type *ObjectType*.

Save

An AcCloseSave constant indicating whether changes should be saved. Possible values are acSaveNo, acSavePrompt (the default value), and acSaveYes.

Example

The example iterates the AllTables collection to determine if a table is open. If it is, it prompts the user to close it.

```
Public Sub CloseTables()

Dim tbls As AllTables
Dim tbl As Variant
```

```
Set tbls = Access.Application.CurrentData.AllTables
For Each tbl In tbls
    If tbl.IsLoaded Then
        If vbYes = MsgBox("Close " & tbl.Name & "?") Then
            DoCmd.Close acTable, tbl.Name, acSavePrompt
        End If
    End If
Next

End Sub
```

Comments

▶ If the object to be closed is a form with a required field that is blank, no error or warning will be displayed, and any changes will be aborted. This contrasts with forms closed by the Close button, the Close macro action, or the File | Close menu item, all of which display a message box in this case.

▶ Close is typically used with all of its optional arguments omitted to close the object from which the code is running. The optional arguments are typically supplied when the Close method is used to close some other object.

▶ No error is generated if *ObjectName* is not open or does not exist. Instead, the method call is simply ignored.

CopyDatabaseFile

The method is intended to copy the current database to a backup file. However, it consistently returns runtime error 2046, "The command or action 'CopyDatabaseFile' isn't available now."

CopyObject

Copies a database object into the same or another database.

Syntax

```
DoCmd.CopyObject([DestinationDatabase][, NewName][,

                SourceObjectType][, SourceObjectName])
```

with the following parameters:

DestinationDatabase

   The path and filename of the Access database to which the object is to be copied. If the current database, the argument should be omitted.

NewName

   The name to be given the copy of the object. If it is to have the same name as *SourceObjectName*, this argument can be omitted.

SourceObjectType

   An AcObjectType constant indicating the type of object to copy. Possible values are acDataAccessPage, acDefault (the object selected in the Database window), acDiagram, acForm, acFunction, acMacro, acModule (a VBA module), acQuery, acReport, acServerView, acStoredProcedure, and acTable.

SourceObjectName

   The name of the object to be copied.

Example

```
Public Sub MakeBackupCopy()

    ' Make backup copy of Purchases table
    DoCmd.CopyObject , "tblPurchases Backup", acTable, "tblPurchases"
    ' Disable warnings
    DoCmd.SetWarnings False

    'Run update query to multiple prices by 10%
    DoCmd.OpenQuery "UpdatePrices"

    ' Turn warnings back on
    DoCmd.SetWarnings True

End Sub
```

Comments

▶   Although all arguments are optional, either the *DestinationDatabase* or *NewName* argument must be provided. This is because Access must make a copy of the object either in the same database (in which case it needs to name the copy something other than the original object) or in another database (where it can presumably use the object's original name).

▶   The default action of the method (if *SourceObjectName* is not provided and *SourceObjectType* is *acDefault* or is not provided) is to copy the object selected in the Database window. This can be controlled programmatically with the DoCmd.SelectObject method.

▶   The CopyObject method is particularly useful before executing a query that may change multiple records in a table, such as an update query.

▶   If warnings are on (see the SetWarnings method) and the object indicated by *NewName* already exists (that is, if the method is attempting to assign the copy a name that has already been assigned to an object), Access will prompt whether to overwrite it. If warnings are off, Access will simply overwrite the object named *NewName*.

DeleteObject

Deletes a database object.

Syntax

```
DoCmd.DeleteObject([ObjectType][, ObjectName])
```

with the following parameters:

ObjectType

An AcObjectType constant indicating the type of object to delete. Possible values are acDataAccessPage, acDefault (the object selected in the Database window), acDiagram, acForm, acFunction, acMacro, acModule (a VBA module), acQuery, acReport, acServerView, acStoredProcedure, and acTable.

ObjectName

The name of the object of type *ObjectType* to be deleted.

Example

The example cycles through backup tables (tables that include "Backup" in the filename), prompts the user whether each should be deleted, and deletes the table if the user responds affirmatively.

```
Public Sub DeleteBackupTables()

   Dim tbl As Variant

   ' Iterate tables
   For Each tbl In CurrentData.AllTables
      If InStr(1, tbl.Name, "Backup", vbTextCompare) > 0 Then
         If vbYes = MsgBox("Delete table " & tbl.Name & "?", _
                           vbYesNoCancel Or vbQuestion, _
                           "Confirm Table Deletion") Then
            DoCmd.DeleteObject acTable, tbl.Name
         End If
      End If
   Next

End Sub
```

Comments

▶ If no object type or object name is specified, Access deletes the object selected
  in the Database window. This can be controlled programmatically with the
  DoCmd.SelectObject method.

▶ If *ObjectName* does not exist, Access generates runtime error 7874.

DoMenuItem

This method executes a command that corresponds to a menu item. However, its
syntax and usage assume menus for Access 1.0, Access 2.0, and Access 95. It was
replaced by the DoCmd object's RunCommand method (documented later in this
appendix) and should be avoided.

Echo

Controls whether the Access interface is repainted.

Syntax

```
DoCmd.Echo EchoOn[, StatusBarText]
```

with the following parameters:

EchoOn

An Integer or Boolean that indicates whether interface repainting is on.

StatusBarText

A String containing the text to appear in the application's status bar as a result of the method call.

Example

```
Private Sub Form_Load()
    DoCmd.Echo False, "Application loading..."
    DoCmd.Hourglass True
    ' Load images for opening screen
    DoCmd.Echo True, "Screen update turned on..."
    DoCmd.Hourglass False
End Sub
```

Comments

▶   DoCmd.Echo is a "compatibility" command. It is identical to the Application.Echo method, whose usage is preferred.

▶   Typically, the Echo method is called to turn off window repainting in operations that draw or write frequently to the application window, thereby improving the application's performance and eliminating screen flicker.

▶   Since only a call to Echo can turn window repainting back on once it has been turned off, it's a good idea to create an Autokeys macro that allows window repainting to be turned back on in the event of an error.

▶   Functions that produce a user interface, such as the MsgBox or InputBox functions, should not be called when screen repainting has been set off.

FindNext

Finds the next record that meets the criteria defined by the FindRecord method or the Find dialog box (available by selecting Edit | Find).

Syntax

```
DoCmd.FindNext()
```

Example

See the example for the FindRecord method.

FindRecord

Searches for the first record that meets designated criteria.

Syntax

```
DoCmd.FindRecord(FindWhat, Match, MatchCase, Search,
                 SearchAsFormatted, OnlyCurrentField, FindFirst)
```

with the following parameters:

FindWhat

The Variant containing the data to search for. It can be text, a number, or a date.

Match

A member of the AcFindMatch enumeration that defines where in the field Access looks for the match. Possible values are acAnywhere (the search value can be found anywhere in the field), acEntire (the search value must match the entire field), and acStart (the search value must match the start of the field). The default is acEntire.

MatchCase

A Boolean indicating whether the search is case sensitive (True) or not (False).

Search

A member of the AcSearchDirection enumeration indicating the direction of the search. Possible values are acDown, acSearchAll, and acUp.

SearchAsFormatted

A Boolean that indicates whether to search for data as it's formatted (True) or as it's stored in the database (False). The default is False.

OnlyCurrentField

A member of the AcFindField enumeration defining the fields to be searched. Possible values are acAll (all fields of the record) and acCurrent (only the current field). The default is acCurrent.

FindFirst

A Boolean that determines where in the database the search starts. If True, the search starts at the beginning of the database. If False, it starts at the record after the current record.

Example

```
Private Sub cmdFind_Click()
    On Error GoTo Err_Hand:

    Dim strSearchString As String

    strSearchString = "Street"

    If Me.cmdFind.Caption = "Find" Then
        Me.txtAddress.SetFocus
        DoCmd.FindRecord strSearchString, acAnywhere, False,
        acDown, , acAll, False
        Me.cmdFind.Caption = "Find Next"
    Else
        If Not Me.Recordset.EOF Then DoCmd.GoToRecord , , acNext

        If Not Me.Recordset.EOF Then
            DoCmd.FindNext
        Else
            Me.cmdFind.Caption = "Find"
            DoCmd.GoToRecord , , acFirst
        End If
    End If

    Exit Sub
Err_Hand:

    ' search failed, go to beginning of file
    DoCmd.GoToRecord , , acFirst

End Sub
```

Comments

► To search for additional records that match the search criteria, use the FindNext method.

► You're responsible for tracking and handling the record pointer between calls to the FindRecord and FindNext methods.

GoToControl

Moves the focus to a particular control on a form.

Syntax

```
DoCmd.GoToControl ControlName
```

where *ControlName* is the name of a control on the active form.

Comments

▶ The GoToControl method does not allow you to designate a control on a form other than the active form.

▶ The GoToControl method has been superseded by the SetFocus method, which is much more flexible.

GoToPage

Moves to a designated page of a multipage form.

Syntax

```
DoCmd.GoToPage PageNumber[, Right][, Down]
```

with the following parameters:

PageNumber
    A valid page number on the current form.

Right
    A horizontal offset in twips indicating which part of the page you want displayed.

Down
    A vertical offset in twips indicating which part of the page you want displayed.

Comments

▶ If *PageNumber* is omitted, the focus remains on the current page.

▶ The *Right* and *Down* arguments have an effect only if the page exceeds the visible area of the screen.

▶ The GoToPage method is little used, in part because it's been replaced by the Form.GoToPage method, and in part because the Tab control offers a superior method of presenting multipage form data.

GoToRecord

Moves the record pointer to a particular record.

Syntax

```
DoCmd.GoToRecord [ObjectType][, ObjectName][, Record][, Offset]
```

with the following parameters:

ObjectType

An AcDataObjectType constant indicating the type of data in which the record pointer is to move. Possible values are acActiveDataObject (the currently active data object, which is the default value), acDataForm (a form's data), acDataFunction, acDataQuery (a query's data), acDataServerView, acDataStoredProcedure, and acDataTable (a table's data).

ObjectName

The name of the object of type *ObjectType*.

Record

An AcRecord constant indicating the record to go to. Possible values are acFirst (the first record), acGoTo (go to the record specified by the *Offset* argument), acLast (the last record), acNewRec (a new record), acNext (the next record, which is the default value), and acPrevious (the previous record).

Offset

The number of records to move backward (if *Record* is acPrevious) or forward (if *Record* is acNext), or the record number to go to (if *Record* is acGoTo).

Example

See the example for the FindRecord method.

Comments

▶ When used with acGoTo, *Record* represents the position of the record in the current recordset. This is not a permanent value, but rather it changes when records are added and deleted and the recordset is sorted.

▶ The GoToRecord method corresponds to selecting the Edit | GoTo menu option.

Hourglass

Displays the hourglass mouse pointer.

Syntax

```
DoCmd.Hourglass HourglassOn
```

where *HourglassOn* is a Boolean that indicates whether the hour glass is on (True) or off (False).

Example

See the example for the Echo method.

Comments

▶ Remember to turn the hourglass off at the appropriate time. It will not turn itself off automatically.

▶ The actual icon used by Access is defined by the Busy pointer on the Pointers tab of the Mouse Control Panel applet.

▶ The Hourglass method can be used along with the Echo method, so that the hourglass appears when screen repainting is turned off.

Maximize

Maximizes the current object window in the Access interface.

Syntax

```
DoCmd.Maximize()
```

Comments

The method affects only the window that has the focus. To change the focus from one window to another in order to maximize it, you can call the DoCmd.SelectObject method.

Minimize

Minimizes the current object window in the Access interface.

Syntax

```
DoCmd.Minimize()
```

Comments

The method affects only the window that has the focus. To change the focus from one window to another in order to minimize it, you can call the DoCmd.SelectObject method.

MoveSize

Repositions and/or resizes an object window.

Syntax

```
DoCmd.MoveSize [Right][, Down][, Width][, Height]
```

with the following parameters:

Right

The new horizontal starting position of the window, expressed as the number of twips from the main Access window's right edge.

Down

The new vertical starting position of the window, expressed as the number of twips from the main Access window's top edge.

Width

The new width of the window in twips.

Height

The new height of the window in twips.

Comments

► Although all arguments are optional, at least one argument must be included or an error results.

► If any arguments are omitted, the window's current value is used.

► A twip is 1/20 of a point. There are 1440 twips per inch.

► To size a form so its contents fit exactly, use the RunCommand method of the Application object as follows:

```
RunCommand acCmdSizeToFitForm
```

OpenDataAccessPage

Opens a data access page in the current database.

Syntax

```
DoCmd.OpenDataAccessPage DataAccessPageName[, View]
```

with the following parameters

DataAccessPageName

The name of the data access page.

View

A member of the AcDataAccessPageView enumeration indicating the view in which the page should be opened. Possible values are acDataAccessPageBrowse (the default) and acDataAccessPageDesign.

Comments

The OpenDataAccessPage method was first introduced in Access 2000.

OpenDiagram

Opens a diagram from an Access Data Project.

Syntax

```
DoCmd.OpenDiagram DiagramName
```

where *DiagramName* is a string indicating the name of the diagram.

Comments

The OpenDiagram method was first introduced in Access 2000.

OpenForm

Opens a form in the current database.

Syntax

```
DoCmd.OpenForm(FormName[, View][, FilterName][, WhereCondition][,
            DataMode][, WindowMode][, OpenArgs])
```

with the following parameters:

FormName

A String indicating the name of the form to open.

View

An AcFormView constant indicating the view in which to open *FormName*. Possible values are acDesign (design view), acFormDS (a datasheet), acFormPivotChart (a pivot chart), acFormPivotTable (a pivot table), acNormal (normal view, the default), and acPreview (print preview).

FilterName

A String containing the name of a query in the current database.

WhereCondition

A String containing a valid SQL WHERE clause (without the WHERE keyword).

DataMode

An AcFormOpenDataMode constant that defines the mode in which the form is opened. Possible values are acFormAdd (the user can add new records but can't edit existing ones), acFormEdit (the user can edit existing records and add new ones, acFormPropertySettings (the mode is determined by the form's existing property values, which is the default value), and acFormReadOnly (the form is read-only).

WindowMode

An AcWindowMode constant that determines the state of the form's window. Possible values are acDialog (sets the form's Modal and Popup properties to Yes), acHidden (the form is not visible), acIcon (the form is minimized), and acWindowNormal (the form is opened based on its property settings, which is the default).

OpenArgs

A value to be assigned to the form's OpenArgs property. Typically, this is used to take some custom action in the form's Load or Open event procedure. For example, you might want a multi-page form to open to a particular page. In that case, you'd open the form as follows:

```
DoCmd.openForm "MultiPageForm", acNormal, , , acFormReadOnly, , 3
```

You can then go to the third page of the form by using the following event handler:

```
Private Sub Form_Open(Cancel As Integer)
   DoCmd.GoToPage 3
End Sub
```

Example

The example prompts the user for a sales representative number, then displays a list of his or her customers.

```
Public Sub OpenSalesRepList()

Dim intSalesRep As Integer
Dim sInput As String

sInput = InputBox("Enter Sales Rep Number: ")
If Not IsNumeric(sInput) Then
   Exit Sub
Else
   intSalesRep = CInt(sInput)
End If
```

```
DoCmd.OpenForm "frmRegional", , , "intSalesRep = " & intSalesRep, _
            acFormReadOnly

End Sub
```

Comments

The various arguments to the function, and particularly the ability to override the form's preassigned or default property values (like the Visible property or the EventArgs property), give the OpenForm function enormous power and flexibility.

OpenFunction

Opens a user-defined function in a SQL Server database for viewing in Access.

Syntax

```
DoCmd.OpenFunction FunctionName[, View][, DataMode]
```

with the following parameters:

FunctionName

The name of the function to open.

View

A member of the AcView enumeration defining the view in which to open the function. Practical values are acViewDesign, acViewNormal, and acViewPreview.

DataMode

An AcOpenDataMode constant that defines the mode in which the function is opened. Possible values are acAdd (the user can add new code but can't edit existing code), acEdit (the user can edit existing code and add new code), and acReadOnly (the code is read-only).

Comments

▶ The OpenFunction method was first introduced in Access for Office XP.

▶ To determine what functions are available, you can iterate the Application.AllFunctions collection.

OpenModule

Opens a code module.

Syntax

`DoCmd.OpenModule [ModuleName][, ProcedureName]`

with the following parameters:

ModuleName
   The name of the module to open.

ProcedureName
   The name of the procedure to display in the window.

Comments

▶ Though both arguments are optional, one must be included.

▶ If *ModuleName* is omitted, Access searches all standard code modules in the database for *ProcedureName*.

▶ If *ProcedureName* is not provided, Access opens the code module to the declarations section.

▶ You might use this method to automate opening code modules while programming. You would rarely, if ever, want it to run in code executed by end-users.

OpenQuery

Opens a query in the current database.

Syntax

`DoCmd.OpenQuery QueryName[, View][, DataMode]`

with the following parameters:

QueryName
   A string indicating the name of the query.

View

One of the following members of the AcView enumeration: acViewDesign (design view or SQL view), acViewNormal (open in datasheet view or run an action query), or acViewPreview (print preview). The default is acViewNormal.

DataMode

For queries opened in acViewNormal view, one of the following AcOpenDataMode constants to indicate what the user can do with the query: acAdd, acEdit (the default), or acReadOnly.

Example

See the example for the CopyObject method.

Comments

▶ The OpenQuery method only works with queries stored in an Access database (an MDB file). In an Access Data Project (ADP) environment, use the OpenView or OpenStoredProcedure methods.

▶ This method is most useful for running update queries. Select queries, on the other hand, are most useful when used with Access forms.

OpenReport

Opens a report.

Syntax

```
DoCmd.OpenReport ReportName[, View][, FilterName][, WhereCondition][,
                 WindowMode][, OpenArgs]
```

with the following parameters:

ReportName

A String containing the name of the report in the current database.

View

One of the following members of the AcView enumeration: acViewDesign, acViewNormal (prints the report immediately, the default), and acViewPreview.

FilterName

The name of a query in the current database upon which the report will be based.

WhereCondition

A string containing a SQL WHERE clause without the WHERE keyword.

WindowMode

One of the following AcWindowMode constants defining the state of the open window: acDialog (sets the report's Modal and Popup properties to Yes), acHidden (the report is not visible), acIcon (the report is minimized), and acWindowNormal (the default; the report is opened based on its property settings).

OpenArgs

A value to be assigned to the report's OpenArgs property. Typically, this is used to take some action in the report's Load or Open event procedure.

Example

```
Public Sub PrintCustomerRpt()

Dim strReportName As String

strReportName = "rptCustomerList"

DoCmd.OpenReport strReportName, acViewPreview, , "txtState = 'NJ'"
DoCmd.PrintOut acPages, 1, 2

End Sub
```

Comments

- ▶ Once you've opened the report in preview mode, you can print a selected number of its pages by calling the DoCmd.PrintOut method. This is illustrated in the example.

- ▶ You can retrieve the names of all reports in the database programmatically by iterating the AllReports collection. It is available by retrieving the value of the AllReports property of the Application.CurrentProject object.

OpenStoredProcedure

Opens a stored procedure in an Access Data Project.

Syntax

```
DoCmd.OpenStoredProcedure ProcedureName[, View][, DataMode]
```

with the following parameters:

ProcedureName

A String defining the name of the stored procedure.

View

One of the following members of the AcView enumeration: acViewDesign (design view), acViewNormal (runs the stored procedure and displays the results, the default), and acViewPreview (opens the stored procedure in print preview).

DataMode

A member of the AcOpenDataMode enumeration for stored procedures opened in acNormal view. Possible values are acAdd, acEdit (the default), and acReadOnly.

Comments

The OpenStoredProcedure method was first introduced in Access 2000.

OpenTable

Opens a table in the current database.

Syntax

```
DoCmd.OpenTable TableName[, View][, DataMode]
```

with the following parameters:

TableName

A String indicating the name of the table in the current database to open.

View

One of the following members of the AcView enumeration: acViewDesign (design view), acViewNormal (datasheet view, the default), and acViewPreview (print preview).

DataMode

A member of the AcOpenDataMode enumeration for tables opened in acNormal view. Possible values are acAdd, acEdit (the default), and acReadOnly.

Example

The example code iterates the AllTables collection, opens each nonsystem table, prints its structure, and then closes the open table.

```
Public Sub PrintTableStructures()

Dim tbl As Variant

For Each tbl In CurrentData.AllTables

    If InStr(1, tbl.Name, "MSys", vbBinaryCompare) = 0 Then
        DoCmd.OpenTable tbl.Name, acViewDesign
        If MsgBox("Print table structure?", _
                    vbQuestion Or vbYesNoCancel, _
                    "Print Table Structure") = vbYes Then
            DoCmd.PrintOut acPrintAll
        End If
        DoCmd.Close acTable, tbl.Name, acSaveNo
    End If
Next

End Sub
```

Comments

You can iterate the tables in the current database by using the CurrentData.AllTables collection. It includes system tables whose names begin with MSys..., however.

OpenView

Opens a view in an Access Data Project.

Syntax

```
DoCmd.OpenView ViewName[, View][, DataMode]
```

with the following parameters:

ViewName

A string indicating the name of the view in the current database to open.

View

An AcView constant indicating in which view the ADP view will open. Possible values are acViewDesign (design view), acViewNormal (datasheet view, the default), and acViewPreview (print preview).

DataMode

An AcOpenDataMode constant defining the data entry mode for views opened in acNormal view. Possible values are acAdd, acEdit (the default), and acReadOnly.

Comments

The OpenView method was first introduced in Access 2000.

OutputTo

Exports a database object in a variety of formats.

Syntax

```
DoCmd.OutputTo ObjectType[, ObjectName][, OutputFormat][,
               OutputFile][, AutoStart][, TemplateFile][, Encoding]
```

with the following parameters:

ObjectType

An AcOutputObjectType constant indicating the type of object to export. Possible values are acOutputForm (a form object), acOutputFunction (a SQL Server user-defined function), acOutputModule (a code module), acOutputQuery (a query object), acOutputReport (a report object), acOutputServerView (a SQL Server view), acOutputStoredProcedure (a SQL Server stored procedure), and acOutputTable (a table object).

ObjectName

The name of the object to export. If omitted, Access exports the active object of type *ObjectType*.

OutputFormat

An AcFormat constant indicating the export format. Possible values are acFormatASP (Active Server Page), acFormatHTML (HTML file), acFormatIIS (IIS .htx or .idc file), acFormatRTF (RTF file for Word or other word processors), acFormatTXT (plain text file), and acFormatXLS (Excel workbook file).

OutputFile

The path and filename of the output file.

AutoStart

A Boolean that determines whether the application that handles *OutputFile* should open and load the file. Its default value is False.

TemplateFile

The path and filename of a file to serve as a template for exported ASP, HTML, and IIS .htx files.

Encoding

A Boolean indicating whether the export file is to be encoded.

Example

The following code exports the customer table in each of the supported formats except XML:

```
Public Sub ExportTable()

    DoCmd.OutputTo acOutputTable, "tblCustomer", acFormatASP, _
                "C:\BegVBA\Customer.asp"
    DoCmd.OutputTo acOutputTable, "tblCustomer", acFormatHTML, _
                "C:\BegVBA\Customer.html"
    DoCmd.OutputTo acOutputTable, "tblCustomer", acFormatIIS, _
                "C:\BegVBA\Customer.htx"
    DoCmd.OutputTo acOutputTable, "tblCustomer", acFormatRTF, _
                "C:\BegVBA\Customer.rtf"
    DoCmd.OutputTo acOutputTable, "tblCustomer", acFormatTXT, _
                "C:\BegVBA\Customer.txt"
    DoCmd.OutputTo acOutputTable, "tblCustomer", acFormatXLS, _
                "C:\BegVBA\Customer.xls"

End Sub
```

Comments

▶ The acOutputDataAccessPage constant is documented but not supported as a value of the *OutputFormat* argument.

▶ The acFormatDAP and acFormatSNP constants are documented but not supported by the DoCmd method.

▶ You can generate an XML file (possibly along with an XSD file) by omitting the *OutputFormat* argument and selecting XML from the Output To dialog box. (XML does not have an intrinsic constant in Access 2003.)

▶ If the *OutputFormat* and *OutputFile* arguments are omitted, Access prompts for the export file type and export filename, respectively.

▶ In the case of ASP and IIS files, *OutputFile* seems to require a file extension; otherwise, Access adds an appropriate extension if it isn't already present.

▶ If *AutoStart* is True, the application launched to handle the exported file is defined by the system registry.

▶ The *AutoStart* argument is ignored for IIS and ASP files.

▶ Generally, the exported files appear to be much more robust than in some previous versions of Access. I was unable to get IIS .htx/.idc files to work at all, and ASP pages required minor tweaking (an ADO connection string had to be added to the call to the Connection object's Open method), but all remaining exported files accurately reflected the Access data and did not require modification.

▶ Except for an ASP page, which uses ADO to retrieve live data from the database, all exported files contain static data; they provide a snapshot of the data at a given point in time.

PrintOut

Prints all or part of the active object's data.

Syntax

```
DoCmd.PrintOut [PrintRange][, PageFrom][, PageTo][,
                PrintQuality][, Copies][, CollateCopies]
```

with the following parameters:

PrintRange

One of the following AcPrintRange constants designating the range to be printed: acPages (print a range of pages), acPrintAll (print the entire object's data, the default value), and acSelection (print selected data).

PageFrom

The starting page to print if *PrintRange* equals acPages.

PageTo

The ending page to print if *PrintRange* equals acPages.

PrintQuality

An AcPrintQuality constant indicating the desired print quality. Possible values are acDraft, acHigh (the default), acLow, and acMedium.

Copies

A Variant Integer that determines how many copies are to print. The default is 1.

CollateCopies

A Boolean that determines whether copies are collated. The default is True.

Example

See the example for the OpenReport method.

Comments

▶ The PrintOut method simply prints; it does not display a Print dialog box.

▶ You can print datasheets, reports, forms, Data Access Pages, and modules.

▶ Typically, you'd want to call the SelectObject method of the DoCmd object to select an object before calling the PrintOut method.

Quit

Quits the Access application.

Syntax

```
DoCmd.Quit [Options]
```

where *Options* is an AcQuitOption constant that determines how changes are handled. Possible values are acQuitPrompt, acQuitSaveall (the default), and acQuitSaveNone.

Comments

The Quit method has been retained for compatibility with Access 95. The recommended method of quitting an application is to call the Quit method of the Application object, which has the same *Options* parameter.

Rename

Renames a database object.

Syntax

```
DoCmd.Rename NewName[, ObjectType][, OldName]
```

with the following parameters:

NewName

 A String defining the new name of the object.

ObjectType

 An AcObjectType constant indicating the type of object to be renamed. Possible values are acDataAccessPage, acDefault (the object selected in the Database window, the default value), acDiagram, acForm, acFunction (a SQL Server user-defined function), acMacro, acModule, and acQuery, acReport, acServerView, acStoredProcedure, and acTable.

OldName

 A String containing the old name of the object of type *ObjectType*. If omitted, Access renames the selected object.

Example

This sample iterates the AllTables collection looking for a table whose name includes the substring "Backup". It asks whether the user wishes to restore the original table from the backup and if the user agrees, renames the backup file, thereby overwriting the original file.

```
Public Sub RestoreFromBackup()

    Dim tbl As Variant
    Dim intPos As Integer
    Dim strNewName As String
```

```
For Each tbl In CurrentData.AllTables
    intPos = InStr(1, tbl.Name, " Backup")
    If intPos > 0 Then
        strNewName = Left(tbl.Name, intPos - 1)
        If MsgBox("Replace " & strNewName & " with " & tbl.Name _
                & "?", vbYesNoCancel Or vbQuestion, _
                "Rename Table") = vbYes Then
            DoCmd.SetWarnings False
            DoCmd.Rename strNewName, acTable, tbl.Name
            DoCmd.SetWarnings True
        End If
    End If
Next

End Sub
```

Comments

▶ To rename the object selected in the Database window, you can call the
SelectObject method with its *InDatabaseWindow* argument set to True before
calling the Rename method.

▶ An open object cannot be renamed.

▶ If warnings are set on (see the SetWarnings method) and *NewName* already
exists, Access prompts the user whether he or she wants to replace it.

RepaintObject

Like many of the DoCmd object's object selection methods, RepaintObject allows
you to designate the type and name of the object you'd like to repaint. Practically,
however, only forms require repainting. As a result, it's preferable to call the simpler
and more intuitive Form.Repaint() method, which has no parameters.

Requery

Updates the data displayed by a form or control by requerying the database. It does
this by closing and reopening the query upon which forms or controls are based.
Because of this performance hit, you should call the Requery method of the form or
the individual form control, all of which do not close and reopen the query on which
their data is based.

Restore

Restores a maximized or minimized window to its previous size.

Syntax

```
DoCmd.Restore()
```

Comments

The method affects only the window that has the focus. To change the focus from one window to another in order to restore it, you can call the DoCmd.SelectObject method.

RunCommand

Runs a built-in menu or toolbar command. The result is the same as if the item was selected directly from the menu or toolbar.

Syntax

```
expression.RunCommand Command
```

where *Command* is one of 196 AcCommand constants in Access 2003 that represent menu and toolbar items. For details, see the Access documentation or the Object Browser.

Comments

▶ There is a RunCommand method of the Application object that is identical to DoCmd.RunCommand.

▶ RunCommand was introduced in Access 97 with the aim of replacing the rather esoteric syntax of the DoCmd.DoMenuItem method.

RunMacro

Runs a macro.

Syntax

```
DoCmd.RunMacro MacroName[, RepeatCount][, RepeatExpression]
```

with the following parameters:

MacroName
    A String defining the name of the macro in the current database to run.

RepeatCount
    An Integer indicating the number of times the macro is to run.

RepeatExpression
    A numeric expression that causes the macro to terminate when it evaluates to 0 (or False).

Comments

- ▶ *MacroName* can use the MacroGroupName.MacroName syntax to run a particular macro in a macro group.
- ▶ If both *RepeatCount* and *RepeatExpression* are omitted, the macro runs once.
- ▶ If both *RepeatCount* and *RepeatExpression* are used, the macro runs *RepeatCount* times or until *RepeatExpression* is False, whichever occurs first.

RunSQL

Runs a SQL statement.

Syntax

```
DoCmd.RunSQL SQLStatement[, UseTransaction]
```

with the following parameters:

SQLStatement
    A SQL statement for an action query or a data definition query.

UseTransaction
    A Boolean that indicates whether the query is included in a transaction. Its default value is True.

Example

The following UPDATE query replaces the substring "Street" in the txtAddress field of the tblCustomer table with the substring "St.":

```
Public Sub RunStreetUpdate()

Dim strSQL As String

' Make backup copy of tblCustomer
DoCmd.CopyObject , "tblCustomer Backup", acTable, "tblCustomer"

' Change "Street" to "St."
strSQL = "UPDATE tblCustomer " & _
        "SET tblCustomer.txtAddress =
Replace([tblcustomer].[txtAddress],'Street','St.') " & _
        "WHERE ((InStr([tblcustomer].[txtaddress],'Street')>0));"

DoCmd.RunSQL strSQL

End Sub
```

Comments

▶   An action or data definition query includes the SQL statements INSERT INTO, DELETE, SELECT...INTO, UPDATE, CREATE TABLE, ALTER TABLE, DROP TABLE, CREATE INDEX, or DROP INDEX.

▶   To run other queries, use the OpenQuery method.

▶   The RunSQL method can run against MDB databases only.

▶   If you copy the SQL code from the query window's SQL view, you may have to replace embedded double quotation marks with single quotation marks.

Save

Saves the design, layout, or structure of a database object.

Syntax

```
expression.Save [ObjectType][, ObjectName]
```

with the following parameters:

ObjectType

A constant of the AcObjectType enumeration specifying the type of database object to save. Possible values are acDataAccessPage, acDefault (the active object; this is the default value), acDiagram, acForm, acFunction (a user-defined function for SQL Server), acMacro, acModule, acQuery, acReport, acServerView, acStoredProcedure, or acTable.

ObjectName

A String specifying the name of the database object to be saved.

Comments

▶   The Save method corresponds to the File | Save As menu option. That is, it typically saves such things as the state of an object's design, layout, and structure, rather than the state of its data.

▶   If you specify an *ObjectType*, you must also specify an existing object name in the *ObjectName* argument.

▶   If you omit both *ObjectType* and *ObjectName*, Access saves the active object.

▶   If you omit *ObjectType* but provide an *ObjectName* argument, Access saves the object using *ObjectName*, even if this amounts to a renaming operation. In this case, if SetWarnings is True and *ObjectName* already exists, Access will prompt you to confirm that you want to overwrite the file.

SelectObject

Selects a database object in order to perform some operation on it.

Syntax

```
DoCmd.SelectObject ObjectType[, ObjectName][, InDatabaseWindow]
```

with the following parameters:

ObjectType

A constant of the AcObjectType enumeration specifying the type of database object to save. Possible values are acDataAccessPage, acDiagram, acForm, acFunction (a user-defined function for SQL Server), acMacro, acModule, acQuery, acReport, acServerView, acStoredProcedure, or acTable.

ObjectName

A String specifying the name of the object to be selected.

InDatabaseWindow

If True, selects an object in the Database window. If False, the default, selects an object that's already open.

Example

The following code selects and then copies the tblCustomer table:

```
Public Sub SelectAndCopyObject()

Dim strTable As String

DoCmd.SelectObject acTable, "tblCustomer", True
DoCmd.CopyObject , "tblCustomer Original Table"

End Sub
```

Comments

▶ SelectObject works with any object that can receive the focus. It gives the selected database object the focus and, in the case of a hidden form, sets its Visible property to True.

▶ SelectObject can be used to select a database object before calling a method that only applies to the active object.

▶ The documentation lists acDefault as a possible value for *ObjectType*, although in fact it generates a syntax error.

SendObject

Exports a datasheet, form, report, module, or Data Access Page to one of four different formats and sends it in an email as an attachment.

Syntax

```
DoCmd.SendObject [ObjectType][, ObjectName][, OutputFormat][, To][,
                 Cc][, Bcc][, Subject][, MessageText][, EditMessage][,
                 TemplateFile]
```

with the following parameters:

ObjectType

One of the following AcSendObjectType constants: acSendDataAccessPage, acSendForm, acSendModule, acSendNoObject (the default value, which sends an email without including an object), acSendQuery, acSendReport, and acSendTable.

ObjectName

The name of the object of type *ObjectType* to send, or (if omitted) the active object.

OutputFormat

A constant defining the output format of the exported object. Supported values include acFormatHTML, acFormatXLS, acFormatTXT, and acFormatRTF. If omitted, the Send dialog box opens to prompt for an output format.

To, *Cc*, and *Bcc*

Strings indicating the recipients, copied recipients, and blindly copied recipients of the email. Multiple recipients can be separated by a semicolon or by the list separator defined for numbers in the Control Panel's Regional Settings applet.

Subject

A String specifying the subject line of the email.

MessageText

A string containing the text of the email.

EditMessage

A Boolean determining whether the mail application should immediately open the message for editing after the SendObject method completes. The default is True.

TemplateFile

The path and name of a template to be used for an output HTML file.

Example

The following code sends a variety of Access objects in a number of formats:

```
Public Sub SendEmails()
    Dim strTo As String, strSubject As String, strText As String

    strTo = "ron@howlingwolfconsulting.com"
    strSubject = "The Customer List"
    strText = "Per your request."
```

```
      DoCmd.SendObject acSendTable, "tblCustomer", acFormatHTML, _
                  strTo, , , strSubject, strText, False
      DoCmd.SendObject acSendReport, "rptCustomerList", acFormatHTML, _
                  strTo, , , strSubject, strText, False
      DoCmd.SendObject acSendQuery, "qryCustomer", acFormatRTF, _
                  strTo, , , strSubject, strText, False
      DoCmd.SendObject acSendForm, "frmCustomer", acFormatHTML, _
                  strTo, , , strSubject, strText, False
End Sub
```

Comments

▶ The acSendModule type can only be sent in acFormatTXT, and
   acSendDataAccessPage can only be sent in acSendHTML.

▶ Names or email addresses must be in a format recognized by the email
   application.

SetMenuItem

This method remains in Access for compatibility with Access 95 and earlier versions.
It does not work with the standard Office menu system.

SetWarnings

Turns warning messages on or off.

Syntax

```
DoCmd.SetWarnings WarningsOn
```

where *WarningsOn* is a Boolean that indicates whether warning messages are on
(True) or off (False).

Example

See the example for the Rename method.

Comments

▶ Once you turn warning messages off, they remain off until you turn them back on. Since these messages are often warnings about potentially overwritten and deleted files, and since suppressing warnings amounts to automatically confirming all operations, it is extremely important that you enable warning messages again before your routine terminates.

▶ The SetWarnings method has no effect on error messages.

▶ The SetWarnings method suppresses only modal dialog boxes that allow the user to select command button options (Yes and No, or Yes, No, and Cancel). It does not suppress dialog boxes that expect other forms of user input.

ShowAllRecords

Removes a filter from the current object, which can be a table, query, or a form.

Syntax

```
DoCmd.ShowAllRecords()
```

Example

See the example for the ApplyFilter method.

Comments

The method also requeries the recordset displayed by a form.

ShowToolbar

Displays or hides a built-in or custom toolbar.

Syntax

```
DoCmd.ShowToolbar ToolbarName[, Show]
```

with the following parameters:

ToolbarName

A String specifying the name of a built-in or custom toolbar.

Show

An AcShowToolbar constant defining the toolbar's usage. Possible values are acToolbarNo, acToolbarWhereApprop, and acToolbarYes (the default).

Example

The following code displays the Filter/Sort toolbar whenever a form is activated and hides it whenever the form is deactivated:

```
Private Sub Form_Activate()
   DoCmd.ShowToolbar "Filter/Sort", acToolbarYes
End Sub

Private Sub Form_Deactivate()
   DoCmd.ShowToolbar "Filter/Sort", acToolbarNo
End Sub
```

Comments

▶ acToolbarWhereApprop displays a toolbar with its customary windows. acToolbarYes displays a toolbar in all windows.

▶ The method affects toolbars only, not menu bars and pop-up menus.

▶ You can see a list of the names of available built-in and custom toolbars by selecting the Tools | Customize menu item and clicking on the Toolbars tab.

▶ If the Allow Built-in Toolbars check box in the Startup dialog is cleared, the ShowToolbar method can only be used to control the display of custom toolbars.

▶ The ShowToolbar method is equivalent to selecting Tools | Customize and checking or unchecking toolbars on the Toolbars tab. This means that any changes your code makes remain in effect permanently, even after Access closes and reopens.

▶ To display a particular toolbar with just one or several forms or reports, use an event procedure to display the toolbar in that object's Activate event and to hide the toolbar in that object's Deactivate event.

TransferDatabase

This method is a specialized one that imports or exports a database object to or from another database format. Supported formats include Access, dBase III, dBase IV, dBase 5.0, Jet 2.x, Jet 3.x, Paradox 3.x, Paradox 4.x, Paradox 5.x, Paradox 7.x, ODBC databases, and Windows SharePoint Services (WSS). For details, see the Access VBA documentation.

TransferSpreadsheet

This method is a specialized one that imports or exports a table to or from a spreadsheet. Supported formats include Excel 3.0 through Excel 9.0 and three versions of Lotus 1-2-3 workbooks. For details, see the documentation.

TransferSQLDatabase

Introduced in Access for Office XP, this method transfers an entire SQL Server database to another SQL Server database. For details, see the documentation.

TransferText

This method is a specialized one that imports or exports data to or from a variety of text file formats. Supported formats include delimited text files, fixed-width text files, HTML files, and Microsoft Word mail-merge files. For details, see the documentation.

Index

INTERNATIONAL CONTACT INFORMATION

AUSTRALIA
McGraw-Hill Book Company
Australia Pty. Ltd.
TEL +61-2-9900-1800
FAX +61-2-9878-8881
http://www.mcgraw-hill.com.au
books-it_sydney@mcgraw-hill.com

CANADA
McGraw-Hill Ryerson Ltd.
TEL +905-430-5000
FAX +905-430-5020
http://www.mcgraw-hill.ca

**GREECE, MIDDLE EAST, & AFRICA
(Excluding South Africa)**
McGraw-Hill Hellas
TEL +30-210-6560-990
TEL +30-210-6560-993
TEL +30-210-6560-994
FAX +30-210-6545-525

MEXICO (Also serving Latin America)
McGraw-Hill Interamericana Editores
S.A. de C.V.
TEL +525-1500-5108
FAX +525-117-1589
http://www.mcgraw-hill.com.mx
carlos_ruiz@mcgraw-hill.com

SINGAPORE (Serving Asia)
McGraw-Hill Book Company
TEL +65-6863-1580
FAX +65-6862-3354
http://www.mcgraw-hill.com.sg
mghasia@mcgraw-hill.com

SOUTH AFRICA
McGraw-Hill South Africa
TEL +27-11-622-7512
FAX +27-11-622-9045
robyn_swanepoel@mcgraw-hill.com

SPAIN
McGraw-Hill/
Interamericana de España, S.A.U.
TEL +34-91-180-3000
FAX +34-91-372-8513
http://www.mcgraw-hill.es
professional@mcgraw-hill.es

**UNITED KINGDOM, NORTHERN,
EASTERN, & CENTRAL EUROPE**
McGraw-Hill Education Europe
TEL +44-1-628-502500
FAX +44-1-628-770224
http://www.mcgraw-hill.co.uk
emea_queries@mcgraw-hill.com

ALL OTHER INQUIRIES Contact:
McGraw-Hill/Osborne
TEL +1-510-420-7700
FAX +1-510-420-7703
http://www.osborne.com
omg_international@mcgraw-hill.com

Sound Off!

Visit us at **www.osborne.com/bookregistration** and let us know what you thought of this book. While you're online you'll have the opportunity to register for newsletters and special offers from McGraw-Hill/Osborne.

We want to hear from you!

Sneak Peek

Visit us today at **www.betabooks.com** and see what's coming from McGraw-Hill/Osborne tomorrow!

Based on the successful software paradigm, Bet@Books™ allows computing professionals to view partial and sometimes complete text versions of selected titles online. Bet@Books™ viewing is free, invites comments and feedback, and allows you to "test drive" books in progress on the subjects that interest you the most.

OSBORNE DELIVERS RESULTS!

OSBORNE